D0908616

"The authors' insight into and understanding of what really makes a true leader, and the kind of leadership it takes to sustainably transform their business, makes this essential reading for anyone with aspirations to fundamentally change the way their organisation operates."
Nick Frankland
Chief Executive Officer of Guy Carpenter, Europe

"I know that leadership makes the difference. Over the past few years, I have focused on my ability to lead big change. Frankly, I don't often read management books, but I have found this to be clear and, above all, practical. If you too have a big change challenge – read it – it will help!"
Leslie Van de Walle, CEO
Rexam PLC

"So refreshing to find an approach to change that is not "change management by numbers" – models, templates etc – but gets to the heart of influencing people. I find it intuitive, tangible and great for building team and self awareness and capability".
Ruth Cairnie, VP Commercial Fuels, Royal Dutch Shell.

"This new book's premise is simple but far-reaching: personality – cult leadership doesn't achieve sustainable change. However, how leaders actually lead does have a profound impact on the outcome. This thoughtful and thought-provoking book looks to explain why some succeed and many fail to achieve their change objectives. Blending theory, real-life case studies, and new ideas on leadership practices, it will appeal to both specialists and those who are leading large-scale change in their organizations."
Lucien Alziari
SVP Human Resources
Avon Products, Inc.
New York

"The world in which we now operate requires us to create organizations which have moved on from big, monolithic change to ones comfortable with flexible, responsive, and constant change. Rowland and Higgs first of all recognize that to be successful we have to create the conditions that allow change to operate at all levels in the organization, in effect for the organization to change itself. The demand on us as leaders is for more subtle, nuanced and enabling leadership and this is precisely what they offer; it works for me."
Martin Davidson, Chief Executive of the British Council

"One of the 'changes' that I had made a couple of years ago was – in general – to declare a moratorium on reading about Change for a while. So it was with great pleasure that I rejoined this debate by reading *Sustaining Change*. I particularly liked the thrust of durable transformation and the book's various diagnostics and helpful tips to achieve this end. The text unerringly focuses on the pivotal role of Leaders in the change process, and I found myself with a sheen of sweat on my brow as I took this opportunity to reconnect with the importance of my own role. In a world where it is often true that "Those who can – do; and those who can't – preach" (sic), this book is a refreshing rejoining of the two: serving as it does as both a very compelling call to arms, married with a powerful model and set of tools with which to join the battle"
Reg Bull, Senior Vice President – HR, Unilever

'To all those in the Transcend Consultancy team who have given us the space to write this book'

Sustaining Change: Leadership That Works

Deborah Rowland and Malcolm Higgs

JOSSEY-BASS
A Wiley Imprint
www.josseybass.com

Other Wiley Editorial Offices

John Wiley & Sons Inc., 111 River Street, Hoboken, NJ 07030, USA

Jossey-Bass, 989 Market Street, San Francisco, CA 94103-1741, USA

Wiley-VCH Verlag GmbH, Boschstr. 12, D-69469 Weinheim, Germany

John Wiley & Sons Australia Ltd, 42 McDougall Street, Milton, Queensland 4064, Australia

John Wiley & Sons (Asia) Pte Ltd, 2 Clementi Loop #02-01, Jin Xing Distripark, Singapore
129809

John Wiley & Sons Canada Ltd, 6045 Freemont Blvd, Mississauga, ONT, L5R 4J3, Canada

Wiley also publishes its books in a variety of electronic formats. Some content that appears in
print may not be available in electronic books.

Library of Congress Cataloging-in-Publication Data

Rowland, Deborah.
    Sustaining change : leadership that works / Deborah Rowland & Malcolm Higgs.
       p.   cm.
    Includes bibliographical references and index.
    ISBN 978-0-470-72454-5 (cloth)
    1. Organizational change.   2. Leadership.   I. Higgs, Malcolm.   II. Title.
    HD58.8.R694 2008
    658.4'06 – dc22

                                                                              2008001327

British Library Cataloguing in Publication Data

A catalogue record for this book is available from the British Library

ISBN 13 978-0-470-72454-5

Typeset in 11/16 pt Trump Medieval by SNP Best-set Typesetter Ltd., Hong Kong
Printed and bound in Great Britain by TJ International Ltd, Padstow, Cornwall, UK

Contents

Foreword

Effective leadership is high demand. This interest has resulted in a burgeoning of academic programs in leadership studies and in leadership development activities. There are organizations which devote considerable resources to selecting, developing, testing and promoting leaders. Whilst the impact of this investment is often thought to be less than was intended, and the evaluation of these efforts is necessarily complex and multi-dimensional, nevertheless what cannot be denied is the interest in leadership on the one hand and the willingness of at least some organizations to invest in seeking to secure a stream of potential 'leadership candidates'. This may well be a result of the widely accepted view that leaders play a vital role in 'energizing' change, innovation and success for their organization.

This book on Change Leadership is particularly timely in this context. Based on rigorous research it also reflects the concerns and experience of the authors – one a successful consultant turned Business School academic, the other a successful consultant and former organizational leader. The authors have collaborated on this work over a number of years and presented it at various conferences to which they have invited consultant colleagues, practitioners and academic colleagues. What they do here is set out a well founded model of change leadership and show how they have applied it in practice. On this basis they argue for a change leadership approach based on collaboration and the building of capability.

What you focus on when thinking about the present may be very different from what you think about when looking at the needs for an organization in the future, particularly in a changing world. Whilst the people working in the organization today may not welcome change, the decisions and choices leaders make will often carry fateful consequences for the health of the organization in the longer term. The outcomes of these choices may determine future success or failure. It follows that, whilst focus on the leader as an individual is important in looking at the role and influence that can be brought to bear today, a focus on decision and choice is vital to gaining an understanding of the longer term impact of any leader. Moreover, by seeking to comprehend the evidence base and assumptions on which decisions were based we deal with material open to analysis. In turn, then, this material is more readily accessible for leadership development purposes.

Where 'social influence' models are used this raises the same question about leadership. Which leaders, positioned where in the organizational system, are likely to be most influential? As soon as you accept the notion that social factors play a part, you must immediately question the idea that change is created on a straightforward top down basis. Even where the organization is a relatively simple affair where change involves embracing new technology, then we know that existing power bases become challenged. This is simply another way of accepting that in that context leadership may well come from different sources.

This book presents a cogent and serious attempt to deepen the conceptual treatment of change leadership. It introduces a framework comprising four necessary practices and four 'distinguishing' practices. The latter are associated with successful change in the research upon which the framework is based. The four distinguishing practices are listed as 'attractor', 'edge and tension', 'container', and 'transforming space'. The necessary practices are insufficient of themselves. Success in change comes to those leaders who find the right balance of the four distinguishing practices. Not least of the value of the framework is that by focusing on practices it is easily translated into an action plan for change leader development.

Clearly here the role, style and decisions of senior leaders are under examination. Whilst 'personal leadership' issues are in play here it is also clear that credibility, track record and business impact are at the core of the analysis. Thus we are not simply looking at finding a 'hands-on' leader. As this book demonstrates, one important key to success is finding the right balance of 'order' and 'disturbance' to generate movement and to stimulate sustained change. The change goes beyond the personal leadership dimensions into looking for a senior leader who can be expected to both understand and embrace the decisions and choices which must be made. The key point here is to argue that the leadership role in change is as much as anything an enabling role. Yes, they make decisions. But to what purpose? In *Sustaining Change*, the power of the answer lies in the challenge to leaders which the authors offer. Embrace change to energize others in the making of change. Get the strength of the organization working with you rather than trying to work across the grain of the organization. A story of struggle it may be but it is also a serious attempt to come to terms with the challenge and complexity of the topic. Is change changing, they ask? Yes, and so must change leadership, with this book giving us clues as to how.

C A Carnall, Associate Dean, Executive Programs
and Professor of Strategic Management,
Warwick Business School

Acknowledgments

The writing of this book could not have been possible without the close collaboration of our colleagues, coaches and mentors: we thank Nancy Clay for her invaluable insights into the stories and concepts contained in the book, her comments on the writing, and her dedicated and gifted contribution to its underpinning research effort and consulting application over the years; Roger Bellis for the vital role he played with one of the authors in the initial creation of the Changing Leadership framework upon which this book is based, its research testing, and then its practical development and application within our consulting team and practice; Anjet van Linge, Chris Robertson, and Michael Thorley, for their depth of contribution, insight and critique to the writing of the chapters that describe the Changing Leadership practices – Part II this book would not be the same without them, and also Nick Mayhew for his comments on part of the text; Dana Kaminstein for his input into the theoretical underpinnings to our Changing Leadership framework and his encouragement to 'go for it' in our writing; Jackie Gittins for providing wise, independent, supportive and challenging insight to us on our writing style and how to engage our reader; Ron Rowland for his perspective 'from the field'; June Rowland for her meticulous proof reading; and the editorial team at Wiley for their sponsorship and positive encouragement throughout.

In addition, the research effort and concept development upon which this book has been created has been pioneered, supported and nurtured over the years by many other colleagues and close advisors, and for this we would particularly like to thank: Ian Colville, Angus Fisher, Phil Hadridge, Bill Johnson, and Nel Viersen. The consulting team and research effort have been ably supported by our administrative staff and field researchers, in particular the ever-present, able and willing Katie Jones; and Jill Foulds, Susan Holland, Charlie Sweeney, Tim Price and Adam Miller.

The entire inquiry was stimulated by our work in organisations. Our research journey, its practical application, and the rich feedback loop between the two, could not have happened without the committed support of many organisational leaders who have generously worked with us in trying to wrestle with the challenges of implementing large scale organizational change. Our partnership with them has taught us much. In particular, we would like to thank the following leaders who have closely supported the research effort and collaborated with us in our organisational consulting work, the experiences and stories from which have enabled us to richly illustrate this book: Caroline Boddington, Ruth Cairnie, Ronan Cassidy, Graham Chipchase, Louise Cowcher, Martin Davidson, James Dorrian, Lynn Elsenhans, Peter Erich, Allan Fielder,

Roger Forster, Jackie Gittens, Paul Kane, Mick Holbrook, Nick Kirkbride, Ellen Lamparter, Adrian Loader, John MacKensie, Louise Makin, Andrew Manley, Peter Molingraaf, Jeremy Newsum, Pat O'Driscoll, Bishop Alastair Redfern, Leslie Van de Walle, and Pavita Walker. In addition we thank the following leaders who have not only personally participated in the research process but continue to engage with us in processing its findings: Colin Abrahams, Lucien Alziari, Sir David Henshaw, Jane Kirkwood, Dave Pace, and Josef Waltl.

Finally, this book could not have been written this year without the affirming personal presence, assistance and encouragement from a close circle of family, friends, and helpers, and for this kind of support we would like to thank (in addition to some of those already mentioned): Ron, June, John and Paul Rowland, along with Wendy, Clare, Katharine, Martin and Louise, Lisa Parr, Pete Clay, Dr George New, Valerie West, and Susan Nordhaal. To all of you, your spirit, candour, love and belief meant the world.

1

Introduction

'Much comes from little'

'Is change changing?' The three words stared out at us from the centre of the flip chart. We had written up the question the night before at a team meeting. It was the question that excited us. It was the question that mattered. It was the question that engaged our purpose. As change consultants and researchers, how could we be sure that the advice we shared with clients really made any difference? To what extent was our practice and research shaped by our own personal prejudices, styles, backgrounds, experiences and assumptions? Despite many 'how to' books on leading change on our office book shelves, why were so many of our client organisations still struggling to embrace this well intended advice?

Unbeknown to us then, these three words were to set us on a significant journey of inquiry, a journey that is ongoing; and one which has changed, and is still, changing us. Using a combination of in-depth research and practical experience, the journey has led us to discover a framework for categorising the various ways in which organisations approach change. It has also enabled us to see how leaders of those organisations can implement change in ways that produce a sustainable improvement in performance. As members of a change consultancy firm advising leaders on how to do this, we wanted to make sure our advice was rigorous and grounded. The change leadership field can be a very 'fluffy' one. We wanted to make it more tangible for leaders by examining the relationship between different approaches to change, alternative styles of leadership behaviour, and how a combination of these two can produce success in different contexts. The results coming from our inquiry over the last five years have been startling. In the data we found very strong relationships between change approach, leader behaviour and success; findings that could not have been explained by chance alone.

One little question, 'is change changing?', yet big findings arising from the pursuit of its answer. We are writing this book to share these findings with a world beyond our own personal network and client base, in order to stimulate further inquiry in the field. We say 'inquiry,' because the leadership of change is a subject that cannot be definitively sewn up and solved. It's a vast subject. On the other hand, we believe our story combines leading edge research with conclusive findings that have very practical application to organisational leadership. We have seen how an understanding of the results of our inquiry has made a real difference to how leaders lead change, and how this change in their practice has led to new, sustainably different outcomes. We have therefore also written this book *to help adapt practice,* and not just influence thinking, in the field of leading change. And when we use the word 'change' we are not talking of a project, or a task force, or a programme. We are talking about leading change in the performance of an entire organisation. Typically, this kind of change is of high magnitude and complexity; it requires the alignment, commitment and energy of many people. Given the stakes at play in such big change, how can it be better understood, led and implemented?

A key finding emerged from the early days of our inquiry: leaders who see change as an *ongoing process* that occurs naturally around them all the time, when compared to leaders who see change as a one off event, a thing to be managed, or a programme with a beginning and end, were more likely to be successful in realising the desired change outcomes. Hence the double meaning of our *'is change changing?'* research question. At one level, it is a question about how the dynamics and challenges of change are changing in today's world, for example an increase in its pace, scale, and complexity. At another level, it is about *substituting* the word 'change' with the word 'changing'. Just put a comma in the question

'is change, changing?'

and the meaning shifts. It asks us to reframe the subject of change as ongoing movement, not a once off episode. If we believe that the world around us is never static, and that there is the potential for change in every moment, every encounter, every conversation – if we so choose to see it and act on it –

then how can leaders harness this perpetually available energy in the communities and organisations that they serve?

This book explores the nature of ongoing change, and primarily the type of leadership it takes to harness its continuously available energy. We hope the findings from our inquiry will challenge assumptions about the purpose of leadership, and what good leadership looks like – especially with regard to leading ongoing performance change in organisations. Much has been written, over millennia not just centuries or even the last two decades, about the role of a 'leader' in our social, spiritual, political and economic institutions. Today's wisdom about the subject sits within a world that is becoming increasingly socially fragmented yet globally interconnected. The resultant complexity makes it less easy for charismatic, 'heroic', leaders to individually dictate and control what has to happen. The world has become too big and individual factions within it too powerful. In this context, the growing paradigm about the fundamental purpose of leadership is one that suggests that the leader can only set the overall purpose and framework for what has to be done; then build insight, capability and ownership for the change around them; and finally leave space for others to step in and become jointly responsible for making things happen. This means, as Jim Collins has described 'Level 5 Leadership' in his book *From Good to Great*, a leader giving up one's own illusion of power and control over others, and moving to a less ego-centric mode of leadership.

One leader we recently worked with expressed this paradigm succinctly. She said that the more senior she became in her organisation, the less able she was to exert any direct power over its outcomes, and indeed, as CEO, she ended up hardly making any decisions at all (save a few big ones). 'Quite frankly, I controlled nothing'. This move away from a more 'command and control' style of leadership, to a less directive one, can be very challenging. At times it goes against the very grain of how we have been taught to exercise power and influence. Our egos are often wrapped up with a story that requires us to have personalised and visible power over others. Our inner voice says 'take charge'. Creating space for others can be seen as a soft option, an easy way out. Yet the giving up of one's sense of individual control over outcomes, and 'empowering others', is not simply about issuing one or two directives, and then sitting back and seeing what happens. It entails the leader paying constant and dedicated attention to what is happening in the organisation around them, and it requires intense investment in the building of new capabilities. This is hard work. It requires a combination of dedicated effort, humility, and resolve.

Through this book we'd like to join the prevailing debate about the changing role of leadership. We have certainly found – as change practitioners, researchers, and leaders ourselves – that leaders who are able to reframe their role *away* from being one of personally directing outcomes, and being a constantly present 'champion', *to* being one of setting an overall mandate and then building capability around them, are more likely to succeed in implementing high magnitude change. Indeed, it can be the biggest determinant of success.

Yet in our own practice we were regularly noticing how leaders and organisations can get 'stuck' when trying to implement significant change – even when they think they are making significant progress. We came across very well intended and dedicated leaders trying their hardest to 'drive change' through their organisation. Their efforts typically went like this. After some initial diagnosis, study, and reporting, the case for change gets created – spiced up with juicy hard hitting facts about the competition, financial results, employee opinion data and operational performance. To these leaders it was obvious what had to be done to improve performance – the tricky challenge then lay in convincing other people. So, the top team create a vision of a new future, set against today's reality, and then engage the organisation in working out how to move from today's reality to this new future. Once the change plan is created, it is launched to the organisation and various project teams and steering groups are set up to make sure implementation happens. The top team are encouraged to 'role model' any new desired behaviours, and they go out to the organisation to engage people and get commitment.

After a while, and with usually an inordinate amount of investment and effort expended, people start to wonder why the change 'is not going fast enough'. Perhaps the top team need to sell the case harder and convince better? Should the resistors and people who are not 'getting it' be taken out? Maybe the top team need to put even more measures and tracking mechanisms in place to get greater accountability and ownership, and receive earlier warning signs about the speed of implementation? Doubt starts to creep in, and despite all the projects and programmes that have been launched, people now think that they were not designed or delivered well enough. The steering group then plan to roll out more initiatives, while the organisation is still figuring out how to implement those launched last year.

We had witnessed (and been party to) the above scenario many times. You the reader might have done so too. It feels like a lot is being set in motion yet somehow the cogs are not connecting. And yet we had also experienced examples of large scale change that had been very successfully implemented, leading to sustainable changes in performance. When we reflected on our own practice, some of our consulting interventions in change with leadership teams had worked very well, others, quite frankly, had delivered little impact. What made the difference? We got curious about this, and what's more the leaders we worked with were also keen to get answers and insights to this question. It was as much their energy that led to our inquiry, and their stories of struggles and success are woven gratefully into this book. The original intent of our inquiry was not to generate long lists and 'how to' recipes for leading change, however it has resulted in statistically grounded insights into the relationship between certain change contexts, performance outcomes, and leader behaviour. To our knowledge we have not yet seen this level of rigour in the field of change leadership research.

Our first round of research revealed that there were significant differences in how organisations were approaching and managing change, despite the fact that the choice of change approach was hardly ever a conscious or explicit one; and that some organisations were more successful than others. When we dug deeper into the findings, what struck us was that it seemed to matter how leaders were leading the change – *in fact what leaders did was the single biggest reason explaining why some changes we studied were successful, and others were not.* In this book we will share the original round of research as context, and then focus on our most recent inquiry which was intended to surface with more specificity the leadership practices that made the difference. The resulting framework we have called 'Changing Leadership', as it describes the practices that are needed for ongoing change, or changing.

Our research process throughout has been conducted in close partnership with practising leaders. We hope this book speaks to you and your leadership. It is primarily intended for those leaders who are faced with the challenges of leading significant performance and/or paradigm change in their organisations and communities, *and who recognise that their own behaviour and practice is a key determinant in being able to bring about this change.* We will share the insights, frameworks, and practices that we have found can lead to greater success. We do recognise that the problem with writing about leadership is that its practice can be made to sound too easy, and therefore do not want to over simplify the subject. However we do want to help leaders learn, adapt their behaviour, and guide others – and we feel we have some pointers to help inform that. The challenge of change often requires leaders to reach out for the help of trained coaches and leadership development professionals. This book therefore is also intended to appeal to those who are helping to coach leaders and leadership teams in implementing significant change.

The book is structured as outlined below. If you are a practising leader you may wish to skip Part I and go straight to Part II, which illustrates our findings about the necessary practices to lead big change. If you are a leadership coach, change consultant, or leadership development professional, you may wish to start at the beginning in Part I, which surveys the landscape of change and leadership, describes our research process and outcomes, and connects these findings with other theoretical fields. Part III is about how to practically work with our frameworks and findings, which should hold interest for all. As we were writing the book we did have a dilemma about its style. As co-authors we span the spectrum of academic-consultant-practitioner. Should we on the one hand adopt a scholarly and detached style that conveyed the conceptual rigour behind our work? On the other hand, should we write in a personal and more engaging way that brought relevance to the day to day, and moreover reflected the essence of our consulting practice and our personalities? We decided to take a 'both-and' approach – so while Part I might feel a bit more scholarly we adapt our style through the book to appeal more directly and personally to you the reader.

Part I: Defining Changing Leadership

Chapter 2: Is Change Changing?

This chapter sets out the different approaches to change that organisations can adopt, and shares our research findings about how these different approaches are correlated to success, or otherwise, in different contexts. Our findings have challenged the predominant 'programmatic' approach to change, that assumes change is linear, predictable, and can be 'managed', and instead support change approaches that assume complexity, non-linearity, and the need to view change as an ongoing process that cannot be broken down into simple and separate parts.

Chapter 3: Are Leaders Leading?

This chapter shares our initial findings about the pivotal role that leader behaviour has in determining change outcomes. It traces the overall context for changing views about leadership, proposes a framework for understanding how leader behaviour can impact outcomes, and shares in detail three different ways of leading change that we uncovered from our first stage of research. As with change approaches, we share our research findings in this chapter that reveal how these three different ways of leading change are differentially correlated with success.

Chapter 4: Changing Leadership – A Framework

This chapter introduces the essential leadership practices that we have found from our most recent research are highly correlated with success in implementing big change. Based on the findings from the initial leadership research, where we had such illuminating data about the practices that either helped, or hindered leading significant change, we created a more specific set of practices that were subsequently tested and refined. These practices are defined in this chapter, which concludes with an examination of other theoretical fields that might explain why these leadership practices, both individually and in combination, relate so strongly to leading successful change.

Part II: Seeing Changing Leadership

Chapters 5 to 8: Changing Leadership Illustrated

These chapters take each one of the four leadership practices in our framework and, through illustrations and in-depth change stories, share what it is that leaders practically do to create more successful change. These chapters bring 'Changing Leadership' to life. They also illustrate how there can be a 'dark side' to each of these four practices, which leaders can easily fall into if the intent behind their behaviour is more about satisfying their own ego needs and wants, rather than acting in service of others and the wider context.

Part III: Working with Changing Leadership

Chapter 9: Linking Changing Leadership

Our research identified that those leaders who can display all four 'Changing Leadership' practices are those most likely to produce highly successful, sustaining change. We describe how the four practices are interrelated, and all required in balance within a change process. We share the key strategies that leaders adopt in combining all four practices in order to avoid any one of them becoming either 'over', or 'under' done, and show with some illustrations how the practices can be linked in what we call 'multi-hit' interventions.

Chapter 10: Developing Changing Leadership

Can these practices be learned? This chapter explores the underpinning orientations and beliefs that we have found leaders need to hold to be able to practice Changing Leadership with any degree of authenticity and success. We then share in some detail, for each one of the four 'Changing Leadership' practices, the learning strategies we have found to be helpful in developing the capability to master them. This chapter will enable you to reflect on your own strengths and development needs in Changing Leadership, and provide some practical guidance on how you might go about building your capability to lead big change.

Chapter 11: Where next?

We conclude with a reflection on the insights generated in writing the book, and set out the big questions we still hold in relation to 'Changing Leadership' that merit further inquiry. We have discovered that our inquiry is an ongoing process. Just as the word 'change', can be moved to 'changing', to reflect the ever present ever evolving nature of change, so should our research effort move to a 'researching' one. In this chapter we invite you to join us in this continuing journey.

It has been said that 'we move in the direction of the questions we ask' (Margaret Wheatley). Questions such as 'is change changing?' do not just seek to clarify; they create movement, and movement in a new direction. That small question certainly took us on a big journey. We are grateful for the questions that have emerged along the way, since they have all served as 'tipping points' that helped us take the next step. We are also grateful for the enormous assistance, energy, challenge and enthusiasm provided by so many of our collaborators on this journey. This book is our offering back to those leaders, and to you the reader, based on our own small steps to discover what makes great leaders of change.

Part I

Defining Changing Leadership

2

Is change changing?

'People support what they create'

We commence with a story that set one of us on a journey to learn more about change and its leadership. What story 'stands behind' you as a leader of change?

While still a fresh faced Social Anthropology undergraduate two decades ago I received a very early lesson in change management. We were seated in a university lecture hall watching a film from the early 1900s about the story of a group of white Christian missionaries entering a native African tribal community. The purpose of the missionaries' visit to this tribe was to make the local culture more 'civilised'. Inter-village warfare was rife and was threatening the future of the local population. The missionaries wanted to reduce this warfare and create a more peaceful, productive society.

The grainy black and white film flickered across the screen in the lecture hall. The lecturer stepped back and let it play. On the screen we saw the group of very well intended missionaries, in crisp white linen outfits, entering the African tribal villages, smiling politely, if somewhat nervously. The native Africans in contrast were wearing grass skirts, had war paint on their bodies, and after some initial curiosity and seemingly aggressive posturing, chose to ignore the missionaries. The missionaries looked intent on their purpose – to reduce inter-village warfare. They had a vision of a more peaceful society. And they had one key strategy which they felt would take the natives from where they were today to this more desirable future. The change plan was to introduce the game of cricket. What could be a more civilising influence? It was the perfect vehicle to channel aggression and warfare into a carefully controlled and safe yet still competitive activity.

We saw the missionaries spend painstaking time introducing the natives to the purpose of the game, its rules, play tactics, and equipment. The pitch was laid out in a clearing outside the village. Women and children gathered to watch the proceedings. What transpired though over the course of this ethnographic story was precisely the opposite of what the missionaries intended. *Instead of reducing inter village warfare, introducing the game of cricket actually served to increase it.* We saw the native villagers pick up the sharp cricket stumps and use them as javelins. The collection of cricket balls was raided to gain access to these highly dangerous weapons which when thrown at someone's skull could kill them outright. The missionaries looked on aghast – what was happening? How could it be that their well intended efforts to change this tribe were actually, far from changing things, actually amplifying the current situation?

With hindsight this story is an apocryphal and instructive one for many of today's so called failed change efforts. The missionaries believed that the villagers would easily 'buy in' to their case for change and vision. Why would they want to kill each other? Isn't peaceful living and respect for thy neighbour something everybody aspires to? The missionaries had made big assumptions about people's alignment to the change goal. They had also shown minimal initial curiosity and inquiry into the current local patterns of behaviour and what these practices were serving in that cultural context. They had simply judged them to be in need of change. A minority of the villagers had already been trying to reduce the warfare; however they went unnoticed. The change intervention, the game of cricket, was imposed without dialogue, consultation or testing. It was one simple, blunt tool. The missionaries, while anticipating resistance, had just pushed harder when they encountered it, only serving to increase people's defensiveness and make the current war like behaviours of the tribal villagers even more pronounced. Ultimately, the missionaries had not seen any need to change their own mindset and behaviour at all – they believed their task was merely to bring the change to others.

Perhaps your own 'stands behind me' change story has equal resonance and similar insight. The main lesson we take today from this early 'change management case study' is the fundamental need to appreciate the ongoing and systemic context within which change occurs. It appears that change can not simply be imposed in a one off mechanistic way, delivered through a programme, or be treated as a straightforward episode or event. Such an approach fails to work with and appreciate the current values that people hold. It ignores the insight that every human system is somehow functioning in a way that serves a particular purpose – it makes perfect sense to those who are in it. Just by trying to change how other people function, without acknowledging, inquiring into, and trying to adjust the fundamental reason why they function that way in the first place, will only produce patchy and half hearted results. It will work against the grain and fail to harness the creative energy *within* people to move in to a different future. And it illuminates why so many individuals, teams, and organisations stay 'stuck' in repeating patterns of behaviour that make no sense at all, and can in fact be quite unhelpful. People can maintain an attachment to a way of being that no longer serves them. *Far from trying to change the behaviour, the task becomes one of trying to change the attachment to that behaviour.* Working *on* people to change their behaviour, as the missionaries did by introducing the game of cricket to the villagers, rather than working *with* people to try to understand what their behaviour is currently serving, to reconsider its usefulness, and thereby release that attachment, can only serve to keep people where they are. However it's surprising how many change efforts fail to recognise this. And it's the reason why organisations, teams and individuals can find it so hard to let go of the past.

This chapter is about the different approaches we have seen organisations taking when implementing change, and by change we mean efforts to fundamentally improve the performance and functioning of an entire organisation, which requires the letting go of past attachments and behaviour and moving toward a new and different way of operating. It sets the stage for the rest of the book which focuses more specifically on the behaviours that leaders can adopt in change implementation.

We begin with a brief survey of the change landscape. Is change changing? What change challenges do today's leaders face? Are these challenges any different to those faced a century ago? Are they more complex? In addition, have our *perceptions* of how change occurs changed based on an increased understanding of how the world works more generally? In other words, 'is change, changing?' Perhaps change is really not that different to what it has always been, but rather we are starting to see change through a new lens. We will then share our framework for codifying the different types of change approaches we see organisations adopting and explore the research findings that show which of these approaches seem to work most successfully in different contexts. Finally, we will illustrate through a story how a leadership team, with an increased understanding of the choices they could make in how to implement change, took certain bold steps to 'change the way they changed' their organisation, with significantly improved outcomes.

In the meantime we thank the anthropology film all those years ago for stimulating our initial curiosity into how systems can be successfully, or less successfully, changed.

Is change changing?

The extent, pace, and depth of change in the world in which organisations operate has been the subject of much study and debate. Perhaps the most influential (and prolific) writers on the topic have been Alvin and Heidi Toffler who have now published four books (*Future Shock, The Third Wave, Powershift* and *The Adaptive Corporation*) exploring what happens to people and organisations when their society transforms itself into something new and unexpected. In exploring the extent to which the world is changing at ever increasing rates there is much debate about the degree to which the fundamentals are really shifting. It is not the purpose of this book to enter into this debate. However, two things are clear. Firstly, technological advances, demographic and socio economic shifts and environmental changes are all having a significant impact on the context in which organisations are operating in the 21st Century. Secondly, it is equally clear that some of the fundamentals, in terms of how individuals perceive and react to change, are deep-seated and unchanging. In addition it is also evident that the process of change, and how organisations seek to manage it, has altered little in the face of more significant contextual changes. These key contextual changes, which are faced by organisations today, may be summarised as:

Macro-economic changes: changes in income inequality, with rising levels in some countries (e.g. China, India) leading to related shifts in patterns of consumer spending; changes in the nature and operation of markets (e.g. Globalisation); changes in market regulation; growing interdependence of economies (for example Japan owns 150 to 200 trillion yen of US Treasury Bonds and China has 818.9 billion US dollars in foreign exchange reserves).

Technological changes: developments in computing power and complexity; advances in means of communication; developments in biotechnology.

Changes in production: speed of production; changes in manufacturing location (e.g. shift to the developing world); shortening in product development life cycles; the emergence of mass customisation.

Changes in customers: demographic shifts (e.g. aging population, birth rates) leading to changing markets; growth in immigration; shift in demand from products to services.

Illustrative of the scale of a number of these changes are the following:

- If you took every single job in the US today and transferred them to China, China would still have a labour surplus.

- The US Department of Labor estimates that today's learner will have 10–14 jobs . . . by the age of 38!

- The top 10 in-demand jobs in 2010 will not have existed in 2004.

- In 2002 Nintendo invested more than $ 140 m on research and development. In the same year the US Federal

Government spent less than half as much on research and innovation in education.

- There are over 2.7 billion searches performed on Google each month.

- The number of text messages sent and received every day exceeds the total population of the planet.

- More than 3000 books are published every day.

- The amount of new technical information is doubling every two years. By 2010 it is predicted that it will double every 72 hours.

Against this background of increasing and accelerating pressures for change we are faced with the depressing reality that 70 % of change initiatives still fail to achieve their goals (see Kotter, 1995). This gives rise to the need to ask some fundamental questions about change and its leadership:

- What are the assumptions we make about the context in which organisations operate?

- How do leaders approach change and in what way does change need to change if we are to increase its success rate?

- How can leaders help people within their organisations make sense of the growth in the rate of change and the related increases in complexity?

Is change, changing?

While the pace of change may be increasing in the world, the way in which we perceive the nature of change and how it occurs is itself changing. Insights into this may be found from a closer examination of the world around us, where it has been shown that living systems are able to stay in a state of perpetual motion and adaptation when two states are nurtured and held in balance *at the same time*. One is the force for stability, structure, and order. The other is the force for adaptation, novelty, and experimentation. The first contains 'rules' that govern the behaviour of the system. The second encourages creative implementation of the rules such that the behaviour never seems stuck and fixed. This co-existence of both the force for stability, and the force for change, has become known as 'the edge of chaos'. The system somehow trembles between order and chaos which enables it to keep constantly changing. This realisation that the world is constantly changing before our eyes, and that despite an appearance of stability there is always movement and flow in any living system (which organisations certainly are) holds fundamental importance to the practice of leading change.

For a little over half a century the predominant paradigm in change management thinking and practice has been that people naturally prefer the status quo, are creatures of habit, and adverse to change. The only way to introduce change into this in built inertia is therefore to 'unfreeze' a stuck situation and disengage people from today's way of thinking ('let's go civilise the primitives'). So, the case for change has to be created and sold to people in order to get commitment and awareness of the need to change. Next, new attitudes, policies and practices are put into place. The 'change' is launched and implemented ('let's introduce cricket to create more peaceful behaviour'). Once this has happened, leaders then seek to 'refreeze' the organisation into the desired new habits and practices so that people do not revert back to the old ways. This is usually affected through changes to such systems as performance management, measurement and reward, in order to 'make the change stick' ('less warfare brings more access to western ways').

The 'unfreeze – change – refreeze' sequence is a rather simplistic overview of how organisational change is implemented. However, you might find this recognisable from your own experience. Have changes you have been part of felt like this? What beliefs were present in others, and yourself, that led you to implement in this way? We have found that the dominant assumptions behind this approach to change are: that people don't want change; that it can be managed and controlled; that it is a more or less linear, predictable and sequential process; and that you are either in a static state or a changing state at any one time.

Over the last 10 to 15 years, however, there has been a growing awareness in organisational change thinking and practice that change is not so straightforward and sequential; it is complex, organisations are never static, and that in fact, if we pay close enough attention to what is happening in the corridors, in meetings, in interactions with customers, and managing operations on the factory floor, we will notice that change, or indeed the potential for change, is happening around us all the time. The organisation is in a state of perpetual motion. Culture is continually being recreated in each and every conversation. When leaders see organisations through this lens, they become less prone to staging dramatic, forward planned, sweeping change programmes, and place equal, if not more emphasis, on the power of step by step, frequent adjustments, and the influencing of change at the more micro level of day to day activity, process and conversation; for this is where change happens, and this is where urgency and pace can be created. And over time, and sometimes even a very short space of time, these frequent changes at the local level can add up to producing very big change at the level of the whole system. The leader's task is to set up the macro conditions for this kind of change, for example creating lateral networks of people from different parts of the organisation, establishing a few 'rules' to govern the day to day behaviour of the organisation, and then 'press play and see what happens'.

In summary, this paradigm turns the predominant and more established approach to change on its head. The 'unfreeze – change – refreeze' *change* sequence becomes a 'freeze – adjust – unfreeze' *changing* sequence. The leader's first step is not to 'unfreeze' a static situation of inertia where people are wedded to the status quo. The leader rather seeks to 'freeze frame' the current situation, almost like taking a photograph, in order to map the ongoing micro level changes and innovations that are naturally occurring in the organisation. *What's happening where? Who's connected to whom? Where are we already seeing signs of innovation and adjustment that are working towards a new future? Where might we be stuck, and what deep rules are creating that pattern of behaviour?* Having mapped the patterns, the leader then seeks to adjust behaviour and practice by adapting the rules that are governing any current unhelpful behaviour, making new connections between people, and disturbing the sequence of how things get done. Very often these changes are made at the micro level, rather than launching grand plans for the whole organisation. They can be as seemingly straightforward as changing how meetings happen and how conversations occur. *What if we were to always start meetings on time such that we build a culture of respect in the organisation? What if we were to start listening to each other differently in this meeting in order to be able to work more interdependently when outside of this meeting? If we could become less cynical in this conversation, how could that increase the rate of adoption of best practices between our teams elsewhere in the organisation?* And finally, having made the adjustments, far from wanting to 'refreeze' the situation to make things stick, the leader wants to set the system free, remove any barriers to change, and 'unfreeze' it, in order to encourage the naturally occurring, ongoing, self-organised change to occur, albeit now adapted to an adjusted set of rules. *Can we transmit what we have learned to change in our meetings to others? How can we create more experimentation and innovation across the silos in our organisation?*

Dominant assumptions behind the 'freeze – adjust – unfreeze' approach to change are: that leaders cannot directly control change – they can only create the conditions; that it is process and connections that create change, not predetermined plans and projects; that things don't happen in straight lines – it will be a bit messy; and that change is ever present – if we so wish to see it. When leaders can create an organisation that holds the balance between stability and change, and is set 'on the edge of chaos', they have the conditions under which the organisation can continually evolve, learn and adapt *without the need to impose change on it.*

So, is change, changing? We have contrasted above the more episodic, planned approach to change (which is sequential, and driven through an organisation like a 'programme'), with continuous, ongoing change which holds that the system is in a constant state of stability and change. In our own work with organisations we started to identify this contrast *as the difference between how change gets managed and how change actually happens.* In other words, organisations tend to manage change in a linear, more programmatic fashion. Leaders lay out public project plans, they predict outcomes, they appoint formal task forces, and they launch pre-designed and set initiatives. And yet the way change actually happens is messier, unpredictable, behind the scenes, and more likely to come from random encounters and unplanned events. This requires leaders to be more attentive to diagnosing what is happening *in the present moment* as an opportunity to change the course of events, rather than spending time planning things to launch in the future.

And yet what if leaders can build the skill to master both types of approaches; to be able to 'drive change management programmes' *and* tap into the natural energy and process of how change occurs? Perhaps the reason why 70 % of change efforts 'fail' is that there is an over-emphasis on the more formal, programmatic approach to change at the expense of the messier, less planned, and informal approach?

A framework for understanding different change approaches

While as consultants and practitioners we were starting to draw from these two contrasting ways to view change, we were at the same time thinking that it could not be quite that simple. It felt too binary. Furthermore, change efforts in practice do not neatly fall into one approach or the other – programmatic, or more 'emergent'. The polarity was helpful, though not necessarily practical for helping leaders make choices and take different steps. Our research question 'is change changing?' took us on a path to more fully identify the range of approaches that organisations take when implementing change.

The inquiry led to the development of a framework based on different scenarios, or assumptions, about how we and others saw the world of change changing. The framework contains two axes: the first axis represents two contrasting scenarios of people either believing that change implementation is straightforward, easily managed, and predictable, or, that it is complex, non-controllable, and non-linear; the second axis represents two contrasting scenarios of, on the one hand, a belief that a one look approach to change can work across any situation or culture, or, on the other hand, a belief that change needs to be self organised and differentiated according to local requirement. When combined, these two axes map out four different approaches to the implementation of change.

We were intrigued by this framework, and so were our clients who helped create it and who subsequently worked with it.

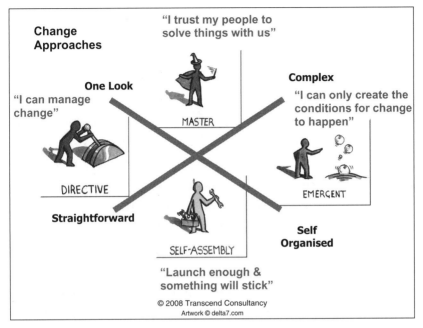

Figure 2.1 Approaches to Change © 2008 Transcend Consultancy

The four change approaches, shown in Figure 2.1, came to be called 'Directive' (straightforward, one look change), 'Self Assembly' (straightforward, self organised change), 'Master' (complex, one look change) and 'Emergent' (complex, self organised change).

While no single change process ever falls neatly into just one approach, and while different approaches might be needed in different parts of the organisation, or at different phases of the change process, for the sake of understanding their distinctions we provide the following summaries. As we describe them, you might start to reflect on the change processes you have been part of, or led, and recognise how they map onto these four different approaches.

Directive (straightforward and one-look)

Directive change is top down and driven from a single source, usually the senior leadership. In this approach both the outcome and goals, and the process or 'how' of the change, are determined and developed by the initiating source. The change is then launched to the organisation, more often than not through a hierarchical 'cascade' process where initiatives are 'rolled out' across the organisation. If the change encompasses several different initiatives (such as a new IT system, factory restructuring, new performance cycle, or leadership behaviours framework) they tend to be led and managed as a set of unrelated projects. Everybody in the organisation has to follow the prescribed steps of the change process. Communications are implemented to get people's understanding and 'buy-in' to the change. In order to guarantee consistency and one look, communications and messages are carefully controlled and are usually accompanied by 'question and answer' statements (Frequently Asked Questions – FAQ's) so that managers can give the same answers to similar questions. Resistance to change is not encouraged, and the drive to alignment is accomplished through a leadership style that says 'the train is leaving the station and there is only one stop, so get on now or stay off'. There is minimal capability building for people beyond technical training or enrolment style events where people are inducted in the necessary vision, changes and behaviours.

When we shared the approaches in the early days with a leader, who immediately identified their own organisation in this Directive approach, he described how his organisation's CEO was trying to implement the change as if he were pulling a lever from on high to connect with and control the rest of the organisation. The predominant assumption behind the Directive change approach is, 'I can manage change'.

Self Assembly (straightforward and self organised)

In Self Assembly change the goals or outcomes of the change are pre-determined; however *how* you go about the change is largely left to local operating units and teams. Because this approach assumes that change is straightforward to implement, it is characteristically accompanied by the launch of 'tool kits' and templated solutions into the organisation, designed from the centre, to assist in local implementation in a D.I.Y fashion. These tool kits can apply to new operating systems and procedures, new HR processes such as manuals for new performance appraisal systems, and even tool kits for how to run meetings, and change behaviour in your local area. It's down to local management as to how they put these together and implement the change. There is usually a help desk available at the centre to assist and support local leaders in their local effort, and 'swot' teams who come out from the centre to the local organisation to help build capability for implementation.

As we were sharing the approaches at one of the research debrief meetings one leader remarked how this approach reminded her of what is called the 'spray and pray' approach to change management (i.e. launch enough initiatives into the organisation and hope that in some way, out there in the periphery of the operating units, some things will take hold which can then bring about the desired change at the level of the whole). The predominant assumption behind the Self Assembly change approach is 'launch enough initiatives and something will stick'.

Master (complex and one-look)

Master change approaches are characterised by having a very clear and strong central framework for the change effort. However leaders then step back to create the space for others to plan what has to be done and to deliver the outcomes. Because this approach is one-look, the framework often uses an overarching statement to convey the essence of the change and its intent to the organisation (for e.g. 'Pathway to Growth', 'Forging our Future'), which everyone in the organisation gets to know about. However, the change does not have prescribed and controlled steps on what has to be done, unlike Directive. There may be certain broad interventions that need to be implemented, such as organisational redesign, or the implementation of new systems. These are accomplished in ways that use extensive engagement and involvement of people in the organisation (often taking a representative group, or cross section, of people from the organisation who will be impacted by the change and instrumental in making it happen), as opposed to the interventions being designed by a central team and then launched. Leaders get out *as a team* into the organisation, and hold events such as 'town hall' meetings where employees have a chance to enter into open unstructured dialogue with the leadership. Extensive engagement is usually accompanied by capability building of the organisation, not just in technical skills or systems implementation, but also in building the leadership capability needed to implement change well. The change effort overall is steered as a connected and interrelated whole, or system, and is accompanied by the creation of formal change agent networks who work laterally across different work streams and parts of the organisation in order to share learning, join up the dots, and manage interdependencies.

When we shared this Master approach with leaders it tended to evoke the need to go and learn more about change and master its associated leadership skills, which would require study, practice, reflection and experimentation. It created insight that the leader would need to give up total control over the change process and learn to work more deeply with the interconnecting forces of the wider system. The predominant assumption behind this change approach is, 'trust your people to solve things with you'.

Emergent (complex and self organised)

Like Master change, the Emergent approach assumes that organisations are complex and cannot be directly controlled. However, this approach does not use a one-look framework and steered process. It is characterised by leaders creating a looser sense of direction for the change, by them establishing a 'few hard rules' to govern what needs to happen, and then stepping back to encourage people around them to experiment and self organise to do the rest ('press play and see what happens'). The loose direction tends to concentrate on the organisation's fundamental intent and identity, 'who are we trying to become?' This is created through leaders tapping into the stories that are being told across the organisation, in encounters with customers, and the conversations in the corridors about where things need to move differently. Leaders then create a shared story for the organisation that encompasses what needs to happen, and this gets disseminated through dialogue and informal communications. The few hard rules are not grand high level statements about goals or behaviours, such as 'focus more on the customer', but rather rules that will govern the day to day behaviour of the organisation at the micro level, such as 'always serve the customer within twenty four hours of taking the order'. Signing up to get involved in the change is done through voluntary mechanisms (not the appointment of people to formal task forces), asking people who would like to get involved, and the work agendas tend to be set by the people themselves – tapping into the local sense of what's needed. Change and innovation are encouraged at the periphery of the organisation, not driven out from the centre. And because this approach holds the systemic belief that everything and everyone is connected, as long as the leaders encourage innovation in the different 'cells' of the organisation, and then open up the informal avenues of interaction between these cells, then change can spread like a virus through the organisation and create movement for 'big change'. Diversity of experience and viewpoints is encouraged since it brings friction and tension. Indeed, far from minimising resistance, tension and different views (characteristic of Directive and to an extent Self Assembly), an Emergent approach actually seeks to amplify disturbance since this is where you find energy for action and change.

This is the change approach that most requires leaders to give up their sense of control and prediction, and leaders consequently thought that this was also the most risky and 'scary' approach. One leader even commented 'so, do you only do emergent change when you don't know the answer yourself?!' It's certainly not the 'when all else fails. . . .' change approach; it can be a conscious and measured, albeit different way of engaging with the organisation in order to implement change. The predominant assumption behind the Emergent change approach is, 'I can only create the conditions for change to happen'.

Change approaches – what works?

We began to have conversations with leaders across several organisations about these four change approaches. Did the framework make sense? Did the approaches sufficiently categorise the requisite variety of ways in which leaders attempt to implement change? Did it enable leaders to make more informed choices about the combination of approaches that could be appropriate for their own change effort? And what combination might work 'best' in a particular scenario? As a team we wanted to investigate further.

And we wanted to do it in a style that reflected our consulting philosophy and practice. To that end we adopted a Collaborative Inquiry approach. In this research model the mind set is one where the researchers and participants work together on the inquiry. They not only jointly participate in data gathering but also in the interpretation of the data and the development of further research questions. Another key question we debated was 'what type of data do we need to collect?' We soon concluded that our question 'is change changing?' would not be answered by simply collecting responses to a questionnaire or survey – we wanted to explore more deeply and tangibly what happens when organisations engage in change. We therefore decided to collect in depth change stories told by the leaders who were actively engaged in the work of change.

To that end we contacted a variety of organisations and conducted in-depth, semi-structured 'behavioural event interviews' with 50 leaders representing 10 different organisations who shared with us 70 separate stories of change. All the interviews were transcribed and then coded for a range of variables, including the extent to which the change story being recounted encompassed the four different change approaches above (the stories were also coded for individual leadership behaviour – the findings from which will be shared in the next chapter).

At two interim debrief gatherings with participants, we felt we 'were on to something'. The curiosity generated was palpable. We did not present the data as neat and conclusive; we wanted to share stories, and to have the participants present share their stories. The data acted as a catalyst to a conversation that these organisations wanted to have happen, and the four approach framework served as a 'lens' through which to have that conversation. Some leaders felt that they had been too 'Directive' in their change approaches to date (which incidentally was the most predominantly used change approach in this first sample), and this explained why so many change initiatives never seemed to stick and really change anything. Others felt they had not done enough to build the skills for leading change in their organisations (which would be contained within the 'Master' approach), and this was why implementation had been patchy. One organisation was seeing how, in their attempt to 'simplify' change, they had in fact made it into a complicated programme that no one in the business owned.

The next stage of the research was to answer the question posed to us by participants: 'what kind of change approach is appropriate in what kind of context?' We had looked at what tended to be *used* in different contexts (for example the use of Directive change when you didn't have much time). However, we were missing the data that told us what kind of change approach was related to *success* in different contexts. Moreover, our initial data, while offering tantalising glances into the power of the 'Emergent' change approach, did not contain as many stories here as the other change approaches. So we went out to gather more data. Ten more interviews were conducted, which resulted in our working with almost 90 change stories as our total 'units of analysis'.

For each change story, we numerically coded the transcripts for evidence of the change approaches, leader behaviour (more in next chapter), and success or otherwise of the outcome. We then examined the data against seven contexts:

Complexity: was this a change story that just changed a few things, such as re-structuring a sales force (low complexity) or a change story that had many things having to change at the same time, such as new strategy, business model, organisational structure, behaviour, and ways of working (high complexity).

Scope: was this a change story that just impacted a few people in one part of the organisation (low scope) or a change story that impacted many people, and also relied on many people getting committed and involved in order for the change to be successful (high scope).

Magnitude: we had a numerical scale for magnitude which was a multiplier of the above two variables. For example at one extreme there was low complexity and low scope (low magnitude), and at the other extreme there were stories with both high complexity and high scope (high magnitude).

Timescale: did the story require a change in outcomes within just twelve months (short term change), within 18 months (medium term change) or more than eighteen months (long term change).

Source: was the change largely the result of external factors, such as changes in the regulatory environment, or new technological, socio-economic trends (externally driven) or more the result of internal factors, such as new leadership team, change in business ambition and strategy (internally driven).

History of change: was the organisation in the change story well experienced in change (ongoing), or was this the first big change that had happened to the organisation for some time (little history of change)?

Driver: was the change story driven by one key player (individually led change) or was the change initiated and led from a collective source (team led change).

We asked the participating interviewees to rate how successful their change story had been in delivering its intended outcomes. This rating was independently validated, and the data entered into what was now quite a considerable Excel spreadsheet. We then subjected the data to rigorous quantitative analysis in order to identify the strength of the relationship, or correlation, between change approach, context, and success or otherwise of the change outcome. The main findings which emerged from this initial analysis, (which have been validated in subsequent studies), were compelling.

Adopting a change approach that assumes complexity is more likely to bring success than the simplistic approaches

Both the 'Master' and the 'Emergent' change approach were found to have varying degrees of positive relationship to success in all of the above contexts that were coded in the change stories. And in no context did either 'Directive' or 'Self Assembly' change have a relationship to success. The only context where adopting a Directive approach to change was at least neutral, rather than negative, was in low magnitude change that was driven by an internal source. This means that in change which leaders can get their arms around, is within their control, and where not many people are being impacted, then it can be led through using a straightforward and pre-scribed approach to change – 'just do it!'. However, the big relationships we found were in high magnitude change, where in fact the Emergent change approach was the most correlated to success – statistically an extremely large amount of the variation in change success (more than a third) for high magnitude change. This means that the bigger and more complex the change, the less the leader can directly control it.

In order to influence the *conditions* that enable the change to be successful, rather than attempt to directly control its out-comes, a leader therefore needs to avoid the temptation to:

- over-engineer the change process from a central group – but rather engage the intelligence, wisdom and energy of the organisation;

- issue prescribed directives – but rather set out the overall framework and guiding principles behind what needs to be done so that people can get committed rather than compliant;

- predetermine the entire change process – but rather, within an overall sense of the 'journey', work more step by step, sensing and adjusting as they go;

- cascade change programmes and initiatives down through the organisation – but rather bring together diverse and informal networks of people that represent a cross section of the population. In this way the interconnections will already start to change the wider system;

- overly structure formal engagement and communications – but rather create the space for open free flowing dialogue and exchange of information.

The Master change approach is strongly related to success in ongoing, longer term change

The Master change approach made the biggest difference between success and failure in the following contexts: where the organisation had experienced a long history of change; where the environment was still continually volatile and the market and competitive landscape kept shifting; and the outcomes were not needed quickly as in a short term turnaround context. It certainly makes intuitive sense that in situations of ongoing change leaders should build the capability of their organisation to master it.[1]

Given these findings it would suggest that leaders within such contexts need to:

- create a single, overarching framework for the change and establish a clear strategic direction, within which people can make sense of the ongoing nature of change and understand how their work relates to that;

---

[1] A somewhat intriguing finding was that in short term change, the Emergent approach was the most successful out of the four. You might expect Emergent change with its self organising emphasis to be the slowest to generate results, however our research indicated otherwise. Given the correlation was not as strong as the others, however, we have not included this finding in the main text. But worth exploring in future research.

- be careful not to plan the change in too much detail for others; the leader's task is to invest in creating the capability to lead change in others around them – since with such ongoing and constant change (a) no one leader will ever be able to see the whole moving picture and figure out all the answers and (b) they could burn themselves out by trying to cope with all the change themselves;

- draw their authority to steer the change through the overarching framework, which can become a consistent mechanism to monitor and track change progress, act as a compass for the overall change effort, and produce a standard set of metrics that helps the organisation to speak the same performance language and share best practice.

Avoid tool kit 'Self Assembly' change in any scenario

In practically every context that we studied, the use of Self Assembly change was more related to failure than to success. In this approach the 'centre' produces tool kits and programmes that get launched to the organisation. One of the authors once worked within a change process where even 'meetings in a box' were issued to the organisation. The process was aimed to create a unified culture and consistent approach to business across a range of different countries. The meeting in a box was sent to each country head for use in their local markets. It was literally a large white plastic box, or tool kit, that contained a video, a meeting guide for how to enrol your staff behind the vision and values, an employee survey to measure current practice against the vision and values, and a guide on how to interpret and feed back the results to staff. It was followed by the launch of a new performance management process that again arrived through the post from the centre, with glossy manuals and self help guides for the local operating units. Nothing changed beyond the fact that when senior regional management went out to tour the countries the manuals were taken off the shelf and put on work desks, and the employee survey generated reams of statistics and reports that provided intellectual stimulation for the regional organisational development managers.

If leaders wish to implement a change approach that needs a degree of self organisation and differentiation across their organisation, but want to avoid the traps of Self Assembly, our findings would indicate that they should:

- not send out standardised tool kits – but rather build local capability in the workplace, on live assignments, using other experts in the organisation out in the field as guides to build skills relevant to the different contexts

- encourage people to try out new things themselves and enjoy experimenting, within some agreed boundaries and direction

- develop the curiosity to innovate in each community, and not just simply spread out best practices. Using similar templates can be helpful, and developing lateral networks and communities of experts can speed up change, however leaders should always be sensitive to developing a sustainable capability in the local organisation

- design any required tool kit by a cross section of the people who will need to use them. At one of our previous organisations we called this 'field ready'. The centre may set the quality standards for the practice, and then facilitate the process of developing the standardised tool kit, however, end users are engaged in this process such that the tool kit is thoroughly tested in the field before it is launched.

Changing how we change – organisational story

Subsequent to this initial research inquiry we have used the findings extensively in our work with organisational leaders. Our aim is not to prescribe, but to facilitate dialogues within leadership teams about the change challenges they are facing; and to help them make explicit choices about the kind of change approach, or combination of approaches, that will most enable them to reach their objectives. We often see leaders embarking on very significant change journeys for their organisations with clearly mapped out performance goals and desired outcomes. They have made assessments of the current state, and developed strategic plans to close the gap. *Yet it is rare for equal leadership attention to be paid to 'how' the change will be achieved.* Our inquiry has identified that the choice of change approach can be fateful in determining the outcome. A key success factor at the outset of any change journey is to therefore make the choice of approach a conscious and explicit one. This should be followed through with consistency of implementation approach, and the building of necessary leadership skills related to the selected change approach. Here's a story to illustrate how this can be done.

The new Vice President, let's call her Rachel, was in the initial stages of forming her new leadership team. She was facing the challenge of setting up a new global business in an organisation which had previously operated along regional and country lines. As part of this change agenda business processes were to be simplified and standardised. The task of moving customers around the world to one business model was not going to be easy. Her business was highly localised and differentiated. There were many different customer offers and ways of doing business in over 50 different countries, which added to the perceived organisational complexity. She wanted to take the business to a new level, and in so doing re-frame its reputation within the larger organisation of which it was a part as a business that could deliver much more value to the bottom line. She realised that this growth in value could only be created by generating a new spirit within her organisation, by the sharing of ideas across the world, and by making the business far less complex. This required her new leadership team to engage differently with the thousands of staff spread out around the world. How could they globalise and standardise the operation and at the same time create ownership and innovation out in the markets? How could they deliver significantly more value at the level of the whole business, without destroying morale and entrepreneurship in the countries?

Rachel had been on quite a leadership journey herself. She openly admitted to being a natural 'pace setter' leader, always testing herself to reach new heights and expecting that others would follow her trail-blazing path. However over the previous two to three years she had learned to recognise that this only got results to the level of her own competence, which arguably were pretty good; however the approach failed to leverage the total capability of the organisation around her. And the more senior she had become, the more she realised that she could no longer directly control the performance outcomes of her business. She realised that she now needed to step back to create an inspiring vision and story for her organisation, and then leave the space for others to excel and deliver within that. At her first few team meetings the agenda therefore covered as much space for *how* the change was going to be led, as it was for setting a strategic plan for the business.

In relation to the change leadership approach, Rachel commented (from her transcript in our research). 'I probably made it very clear to them that I was up for doing something incredibly scary and out of the ordinary, and I knew that a couple of the leadership team would be positive and supportive of doing that'. Some of her team in their previous business had already seen the power of working with a less Directive and a more Master and Emergent change approach. At this particular meeting the rest of the team were introduced to the different change approaches, and, within the context of the overall drive towards globalisation and standardisation in their organisation, most were pretty sceptical about the chances of being able to move away from more directive approaches. However Rachel stayed persistent. She shared some of our research findings, and inquired of her team, 'given we are facing high magnitude change for this business, can we do this through Directive alone? We are leaders of our own business transformation – as long as we deliver the results, can't we experiment with how we do the change?'

During the course of this conversation Rachel turned to one of us present and asked for an illustrative example; what in practice, would their forthcoming extended leadership team meeting event look like if they adopted either a Master or an Emergent approach? Traditionally, these meetings gave the opportunity for the senior leadership team to sell their vision of the future to the next level of leadership down, and to present the current financial and customer data to get conversation about the current state of the business. They then engaged the extended leadership group to develop action strategies and next steps to move the business forward. The event is usually kicked off by the most senior person present. People are sat at pre-ordained tables to mix up different teams; exercises are tightly controlled and structured with detailed instructions and exercise templates to be completed at the tables. There is often a video shown of the boss's boss who cannot be present at the event, encouraging those gathered to be bold and visionary in their leadership. The event is often facilitated by a professional facilitator, and the leadership team engage the group in open forums such as 'Question and Answer' sessions.

A Master approach was suggested as an alternative to this traditional format. In this approach the change intervention would be seen to start with the design process itself and not the event. A design team would be appointed that represents a cross section of the people who are going to be present at the meeting, in order to get a 'microcosm' of the organisation engaged. This would be done not just to build involvement and ownership. It would be done with the systemic mindset that the dynamics and issues that are being enacted in the wider organisation will start to become apparent in the behaviours of the design team process – for example deferring to hierarchy, or fear of taking risks. A Master approach would seek to explicitly surface these through reflective inquiry within the design team and then seek to change any of the current dynamics that are unhelpful. This would be consciously done with the expectation that the dynamics would then start to change in the organisation around the design team. In a sense, the design team process can become a 'practice field' in how to change the wider culture. The design of the event itself would encourage the taking of leadership responsibility in every person present, not just the senior team. It would have space and time to build the capability to do that. Also in the Master approach, Rachel's leadership team would go into the meeting with a clear framework and story for the change. This would have been tested out with people before the event. Finally, the Master approach would have the senior leadership team facilitating the event, not an external facilitator, and this would not mean that the leader just shows up at the event with a deck of slides to deliver in a particular session. The leader's task would be to both share messages and facilitate the whole group in engaging and interactive dialogue.

We then moved on to consider an Emergent approach to the same event. It was pointed out that in using this approach in its purest form there would be no detailed design for the event at all, just a loose vision for the desired outcome, some design principles, and the right people in the room. The meeting could then take over in a truly self organised manner. To illustrate this approach an event was described at which the leader started the meeting with his closing speech. Everyone thought he was crazy. He then asked for some volunteers from those present to spend the next 45 minutes designing a process for the next two days that would get to the outcomes he'd just delivered in his opening address, while the rest of the 100 people in the room went off to have coffee. Whilst this sounded risky, those present at the event said it was one of the most successful they'd ever been to. This particular event epitomises the inherent belief in an Emergent change approach that 'structure will follow chaos', that human beings are naturally self organising, and that after a bit of messiness, the group will start to move naturally into repeating patterns of organised activity – as long as the leader sets up the right conditions for the event, and the few hard rules about how people should interact. It really is about giving up control.

Another important condition for Emergent change is diversity – it is important to get a representative sample of the whole organisation present, and especially to engage the voices of the people who are closer to the periphery of the organisation. To that end, we pointed out to Rachel's team that they wouldn't even start with the premise that the forthcoming event be just for the next layer of leaders beneath them in the hierarchy. They would go deeper into the organisation and invite people who are closer to the customer, or closer to other interfaces that they have within the wider organisation. And these people would not just show up to the event to be respectful of the hierarchy, the event should be designed to have the space where 'every voice is equal'. We then advised that while the leadership team would front this event, as with the Master approach, there would be space designed at the event for any of the leaders present to step up and volunteer to lead the agenda.

When the team started to talk we sensed that the descriptions had given them a tangible sense of what might be different in the change process as a whole, it had not just helped them picture how they would approach their forthcoming extended leadership team event. Over the course of an hour the team dug deeper into what it was they needed to do. The conversation was a vital one, and it established the course of their entire change journey together. Most powerfully at one point, the leader who had been most vocal about why he thought they could 'never do anything other than Directive change', openly admitted that his resistance to any other approach was actually down to his own fear of moving into unknown territory, and giving up a sense of control. 'So', Rachel inquired, 'what else is this telling us?' There was silence. One person volunteered, 'how can we talk the words about being innovative and taking the business to a new level if we're not able to do those things ourselves?' The dialogue then deepened and moved *from* 'how should the change be implemented?' *to* 'how do we need to change as leaders?' The team had reached the biggest insight of all. . . . that the organisation can't change around them unless they themselves change, because they *are* part of the organisation they are trying to change. It's all connected.

The outcome of this dialogue was that the leadership team consciously chose a Master change approach in order to align the organisation to a global agenda of standardisation. They also chose to seek out relevant opportunities to stimulate

Emergent approaches, recognising that not all could be controlled from the centre, and that they needed to encourage lateral connections and spontaneous informal networks across the globe. Subsequent to this meeting the leadership team launched themselves whole heartedly into implementing these approaches to change, more of which will be shared in subsequent chapters. Suffice it to say that their forthcoming extended leadership team event was a resounding success. The design process involved a good cross section of the business community and engaged people called 'wild cards' who were key business contributors beneath the hierarchical leadership layer – their contribution both to the design process and their attendance at the event itself was a transforming one. Prior to the event, all of the countries were involved in a process to jointly create the vision and story for the new global organisation. When participants walked into the room at the event and saw their contribution posted up all around the walls, enormous excitement and ownership for the change agenda was created; it conveyed a strong message that 'the leadership team are really listening'. The rest of the event was courageously facilitated by the leadership team. They took risks with their own leadership style in front of the group which again conveyed the strong message that they expected others to step up and start leading differently too.

Three years into the business transformation, Rachel was recently asked by us to come and share her story with another of our clients. When asked what her key learning had been from the three years, she replied, 'all the best moments came when we were out of our comfort zone'. Rachel and her team had consciously pushed out their boundaries in how they had led the change. This had required them to take personal risks in front of their organisation, put their toes into hot water, give up personal control, and let others find the answers with them. They became accustomed to a leadership style that clearly framed the required change, yet still allowed space and messiness within that for commitment and ownership to be built. Since these early days the business has consistently delivered on its targets, and indeed surprised their parent organisation with unexpected levels of performance.

Summary

In this chapter we have explored the landscape of change – is it actually changing, and/or is it that our perception of how change occurs has changed. Aided in recent years by the transfer of insights from the study of living systems, we showed how organisational thinking about change has changed. These disciplines show organisational leaders that the world is startlingly complex and dynamic, and that those living systems which are able to stay in perpetual motion have an equal and co-existing balance of the forces for stability, or structure, and the forces for change, or experimentation. By setting up these conditions you can transform the behaviour of a system without having to personally direct and control it.

Within this context we shared our framework of four contrasting change approaches, which are based on different assumptions about how change happens and can be led. Directive change is top down and one look, and assumes that change can be managed. Self Assembly change sends out tool kits for local implementation, and assumes that if you launch enough initiatives, some things will stick. Master change is one look yet assumes complexity in the organisation, and holds the belief that you need to trust and engage the system to bring about change. Emergent change assumes complexity and that change should be self-organised, and therefore the leader can only create the conditions within which change will naturally occur. We shared our research findings into these approaches that show compelling evidence that in high magnitude change, the Master and Emergent approaches (which both assume complexity), are the most successful.

Based on this we hypothesised that the main reason why so many big change efforts fail is because they have overly adopted a Directive or Self Assembly approach. Finally, we shared a story of how a leadership team can work with the change approaches framework to make conscious and explicit choices. This led to insights about themselves and their own leadership which enabled them to implement change in a different way as they engaged the rest of their leadership community in the change effort. It is to the critical variable of leadership behaviour that we now turn.

3

Are leaders leading?

'Lead less, change more'

In the previous chapter we have seen how communities and organisations can stay 'stuck' in repeating patterns of behaviour despite large investments being made to try to change things. The same can be said for leaders and leadership. It is easy to talk about leading change differently while finding yourself walking in the same way you always have done. Sometimes it takes the powers of observation of those around you to help you see the repeating patterns.

It was day four of the 'Leading Business Transformation' workshop. We were working with a group of senior managers who were in the initial stages of a significant change process to move a much localised operation into a global one. The change was going to require many things of the organisation: interdependent working across functional and geographical boundaries; the elimination of multiple, local products and the speedy development and commercialisation of fewer global ones; a mindset change from spending money to earning money; and senior managers being able to think and act as corporate leaders for the enterprise, not just as sponsors for their own specialities and local ideas. Change of this scale and complexity could not be led by the senior executive leadership team alone. They needed the coalition of leaders beneath them, who were critically more in touch with the operations, to be able to lead the effort and implement the new systems and ways of working. This programme was designed to start to develop these skills.

The first three days of the programme had set the stage for the new vision, engaged the leaders in understanding the strategic choices, and begun to build a deeper sense of why the change was necessary. The week's programme was centred on major change projects, for example designing a new global product commissioning process, and creating a more commercial approach to marketing and income generation. Participants had been digging into this work to picture what success would look like, where they were today, and what was needed to close the gap. They had also been introduced to the different approaches to change in order to create implementation plans more likely to work. All this had been accomplished, and yet there still didn't seem to be real movement happening in the room.

In the course of facilitating the event we reflected on what was still needed to be done and how we could facilitate that. The participants appeared to be picking up new frameworks and words about change and leadership, yet we had a strong anticipatory sense that once they left this programme in two days time nothing would change. On the morning of the fourth day we decided that it was time *to help the leaders see how they had been leading in the room there that week*, and, to explore how these practices, *if lived outside of the room in the wider organisation* would negate the change process; far from enabling movement towards the expected new ways of working, their current leadership style could only serve to keep things where they were (remember the missionaries from Chapter 2). We sensed that they were talking the language of change but leading in a way that served no change. We took a risk with the group to share our observations about the behaviours and dynamics which had been noticed over the first three days. When we initiated the intervention people started listening, really listening, and there was silence.

We had seen three particular repeating patterns of behaviour that appeared to be unhelpful for the organisation's change goals. The first we labelled 'tell me, but don't tell me'. The group had been unprepared to take risks and lead until someone had clearly told them what to do. However, when clarity was provided from the 'leader', they said they did not like what they had heard and wanted to be left to do their own thing. These extremes of dependence and independence were not going to facilitate interdependent working in the new global structure. The second dynamic we had seen that week was extreme cynicism, which appeared to stem from the fact that it was culturally acceptable to say one thing at meetings and then say and do something else after the meeting – leading to people not trusting the directives and formal language that came out of meetings. It was causing significant disquiet. Cynicism was a perfectly understandable response to the repeating situation, yet how was this 'stuck' pattern of behaviour going to enable them to be open to new ideas and accept different ways of seeing things? Our final observation was that there appeared to be a complete lack of listening behaviour in the room. During small group exchanges some people even walked away when someone else was speaking. No one seemed to be prepared to really hear what other people were saying, to build on what was being said, and to generate new thinking and ideas that no single individual could have thought of alone. Again, this behaviour had to be serving something in that culture; it wasn't that these people were 'bad' people. Yet how was non-listening leadership going to transform an organisation into one which required 'joined up' working and superb team work across the supply chain? In closing, the group was reminded of the intent behind our intervention – which was to help them succeed. Enough evidence had been seen over the previous three days to indicate that there was the capability and the capacity to make these leadership changes, if they were determined to do so.

The immediate reaction to these observations was complete silence. It felt an important silence, not a threatening or awkward one. Gradually, the participants started to talk, and the talk centred on their own personal leadership. They either owned up to their own behaviour that week, or courageously shared what they had noticed about others' behaviour. When the conversation started to drift towards generalised statements about the organisational culture at large, the group self-regulated and pulled the conversation back to what was happening right there, right then, at that event. What really was this change all about? Was it about producing new mission and vision statements and lengthy papers about the new product development process, or was it actually about their own leadership, and confronting their own behaviour? Were they able, even willing, to change their own leadership practice? What would they be giving up? What were they prepared to risk? The group was invited to take a risk in the remaining two days and adjust their unhelpful behaviour, starting from that point in time. If they could use this learning environment to practice how to lead differently, then they held the potential to transmit that to the organisation from the following week, and in so doing start to change the organisation and the systemic context around them. While people are shaped by their environment, they can also shape that environment. Leaders would be leading.

From that moment on the 'Leading Business Transformation' week ceased being a programme *about* leading change and it became a programme *that was* changing leadership. Five months after that week we were present at a reunion of the programme, designed to share learning and progress. The one hour intervention described above had been for many the most impactful moment of the week. It had forced them to look in the mirror at their own leadership. And it subsequently inspired them to lead quite differently with their teams and in the organisation.

Why the big focus on leadership?

It is generally recognised that leadership matters. Our research findings took this one step further and identified that *what leaders do makes the biggest difference between success and failure in implementing high magnitude change, in fact it accounted for 50 % of the variance. Put another way, if leaders do not reflect on and pay attention to their own leadership behaviour they could reduce their chances of successfully implementing high magnitude change by a half.* That's a big swing factor. Our finding has validated the general awareness of the supposition that 'leadership counts'. It demonstrates that it has a statistically significant relationship to success.

However, simply knowing this statistic does not alone help 'changing leadership'. If leadership behaviour does explain half of success in leading change, what kind of leadership is that? In this chapter we share the initial findings from our research inquiry into the leadership practices that did make the most significant difference in being able to lead and implement change. They provide some important pointers. The relationships we found between leaders' behaviour and success in change were even more statistically significant than those we shared for the change approaches in the previous chapter. And since they were so significant, they led to an additional and deeper level of inquiry into leadership practice that we share in the remaining chapters of the book.

Developing views of leadership

The contextual scene for the subject of leadership is an important back drop to our own inquiry's findings. As with change, people's perceptions of leadership and what leadership is for have been shifting significantly in the last few decades. The literature on leadership is widely seen as vast and confusing.

However, if we consider leadership as a long line of study it could be argued that societies have had an interest in leadership which stretches back over millennia. Considering all issues and views could be the subject of a book (or even several) in its own right. Below we aim to chart the key developments in this debate over the course of the period during which researchers and practitioners have more systematically studied leadership as a significant aspect of organisational behaviour (arguably beginning in the early 1930s).

The purpose of leadership

Thinking about leadership has been dominated for a significant period of time by the view that the purpose of leadership is to *deliver results*. In much of the literature this perspective has been focused on the specific delivery of financial results. During the 1970s a somewhat different view of the purpose began to emerge. This saw, in some cases, a shift from seeing the purpose as delivery of results to that of *effecting a transformation* in the organisation. Books started to be written from this time on by current or former CEOs talking about the story of 'how I transformed x, y, or z company'. In essence, this view saw the purpose of leadership as being to bring about significant change within an organisation, in order to deal with significant changes in the business environment.

Many examples of effective leadership, from the business world, began to lose credibility when 'successful' CEOs left an organisation only to see a significant dip in performance. This, in part, led to a view about the purpose of leadership being concerned with the delivery of sustainable performance.

This view, which began to emerge in the late 1980s, positioned the purpose of leadership as being the *development of capability*. Building individual and organisational capability here is seen as central to the delivery of sustainable organisational performance. Today the thinking about the purpose of leadership is more concerned with an *integration* of the above views. This viewpoint sees leadership as enabling results to be delivered through the development of capability; importantly, the capability to effect change and transformation.

The focus of leadership studies

The focus of leadership studies has shifted notably over the period in two ways. Firstly, our approach to leadership studies has begun to move away from a focus on top leaders, which has traditionally dominated research in this area, to a more distributed view of leadership within an organisation. This has moved the attention away from leadership being purely associated with *position* within an organisation to it being seen to be concerned with the *process* by which anyone who needs to engage followers in the organisation achieves such engagement. In part this shift responds to the critique that leadership studies have been in essence little more than studies of the traits and behaviours of white, male American CEOs.

The second related shift we have seen under this heading is a move from seeing leadership as an *individually centred* phenomenon to being more of a *collective activity*. Hence leadership is now being seen by many as a team game.

Sources of power

In broad terms the relationships between leadership and power have been under-explored in research into leadership. However, it is evident that there have been underlying assumptions made about the source of leadership power. From the early studies of leadership until the 1970s the dominant assumption about power tended to be that a leader's power was derived from their *position* within the organisation. In the course of the 1970s the power base tended to be seen as being less concerned with positional power and more concerned with *personal* power. This tended to be illustrated by a growing focus on the charismatic aspects of leadership. More recently, as organisational life has become more complex, the power of the leader is being seen to be more concerned with the ability to create *connections* within the organisation. This is clearly linked to the development of the view that the purpose of leadership is to build organisational capability.

The nature of effective leadership

It has been suggested that the extensive literature on leadership, and changing schools of thought and models, contain much re-working of earlier concepts. Perhaps the frustration with the inability of leadership research is rooted in a paradigm which suggests that there is a fundamental truth which is yet to be discovered. However, if we shift the lens through which leadership is observed, to one which explores the relevance of earlier work in today's context we may gain new and useful insights. Viewing leadership through this lens suggests a potential change in the measure of leadership effectiveness from hard business results to the impact of leaders on their followers. This view resonates with the view that leadership, in a change context, requires focus on building the capability of people within the organisation to deal with continuing change. Researchers and writers exploring leadership in this way have identified two common strands which are: (i) the focus of study is on what leaders actually do; and (ii) the determinant of effectiveness includes the leader's impact on followers and their subsequent ability to perform.

Having reviewed the development in thinking about the nature of effective leadership and, in particular, having looked at the literature from a 'sense making' rather than discovery perspective, a pattern is beginning to emerge. This pattern shows a shift from a focus on the qualities and characteristics of the leaders – a 'Heroic' leadership framework – to a focus on the process of leadership and how leaders interact with followers to achieve successful outcomes – an 'Engaging' leadership framework. The changing patterns of thinking about leadership outlined above provided us with some prompts for our own inquiry into change leadership behaviours.

Leading change – findings from our research inquiry

What we had not witnessed so far in the leadership debate was any systematic research into the relationship between leadership practices, differing approaches to change, and success in bringing about change. While the general trend in thinking appeared to be away from 'leader as charismatic hero', to, 'leader creating great organisations', we wanted to examine the validity of this assertion and beyond that to uncover the concrete leader practices that made the difference. We have described in the previous chapter our research methodology that involved the grounded use and detailed coding of semi-structured interviews eliciting actual stories of change and specific leader behaviours within that. We subjected the transcripts to both quantitative and qualitative analysis. After review of an initial sample of transcripts, we identified nine different leadership practices that the interviewees were repeatedly adopting to implement change. These became our coding framework for all 90 change stories. Just as we had coded each change story for evidence of the four change approaches, so we coded each sample of concrete behavioural data into these nine different leader practices. When we conducted a quantitative factor analysis of these different practices they grouped into three overarching clusters, which we called:

- Shaping

- Framing

- Creating Capacity

These three factors, which had originated from stories of leaders in the field, not our theoretical conjectures, became instrumental in helping leaders to learn to lead change differently and more successfully.

Just as each change story had contained elements of more than one of the four change approaches, so did individual leaders exhibit behaviours from across all these three factors. However, for the purposes of illustration, we will describe them separately and add illustrative quotations from our original inquiry.

Shaping leadership

Leaders who displayed Shaping behaviour were characterised by the following set of practices.

Likes to be the 'mover and shaker'

The Shaping leader is very personally present throughout the change effort. They make themselves visible. They tend to be vocal at key meetings and engagement events, firmly placing their vision for the change and what has to be done into all interactions. They use communications to clearly lay out their personal sense of what's needed. They are often described as a change 'champion', and deliberately adopt behaviours that will catalyse disturbance and change. They take every opportunity to be out and about mobilising the organisation.

I wanted to make sure my club got the best possible deal and I put my body across the line on this one at every opportunity.

Sets the pace for others to follow

The Shaping leader's vision of what has to be done determines what people do and when. They are very clear on milestones, targeted achievements, and the importance of maintaining urgency and momentum. More often than not they will have figured out the change plan in advance of others, even detailing what others need to do in the next 30–60–90 days. They bring their experiences of change that they personally led in other contexts into new ones. They tend not to make explicit the behaviour required, since they believe people are more likely to follow their own behaviour than their words.

Just do it!

Expects others to do what they do

Shaping leaders will try to shape the behaviour of others. They will overtly demonstrate new behaviours and experiment with different, counter cultural ways of doing things in front of others and reward those who follow their example. There is strong implied encouragement to others to take risks and do things differently – along the lines of the new behaviours and practices they are modelling.

I think everyone's aware of it, I have given them, I have shared with them my personal route map for coping with this and most people seem to embrace that so I shall put that down to a bit of leadership.

Is personally persuasive and expressive

Leaders who demonstrate shaping behaviour have clear views and theories about how successful change happens and they use these reference points to influence what has to be done.

They plan for people resisting or rejecting change and express strong feelings and enthusiasms for certain ideas and courses of action in order to influence people to get on board. They tend to use all interactions with others to advocate their change vision. The interactions and style of engagement are closely centred on them as the leader.

It was a matter of trying to influence relationships and get people to do it as opposed to this is a corporate initiative.

Holds others accountable for delivering tasks

This set of behaviours is about the actions taken to direct or measure the performance of others in the change process, such as agreeing outcomes or deliverables with an individual and measuring the progress or impact of change. There is a strong focus on getting complete clarity as to who needs to do what and then ensuring that people know how their actions will be tracked and regulated.

I think it was very important along the journey for both myself and the management team to keep our finger very closely on the pulse of the key milestones and the key performance indicators of how our business was running. We did this on a regular basis.

Personally controls what gets done

Activity and performance tends to be monitored by the leader themselves. They display close personal attention to who is doing what and then intervene to make adjustments if they feel it's necessary. They consider how an individual might react to their intervention or the change and based on this adjust their approach to them and if necessary take action to support them in order to get the task accomplished.

I thought I had everything sorted, I communicated it, and I had plans all over the place.

The predominant assumption behind this group of Shaping behaviours is, 'without me, nothing will happen'. It is the most leader-centric of the three leadership factors. The leader will bring attention to themselves as an individual. Whether conscious ('I need to get others moving in my direction') or unconscious (e.g. the leader is unaware of a strong need for personal affirmation), it is primarily personal needs that drive their behaviour.

Shaping leadership in action

We once worked with a leader who was heading up a major change process to move a localised and independent country based organisation to an organisation run along regional business lines. At the same time, market research showed that the organisation had to get much closer to its customers. We will call the Vice President Paul. He is a good example of some of the Shaping leadership practices we have just described.

Paul was a very charismatic and gifted individual who cared deeply about his work and how it should be accomplished. He regularly assembled his newly established leadership team to plan the change. People were in awe of him; his insights and powers of analysis into people, organisational and business issues were second to none. He had just completed another assignment in a different region where he had been introduced to quite radical change management methodologies, which he brought into this change process and it kick started a whole new way of leading and implementing change in the organisation. It created an entirely new language, and Paul was an expert in role modelling these behaviours and techniques to others. The approach often took people into very open and confronting conversations with each other. Members of his leadership team would come up to one of us who was acting as a change coach to the team and ask, 'how can I become more like Paul? He's so good!' Or, 'do you think I really have to behave in the way that Paul behaves and expects us to?' Others in the organisation who were not part of Paul's circle, or had not engaged with him, felt a bit left out, 'what's this new language developing over there and what's all this crazy behaviour?! How does it all connect?'

Another notable feature of Paul's leadership was how he got out and about into the organisation, and he especially focussed his presence out in the operations at the 'front line' of the organisation. When he was out at these locations he would personally role model customer-oriented behaviours, get kitted out in the uniforms of staff serving the customer, and spend a day personally and visibly championing how the organisation needed to behave differently. It was mesmerising, and word would spread round the organisation about what he was doing and where he was going to go next. It created a spirit and a momentum, and people were keen to follow him around. Very soon the change process started to be known as 'Paul's change process', it became strongly associated with his name, a legacy which continues to this day.

Framing leadership

Leaders who displayed Framing behaviour were characterised by the following set of practices.

Helps others see why things need changing and why there's no going back

Leaders who frame spend their time considering the sources or origins of the need for change – whether internal or external to the organisation or both – and they then help to draw these critical starting points to the attention of others. They access benchmarking data, pay close attention to what's being said and done around the organisation, and share these patterns and signs as data, or a 'mirror', to the organisation that help to raise people's awareness of the need to change. Their starting points are therefore drawn from data in the wider system, not their personal theory or opinion.

The rate of change is being driven by customer expectations growing at a far faster rate which of course is driving the organisation to adapt much faster so one of the important pieces I set up was having people who have got antennae which reach out into the market place to sense and listen, distil that information, bring it back in and use it constructively to adapt the organisation to move on.

Works with others to create a vision and direction

Leaders who frame typically determine the 'corner jigsaw pieces' of a vision, in other words the essential parts that need to be present to make sense of everything else, and then work with their leadership team and the wider organisation to work out the 'jigsaw edges', and then how to complete the picture. The corner pieces they set out are typically the broad sense of direction or vision for the future, any key performance expectations, and the guiding principles behind the change; in other words not just what needs to be accomplished but also a sense of how things should get done to determine success. They then hold this frame consistently throughout the change effort – it lives beyond themselves as leaders.

I see my role as a leader as not to provide the detailed answers but to provide a framework and context for people to make sense of the world.

Shares overall plan of what needs to be done

This set of behaviours relates to how a leader sets out the broad course, or phases, of the change to help the organisation navigate the journey. It is not micro management, but rather like setting out the chapter headings of a book. The framing leader will outline the broad phases of what has to be done to help give a sense of the forthcoming agenda and its key milestones. They also provide a sense of what the journey is going to feel like at different stages, in order to manage emotional and behavioural expectations. While not micro managing, the leaders we studied did put in place sound project management processes to steer the change. In framing leadership the agreed and widely disseminated journey guides people on what has to be done, not the leader personally checking up on things.

It was broken down into dates and time lines, so by this time we will have done this and by this time we will have done that and the work, the enormous change was broken down into seven chunks and this was the initial presentation to all the troops. This is a journey that we are going to go on, the detail will follow.

Gives people space to do what needs to happen, within the business goals

Once the case, vision, principles and plan have been established, the framing leader steps back to enable others to take ownership and accountability for implementing the change. They would do this either through formal project teams and the current organisational structure, or through encouraging volunteers, task forces, and the informal organisation to take initiative. They encourage the organisation around them to take on the change and do not feel they have to be personally present in order to get things going.

In order to do this we created a wider body, the extended management team which was around 25 of our departmental and functional group leaders. Each of those people had a role, a very clear role, in order to lead the transformation forward and make sure that it really lived in our business. So the people who were doing the majority of the work could actually see where their piece fitted and what they were doing, how it met the end game of where we were trying to get.

Seeks to change how things get done, not just what gets done

Finally, the framing leaders in our study paid close attention to the organisational behaviours and culture. Their thoughts, observations, and analysis of these factors influence how they lead the change – what needs to be done, at what kind of pace, in what kind of way. They do not just use these insights as private observations but seek to bring the cultural dynamics to the attention of others in order to encourage new ways of working. Their attention to changing ways of working is strongly focussed on the work that has to be done, rather than launching separate and unrelated programmes about changing behaviour.

The guy who was leading the change had a very adept understanding of where we were in terms of culture and where we needed to be in order to live the change that was needed. And he believed that by getting people involved in that process, by giving them the tools to do it themselves, was the way to move the culture from where it was to where it needed to be.

The predominant assumption behind this group of Framing behaviours is, 'with clear boundaries, people can be free to contribute'. The Framing leader acts as a firm yet guiding 'architect' behind the change process. They first work to create a design and some essential rules, build understanding for that, and then let others construct the building.

Framing leadership in action

David had been appointed to lead a major turnaround in a global business. He inherited an overstretched organisation that was chronically underperforming, and yet the tensions and shortfalls in plan were unable to be openly confronted. And the very fact that they could not be confronted was also unable to be confronted. Suddenly a few major visible events in the market place burst the bubble and the reality of the underperformance became clear. David stepped in to take command. He knew he had to act quickly to restore market and investor confidence. Yet he knew that fundamental change can take time. How was he to pull off this turnaround in a way that created whole hearted organisational commitment to a completely different way of running the business? This could not become a 'quick fix'; it had to produce a sustainable, longer term business.

In the first two weeks David met several times with his top leadership team to get the collective facts of the poor performance scrutinised and understood. He made it safe for people to talk, and asked a few simple straight questions to everyone over and over again. The starting points for change were clearly established. The team also developed a few hardnosed 'non-negotiables' relating to how the business should be run in the future, and these were expressed as a set of 'from – to' statements, in other words, concrete definitions of today's reality and actionable descriptions of a different future for the business. These statements covered both the 'what', i.e. the business strategy, and the 'how', i.e. the operating philosophy and behaviours, that needed to change. The corners of the jigsaw were clearly established. David then convened a meeting of his top 100 leaders. In the week prior to the conference the finance people were advising him to open with the hard hitting facts about the underperformance and his personal theory of what had to happen. David decided not to do that. While reality had to be confronted, he wanted to do it in a way that did not have him placed as the 'guy beating us over the head'. He needed his organisation alongside, not getting defensive, owning the problem with him, and not becoming dependent on him to figure out how to get out of the crisis.

He opened the meeting with a metaphor, a metaphor from a well known children's tale that told the story of the three little pigs and the big bad wolf. The attempts of the wolf to destroy the construction of the pigs' house provided a simple metaphor that encapsulated the essence of what had to change in the organisation. The big bad competitor had found it very easy to destroy the rapid expansion of a business built on a flimsy operating platform. Needed now was not quick new market entries but rather a more concerted and disciplined effort to grow the business, building operational excellence brick by brick. The moment in which David shared the metaphor became the single biggest memory people had of that meeting (it even lingers in the minds of people today), and it influenced what people did back in their operations to turn around the company. The powerful metaphor was aided by the set of 'from – to' statements, against which the whole two year change process was tracked and measured. The metaphor and the statements guided people in nearly 60 countries around the world to implement a fundamental organisational re-design. They helped influence the needed change in mindset and behaviour, and they guided how essential work processes had to change. In summary, the change process was framed and catalysed by a vivid, relevant, and enduring metaphor, combined with some strong guiding and enduring statements. It had not been catalysed by the personality of the leader.

Creating Capacity leadership

Leaders who displayed Creating Capacity leadership were characterised by the following set of behaviours.

Develops people's skills in implementing change

Creating Capacity leaders spend time helping others to learn; and not just learning about a new system or technical skill, they focus on helping people learn how to master change and transition, both for themselves and the organisation at large. Leaders in our study who were seen as being strong on creating capacity acknowledged that high magnitude change creates extraordinary demands, and they invest time, money and effort in equipping both the organisation and the people within it to deliver change. They consciously plan which different groups of people require different kinds of change skills, and target development interventions accordingly.

I spent all of my time in the subsequent 18 months focusing on people capability, communication abilities, the emotional side of the change so I was working with the management team on a monthly basis, then the extended management team and then really with groups out from there really testing and sensing how this whole people, communication, change piece was playing out.

Lets people know how they are doing and coaches them to improve

This category is about the time and effort leaders put into feedback and coaching – both with key individuals and their teams. Practices included setting aside dedicated and ongoing one-on-one time with members of their team – working through not just *what* their team member is accomplishing but also *how* it is being accomplished. The Creating Capacity leader knows that these two elements are related and therefore seeks to accomplish greater performance improvement by building people's capability to approach the task differently.

I spent an awful lot of time with X, essentially trying to coach on what the appropriate leadership style was for where we are in this change process, how do you adjust that, how might it shift with different audiences.

Gets people to work across organisational boundaries and along key processes

A Creating Capacity leader spends time engaging the organisation in processes to map out how critical work gets accomplished, so that operational excellence is improved and greater value created. Such interventions in themselves enable different organisational groupings to get together and improve how they connect with each other across organisational boundaries. Practices include: creating formal teams; informal alliances and networks to support change; holding large group gatherings at which a cross section of the organisation gets together to figure out how to transform how they create value together; and implementing information sharing and best practice exchange processes that built greater collective wisdom about performance and the capability to improve it.

I set up a sort of learning set where we maybe have a dozen people who are interested in applying the methodologies and apply change in their own departments . . . we had a whole day with heads of departments doing process mapping . . . you could see the light switch on and they went to pull together some of those leaders and it gave them an ongoing support network.

Makes sure the organisation's processes and systems support the change

This set of practices is about leaders taking action to reconfigure processes and systems that in their current state are proving unhelpful to the change. The current processes could be holding up the free flow exchange of information to those that need it, or they could be encouraging behaviours that reinforce a steady state scenario. In this respect Creating Capacity leaders know that reaching improved performance outcomes is not just about developing the skills and behaviours of their employees, but also changing the underlying systems and structures that create the behaviours in the first place.

When I arrived I saw the current issues in the business but looked deeper and deeper to see what the real infrastructure issues were sitting under that in terms of the hardware and how that was operating but as importantly the organisational infrastructure and mind set and how is that really working.

The predominant assumption of a Creating Capacity leader is, 'we cannot change unless we learn and grow'. Big change in particular requires the creation of new capabilities and structures if improved performance outcomes are to be sustainable.

Creating Capacity leadership in action

We return to Rachel from Chapter 2. She was the leader creating a new global organisation. Her leadership team had decided to go with the Master change approach, supplemented by harnessing the Emergent change processes naturally occurring in the organisation. She realised that she was going to have to help her team to learn to lead change differently, *and* it was going to need the organisation at large to become more capable of implementing change. The strategic change of direction towards standardisation and simplification would require some businesses to close, some to expand into other regions, and some to be re-positioned with the customer. This agenda could not be controlled centrally from her global leadership team – it required excellent change leadership skills in the local operations. Moreover, as the business was globalised, 'silos' had been created within the organisation that had created divides across key lateral interfaces. Making this new structure work was going to require a change in mindset and behaviour.

Rachel did a number of things to create the capacity of her organisation to change. Firstly, she invested in developing herself and her leadership team. One of us helped as a 'team coach' in the initial two years to build the ability of the leadership team to experiment with new behaviours and change approaches. They learned to direct and control less and create more unstructured space for the organisation to lead and own the change with them. At the same time the team realised they had to develop more 'edge' in their leadership in order to challenge and improve performance, both as peers and with their teams. The team implemented a peer coaching process. At each two monthly team meeting time was dedicated to the team giving live feedback to one of their colleagues about their leadership and how they thought it could be improved. This was a challenging yet very powerful process, especially when the team leader herself took the seat – it not only helped the individual leader to improve how they were leading the change in their business, it also had a deep impact on building trust, honesty and openness in the top team itself. Not surprisingly, this impact was felt in the wider organisation. Rachel was not developing her team for the team's sake.

She encouraged her team members to take the change leadership insights and tools they were using within her team to their local business teams in order to build wider capability to implement change effectively. This started to have a discernible impact on local business outcomes. In addition, Rachel and her leadership team encouraged the use of lateral networks of leaders across the different countries to tackle shared business challenges together. One globally networked team alone delivered tens of millions of dollar savings on margin optimisation in the course of one year. These lateral connections could not have been developed so successfully unless her top leadership team had invested in the development of their 'extended leadership team', a large coalition of around 90 leaders who met once a year. The design and processes used at these events had set the foundation for global trust, mutual support and shared business insight. Stakeholders from interfacing organisations were invited to these events, which helped to transform the ongoing relationship between Rachel's organisation and the interfacing businesses in getting the work accomplished.

More recently, Rachel has invested time visiting her local markets and spending one-on-one time with each of her extended leadership team members. She asks to see each of their development plans and coaches them on how to transform their business by transforming how they as leaders approach their business.

Shaping, Framing, and Creating Capacity leadership – what works?

We analysed our research data to find out how these three leadership factors related to successful change outcomes in different contexts. The findings here were compelling, and the correlations with change success even stronger than those we had found for the relationship with change approaches. The main messages are as follows.

Leadership behaviours that centre on the position, role and power of the leader and their abilities – in other words the Shaping leadership factor – do not appear to be related to successful change. Indeed, such behaviours are related to change failure

Our research found that Shaping leadership behaviours were ineffective in supporting successful change, *and in particular high magnitude change, where shaping leadership accounted for over half of the reason why these change efforts fail.* It certainly made sense to us that in situations where the change is highly complex, requiring the whole organisational system to transform, that a leader-centric approach to change will not succeed. The change effort would become too associated with the individual leader, and not guided by a broader vision which can capture the 'heads, hearts, and hands' of many. Shaping leadership tends to develop a leader dependency – when the leader is not there, or the leader moves on to a new role or their priorities change, it is highly likely that the change effort will stall or fizzle out all together. It is not sustainable. Leader-centric behaviour therefore does not work in high magnitude change.

We found negative relationships between Shaping leadership and other contexts. In change that is longer term, in other words requiring results to be built up sustainably over time, Shaping leadership was linked to the failure of change efforts. The same negative relationship existed in change which has an external source. A leadership approach driven by personal presence and force of persuasion alone is unable to tune into the wider environmental issues that require the organisation's attention.

In our qualitative analysis of the research transcripts, we found evidence that leaders who adopt Shaping behaviour are more likely to reinforce the existing context than transform it. Their practice does little to engage people to figure out *for themselves* the essence of the change, and while their persuasive power was found to impact on others, it felt more like influence *over* people rather than influence *through* people. They tended to create factions who either supported them in the change, or who resisted their effort. The change became personalised, it lacked the call to a wider and higher purpose that would have created collective spirit and ownership.

Framing leadership alone accounts for over half the reason why high magnitude change succeeds

The correlations between leaders who can frame, and the success of their efforts in implementing high magnitude change, were some of the highest in our entire research inquiry. Moreover the leadership factor of Framing was strongly related to success across most contexts. This would suggest that organisational change benefits from leaders who can create collective sense and meaning for a change effort, drawing from the signs they see around them about what needs to change and what might be. It is a guiding, rather than controlling style. *Fundamentally, they are acting to create power and purpose in the organisation around them, rather than draw power and benefit to themselves.* As part of our inquiry we looked up the meaning of the verb 'to frame'. It is derived from an Old English word, 'framian', which means 'to act in service of'. A picture frame acts in service of the picture – it gives it meaning, dimension, and perspective. A Framing leader does just the same thing for the organisation – they are there to serve a collective purpose that goes beyond their personal needs.

Much literature has emphasised the importance of a leader's ability to 'make sense', or create meaning in the organisation for the situation in which people find themselves. And this becomes more important in major change where uncertainty and ambiguity is high. Uncertainty can disable people and impact their ability to engage whole heartedly in the work, leading to distraction and performance slippage. Our qualitative analysis of the transcripts showed that leaders who could create meaning in their organisation developed an overarching frame, or picture, for the change effort that acted as an enduring and compelling call to arms. The starting points for change flowed from collectively held beliefs and facts about the environment, not personal theory or per-suasion alone, and when the leader created clarity for the change journey and its major milestones, the change process became actionable. People could see what they had to do within the context of the frame. The change journey provided a navigating map.

This wasn't a warm fuzzy strategy about a turnaround. It ended up being a very hard nosed and specific strategy with 10 work packages.

I made these 10 things all that there was in the business. If you weren't doing one of these 10 things then you shouldn't have been doing anything.

When we looked at the relationship between leadership practice and the four change approaches, we found that Framing leadership was the most dominantly used style in the Master change approach. Given that the Master change approach seeks to establish a clear unifying direction and set of boundaries, and then create space for the organisation to get engaged with the change, the relationship to Framing made sense.

In short term change Framing leadership is the most effective leadership practice

While Shaping leadership was the most used style in change stories where quick results were required, it was Framing leadership that explained most of the success in this context. The temptation is clearly to take strong personal charge, yet it was the adoption of leadership behaviours concerned with guiding and enabling others that was more likely to achieve the change goals. In particular, we found that the Framing practice associated with establishing the starting points for change created urgency and impetus for the change effort. In David's story above there were only six weeks between the new leadership team being established and the implementation of a completely redesigned organisation.

Creating a sense of the case for change helps if it's urgent. The more audacious the goal the harder people will run.

In longer term change, and where the change is ongoing, Creating Capacity leadership is related to success

In our research this set of leadership practices alone accounted for 45% of the variance between success and failure in ongoing change. It makes intuitive sense that in times of constant change, leaders had better build the capacity to implement it as a core competence. When we looked at the relationship between leadership practice and the four change approaches, we found a strong correlation between Creating Capacity and Emergent change. They share characteristics such as the establishment of organisational networks, the building of lateral connections across critical organisational boundaries, and an emphasis on working on the underlying organisational structures, rather than directly controlling the behaviour of others. As leaders become more senior the less able they are to directly control performance outcomes; the task becomes one of creating capability in the organisation around them to deliver.

My role was to listen, sense, coach and guide. I did not make business decisions. One of the fascinating things about all of this is that frankly I controlled nothing.

In ongoing change, this task is never over. Creating Capacity is not simply about restructuring the organisation, and then launching a few development programmes in the hope that things will change. It's about the constant paying of attention to what's going on around the organisation, noticing energy breakthroughs, addressing where the organisation or people seem to be 'stuck', and helping people to take risks in change to break any stuck behaviour.

What about culture?

During the research debriefs throughout our inquiry, participants were asking us questions about corporate culture, its relationship to successful change, and the connection between corporate culture and the style in which leaders in different cultures were more or less likely to be successful. For example, were autocratic cultures more likely to develop Shaping leadership, how would Creating Capacity leadership work in cultures that emphasised results above learning? And what change leadership style would work best in what kind of culture? We decided to investigate this subject further.

In order to explore the relationship between organisational culture and change leadership it is necessary to be clear as to what is meant by organisational culture. This is an area of considerable debate and a voluminous literature. Whilst it is beyond the scope of this chapter to explore this vast literature it is necessary to establish a frame for considering organisational culture. There are numerous definitions of culture that have been produced over the years. In searching for an appropriate definition we found the frequently used colloquial description of culture as '*the ways in which things are done around here*', and, as a form of *social glue* that holds a group of people together, to be the most helpful.

The difficulty in pinning down the nature of culture has led to challenges in finding ways of assessing or measuring an organisation's culture. Although many different approaches are adopted a framework developed by Rob Goffee and Gareth Jones which has been widely used in practice seemed appropriate for our research. In this framework they use two dimensions to describe the way human beings form groups and how they relate to each other: *sociability*; and *solidarity*. They define Sociability as: *'a measure of friendliness among members of a community'*. This measure considers how people relate to each other. High levels of sociability are likely amongst people who share similar ideas, values, personal histories, attitudes and interests. Solidarity is defined as being: *'based on common tasks, mutual interests, and clearly understood shared goals that benefit all the involved parties'*. This measure considers a community's ability to pursue shared objectives quickly and effectively, regardless of personal ties.

Goffee and Jones do not claim that there are 'right' or 'wrong' cultures and most organisations are characterised by several cultures which coexist and which can change over time based on their life cycle. However certain kinds of cultures may be more or less appropriate for different business contexts. The latter point begins to establish a relationship between change and culture. There is broad agreement that organisational culture has a major impact on the ability to implement change effectively. While our sample using the Goffee and Jones instrument was too small to draw typological conclusions, we did find some significant findings at the level of the two overall dimensions they employed.

The dimension of Solidarity shows strong links to change success across most contexts. This would suggest that for change to be implemented successfully there is a need to build a culture focussed on a clear and shared sense of the organisation's key goals and tasks. When faced with significant change, a focus on the 'friendliness' of an organisation is not enough to build success. So how can leaders build a culture of 'solidarity'? We discovered that our Framing leadership factor was strongly linked to the cultural dimension of Solidarity. Combined, they accounted for over a third of the variance between success and failure across most change contexts. The findings suggest that Framing behaviours such as establishing the starting points, clarifying the change journey and milestones, and setting and using clear values to underpin the change process can contribute to a Solidarity culture where there is urgency for change, clear goal and task alignment, and a desire to continually improve performance. We also found that Shaping leadership practice is negatively related to the cultural dimension of Solidarity. This was further confirming evidence that Shaping leadership does little to build the alignment of an organisation to implementing significant change.

Summary

In this chapter we have added confirming data to the general recognition that 'leadership matters' when implementing change. It accounts for half the reason why high magnitude change either succeeds or fails. In this respect, leaders would be advised to pay as much attention to their own behaviour and practice as they do to planning the change for the organisation 'out there'. If leader behaviour is such an important aspect of implementing successful change, then what kind of behaviour makes the difference?

We have explored the changing perceptions of the role of leadership and the general recognition that the charismatic heroic leader does not necessarily create sustained greatness in an organisation. Rather, the more humble, modest, and enabling leaders are better placed to create an organisation that day by day moves an organisation towards its future. These kinds of leaders give others the freedom and space to excel, though within a highly disciplined framework. They inspire people through standards of excellence rather than charisma. They seek power through people and not over people.

Our own research inquiry has validated this growing perception. It has statistically proven that leaders who adopt what we call a Framing leadership style are much more likely to be successful in the implementation of big complex change. They work *with* the organisation to help people see why change is necessary, they establish a firm overall direction, a set of guiding principles, and a high level sense of agenda and journey for the change process, and then leave space for people to get on with it.

We have contrasted this approach with the Shaping leadership style which was strongly negatively related to success in implementing big change. This style, which is very leader-centric, tends to either create dependency in the organisation on the individual leader or indeed create factions who want to resist the leader. It can lead to bursts of energy and momentum, however ultimately leads to patchy and half hearted implementation. The change is associated with the leader, it is not owned by the organisation. The higher the magnitude of change therefore, the less your personal style and effort makes a difference, and the more your framing ability will lead to success.

Organisations that are faced with ongoing change benefit from leaders who adopt a Creating Capacity leadership approach. This is about building the capability of people in the organisation to lead and implement change, creating rich networks in the organisation that facilitate innovation and movement, and adjusting the underlying organisational structures and processes to enable faster movement towards the change goal. Leaders who use this style recognise that their task is to build the capability of the organisational system (i.e. talent, structure, energy, innovation processes) to generate the performance outcomes rather than directly control the performance outcomes themselves.

Finally, we have discovered that a high Solidarity organisational culture is related to successful implementation of change, and that Framing leadership helps create the clear goal and task alignment associated with this dimension of culture. Leaders aiming to implement successful change do not need to pay attention to the Sociability dimension, or friendliness of the culture. While this might create a happy working environment, it's more important to create pride and confidence in meaningful work directed towards a shared endeavour.

4

Changing leadership – a framework

'Never confuse movement with action'

Hemingway

We continued our quest to discover what it was that leaders did to move an organisation to a different place. Many leaders attempt to implement change by creating a lot of new action in their organisations. However we could see that more activity by itself did not guarantee that an organisation would break out of its cycles of repeating patterns, or habitual routines. People can just get busier. Initiatives, work streams, programmes and events create a lot of noise and apparent 'change' and make senior executives feel that 'things are happening'. Yet deep down, the organisation, while in motion, can feel just the same. New words and language enter the organisation without the work changing. People's behaviour looks eerily familiar. And the organisation's customers and partners still experience the organisation in exactly the same way – perhaps just a little more stressed. For some reason, certain change initiatives expend an enormous amount of effort for very little return.

Insights were emerging from our initial research inquiry as to why that might be the case. Certainly the choice of change approach made a difference. However the most compelling finding was that *what a leader does makes the biggest difference to successful change, not what they say or plan.* One of the factors we studied in the stories was the leader's personal theory about how change should happen. And yet this theorising leadership style made absolutely no difference to the outcome. There was little correlation between a leader's theoretical understanding about change and whether or not they were then successful in implementing it. It was what they chose to do that made all the difference. To be successful in change implementation, leaders therefore have to pay acute attention to their own style and practice. And yet we frequently observe that the more senior leaders become in their organisations, the more that attention is paid to the quality of their thinking and the rigour of their planning – not to the quality of their behaviour and what they do. We are not saying that thinking and planning are not important. We are saying that leaders should pay equal attention to *how* they go about their work – how they engage with others, how they set up meetings, how they have conversations, how they create meaning in the organisation for the change process – in order for any change to be successful. This requires leaders to have a heightened awareness of the dynamics in the organisation and why it might be 'stuck' in repeating patterns; the self awareness and humility to recognise that certain elements of their own leadership practice has created that; and the courage to then act on this insight and adapt their behaviour in order for the organisation around them to change. For when a leader's behaviour moves, it can have a wonderfully surprising impact on moving the wider system around them.

Another related theme we were noticing in our inquiry was that *the successful leadership of change seemed to be about leading in the moment.* The power of the present was all important. The leader needed to pay constant attention to clues in the current environment – for example how people were reacting to the change, who was showing up to what type of meetings, what kind of emails were being written (and not written), what range of emotions were being expressed or avoided – and then take action based on these clues. Leaders who exhibited strong Shaping style behaviour appeared to let their own personal needs and agenda dominate how they took action. It created 'situational blindness'. Whereas leaders who could Frame and Create Capacity, and who did not need to impose their personal agendas, were more able to tune in to the wider system and could therefore tap into and influence its energy. The close paying of attention to the present included an awareness of the power of process. People's mindsets and behaviour are influenced by how the present moment is structured – for example the diversity of people present in a conversation, the degree of interaction available to deal with the ambiguity of a changing agenda, the physical space in which people meet, how the organisational hierarchy is represented in a conversation, and how information is displayed as people talk.

So, creating movement to get to a different place is about changing the way in which things happen, it is not simply about generating more action to make people busy. It's about working on the deeper processes that structure behaviour in order to create new results. And what leaders do personally to enable this shift in process seems to be important; yet the senior leaders we were working with could not always be physically present around their organisations to make this happen, the scope of their roles was too large. Moreover, the change effort was going to live or die based on their ability to create committed leadership throughout their organisation – the change could not rely on their efforts alone. We became more and more curious about the question of how senior leaders can generate large scale transformation in a way that creates sustainable conditions for the organisation to keep moving in a self organised fashion, without the leader having to heroically carry the load.

We knew, from our research findings into change approaches, that leaders who assume that change is complex and can not be simplistically directed or controlled are more likely to have successful implementation. So what kind of leader behaviour can move 'complex systems'? The risk of working with complexity (or assuming that the world is non-linear, comprised of multiple interacting parts, and yet related in one connecting system), is that you can make things complicated. Complicated systems are rich in detail, which you can easily get bogged down in. Complex systems are rich in structure, which when mapped can be startlingly simple. At its most straightforward, the study of complexity is the study of the dynamics of the diverse linkages and interactions among people, technology and systems over time. This dynamic approach conceptualises organisational systems as sets of agents, or individuals, processes and mechanisms that generate novel and emergent outcomes from the interaction of the agents. We knew that a Shaping leadership style did not generate novel and emergent outcomes. A combination of this leader-centric behaviour, and a mechanistic change approach, seemed to generate a 'stuck' organisation, not a healthy adaptive one. When individuals take charge, others around them stay frozen. They abdicate their own responsibility for making change happen and put that onto the Shaping leader.

We now knew that the two factors of Framing and Creating Capacity leadership were producing different outcomes. They were leading to movement and successful change. They had given us some important clues. And yet we wanted to move beyond working with two separate factors and a list of behaviours. In using them with practicing leaders we began to develop curiosity around a set of questions that were to give shape to the next stage of our inquiry.

- What are the interrelationships between Framing and Creating Capacity leadership?

- Can we develop an emerging vision of a more integrative model for leading ongoing change?

- What is it that leaders can do to keep their organisation in a state of perpetual motion and novelty?

- Can we develop a framework for leading change that could embrace both the leader's behaviour and what needed to happen in the organisational system?

- In summary, could we create a practical yet theoretically robust framework that gave leaders choices and options for leading change and which would free them from the burden of carrying the entire load?

The rest of this chapter shares the story and outcomes of our latest round of research and inquiry. This time we focussed solely on the leadership practices associated with successful change – what is it that leaders actually do – rather than examine further the more general change approaches that organisations adopt. We were going to dig deeper into how such practices contributed to change success.

Working more deeply with Framing and Creating Capacity leadership

Before we undertook any more field research, we developed an emerging set of leadership practices for combining the two factors of Framing and Creating Capacity. We did this in a variety of ways. We returned to the original research transcripts of successful change outcomes and interrogated them further. What did we see the leaders doing in these stories? Secondly, we drew on our combined experience over the years of working in large transformation efforts with change leaders we would have called 'world class'. What is it we recalled them doing that set them apart from the rest? We also dug deeper into the latest academic thinking – not just in the field of leadership, but also related theoretical fields that shed light on the dynamics of how systems can either get 'stuck', or can advance, such as the field of group dynamics, positive psychology, complexity theory and once again the study of 'living systems' in the world around us. Finally, we continued to test the emerging framework with practising leaders in our ongoing client work, finding out what was helpful, what made sense, and what was real for them.

Based on this exploration we developed eight leadership practices for change. As we examined these eight practices we started to see that four of them were standard and necessary aspects of leading change, while the other four seemed to be more distinguishing. They appeared to be more distinct and intense activities that truly set apart the leaders who could bring about a sustainable change in the performance of the organisation. The eight practices, as originally defined, are set out below.

The four necessary practices

Insight and Comprehension: creates absolute clarity around the business imperatives behind the change; cuts through organisational complexity to do this; promotes wide understanding of the imperatives in the organisation.

Builds the organisation's blueprint: creates the appropriate architecture of governance, structure and control for the change effort; supplements these formal supporting structures with the building of informal networks and change skills.

Builds capability: develops skills for the change, creates connections along key organisational processes; standardises processes; maintain congruence between these and the organisation's goals, outcomes and measures.

Maximises performance potential: grows the organisation's talent; brings out the best in and trusts people; builds understanding of how the organisation works, how it competes, and what everyone can do to 'know how to win'.

The four distinguishing practices

'Attractor': embodies, and helps to create, a clear and widely held sense of vision, intent, and identity for the organisation; uses this frame to capture and disseminate organisational stories that give meaning to the daily reality that people experience in the organisation, especially during times of turbulence; acts in service of the organisation rather than as traditional 'bosses'.

'Edge and Tension': tests and challenges the organisation; amplifies the disturbance generated by the change process by helping people see the repeating unhelpful patterns of behaviour in the culture, while at the same time staying firm to keep the change process on course; acts as a 'mirror' to the organisation by promoting feedback; positive consequences and behaviour appreciated and rewarded, negative ones managed and appropriately addressed.

'Container': to channel the edge and tension into a positive force, manages the anxiety and turbulence that change brings. Does this by, articulating the 'few hard rules' within which people can channel their energy and operate freely; has visible

self confidence and takes a stand on issues that matter; is accessible to others and provides an affirming presence.

'Transforming Space': can slow down the busy-ness of an organisation and promote learning and inquiry, *in the moment,* as a foundation for self awareness, growth and improvement; promotes unstructured and courageous dialogue that can take people to a different place; sponsors networks of change agents to support and facilitate energy and commitment.

The first four necessary practices are those 'needed to play' as a change leader – without them, you don't get past first base. The second four distinguishing practices are those 'needed to win' – without them, your change effort won't get you to where you want to be – as effectively and effortlessly as you would like. While much of the existing leading change literature focuses on the first four, we were more intrigued by the 'needed to win' practices. We observed them less frequently in the change leaders we studied and worked with, yet when used, created the most profound and lasting impact on the change outcome. In particular, they seemed to be able to serve well the leaders who were faced with the scale and complexity of high magnitude change. The rest of our inquiry therefore centred on these four.

Before subjecting the four practices to the rigour of quantified research, we first tested them out in practice. We had deliberately chosen different kinds of words to describe them – did this language draw attention to new possibilities? Did the words create a helpful frame of reference that brought new meaning to the change leader's task? Were the four practices helpful to organisational leaders tackling real world change challenges? Could they provide a framework that helped navigate change more generally, as well as promote development in individual leader practice? Most importantly, when applied, did they seem to produce different outcomes?

Introducing the Changing Leadership framework

We worked with several organisations and leadership teams over the course of a year, introducing what we now call the four 'Changing Leadership' practices into their change effort. The framework started to resonate and challenge; it served as a check on current practice, helped provoke learning, and changed the way in which leaders approached the change task. Below are some highlights of how the four practices started to impact their change activity.

Attractor: the energy generated in Attractor leadership creates a magnetic pull in the organisation, not magnetism in the leader. For example, when building shared vision for a change effort, leaders were learning how to move away from developing and launching personal bold visions from on high, and move towards implementing processes that engaged the stories and ideas of the organisation around them. In this way a collective story, spirit and energy gets generated; and the process of creating shared vision becomes the Attractor, it generates something like a field of energy. The words or language that are produced are simply an output. Having said that, leaders became more aware of the language and symbols they used in their communications – a simple change in language can reframe the sense, or meaning, that people place on the purpose of change. They began to appreciate the importance of 'contextualising', or providing a frame for the change, such that people could find positive energy in the current circumstances. It pulled people towards a new sense of purpose. One local leader in a public sector organisation simply re-labelled central government targets as 'our pathway to freedom', and almost instantaneously the climate in her organisation switched from brow beaten cynicism to energised innovation.

Edge and Tension: when skilfully done this leadership practice creates ambition, not stress. Leaders learned to get courageous in uncovering and naming awkward subjects that had been kept quiet for the sake of not rocking the boat, or not causing people embarrassment. While such subjects stay hidden it becomes hard to establish the precise starting points for change, or 'current reality', and therefore difficult to sense how far performance improvement can be stretched. Leadership teams learned to becomes less 'polite' with each other, and in its place have more edgy conversations about scary yet vital subjects. They discovered how this made conversations more 'real', alive, and consequential – it helped to challenge assumptions and beliefs present in the team, and paradoxically build more trust. They found that the discomfort generated from Edge and Tension could change things for the better, not lead to collapse and break down. When engaging the organisation at large, leadership teams became more transparent in sharing performance data and confronting the reasons for underperformance. The transparency sparked a desire to improve, not get defensive, which enabled even more challenging standards of performance to be set. Edge and Tension seemed to be enabling an organisation to both find and better perform to its potential.

Container: the stronger the container, the greater the ability a leader has to channel the anxiety created from Edge and Tension, and then convert it into constructive energy. Containment is the fierce yet supportive holding of energy. Leaders learned that this was partly down to their own personal presence. The more they could exude calmness and confidence, despite the fear and anxiety around them that change inevitably brings, the more they could 'hold' people's tension and build belief that it was there for a reason – to move closer towards the organisation's essential purpose. Leadership teams also discovered the importance of setting 'hard rules', or boundaries, within which their organisations should operate. These rules primarily set expectations for the values and behaviours necessary for the healthy functioning of the organisation. They also learned to become firmer at setting rules for the day to day running of the business, which could be as straightforward as conduct in meetings, or how and in what style their teams should engage the rest of the organisation. Indeed one way to channel energy in a change process is to build social networks across the organisation; and leaders became more aware of the importance of nurturing these networks to enable faster adoption of new ideas and ways of working. In a sense the networks became self organising structures that carried and sustained the change process.

Transforming Space: the essential prerequisite for working with Transforming Space is the acute paying of attention to the current moment. Leaders learned how to notice the dynamics of what was happening in front of them – in meetings, in conversations, during their walks around the organisation. And they began to spot the opportunity for making change happen in that moment, and not simply talking about it as if the change was going to start some other day. They took greater risks in conversations to bring attention to some of the limiting assumptions that were being displayed, then processed those with people, and in so doing created greater awareness among all present of what might be holding the change back – critically in their own behaviour and practice. This ended up with quite startling 'aha' moments. Leadership teams also paid closer attention to the qualities of the physical space in which they held meetings and conversations. It is hard to create movement 'in the moment' when people are stuck in rigid seating arrangements in standard meeting rooms that are traditional and uninspiring. Activities were designed to become more interactive and engaging, diverse groups of people were invited to critical conversations, meeting agendas became more self organising, and leaders started to notice change happening in front of them. The change was no longer being talked about, it was being lived.

The more we worked with these four Changing Leadership practices the more we realised they were driven by some fundamental underlying beliefs. Unless leaders held these beliefs it was easy for their behaviour to stay in the more leader-centric Shaping leadership mode, despite their conscious and well intended effort to adopt new practice. In Chapter 10 on how to develop Changing Leadership practice we will examine these fundamental beliefs in more depth. In summary, emerging beliefs we found to be important were:

- by relinquishing power to the situation, and not holding on to it oneself, the 'right' things will happen (trust in the system);

- that the leader is still a responsible agent, can act with agency, and make choices that will impact the flow of events (don't just 'blame' others or the situation);

- a supreme confidence that all is well in oneself and the organisation around you, despite any anxiety and turbulence that exists (we have what we need);

- given this it is perfectly okay to take risks and display the courage to disrupt and disturb, since the organisation will find its way through to improvement (order follows chaos).

Beliefs that underlie Shaping behaviour are quite distinct. They assume that the self is the primary agent to make sense of the world and make things happen. In organisational cultures that promote idealisation of the individual leader this can create pressure on the leader to feel that it is all down to them, that they have to be inspiring, that they have to find the right answers, that they have to persuade and influence, and that they have to take care of and protect the organisation. This is a big responsibility to carry, and effectively disempowers others. Charisma can only obliterate another's sense of responsibility. We saw that leaders who were trying to practice Attractor behaviour, without examining or switching their beliefs, sought to *dazzle* their organisation. Attention had to be drawn to them and their vision, not to the wider purpose of the organisation. Leaders practicing Edge and

Tension who were still holding Shaping beliefs ended up causing *unnecessary stir* and agitation. Rather than holding up the mirror to others to see reality, they would point out the facts themselves, which only served to create defensiveness in others, not the desire to change. Leaders trying out Container behaviour could become quite *protective* and constraining. Rules and boundaries ended up as managerial controls rather than signposts to purpose. The affirming presence of the leader could feel intrusive rather than supportive. And finally, when leaders practiced Transforming Space while still holding Shaping beliefs, their interventions in the moment tended to draw visible attention to them and their needs, not to what needed to happen in the situation. Their behaviour felt self indulgent and caused *distraction* rather than movement.

As the importance of underlying beliefs to Changing Leadership practice became clearer, we realised that our framework was more than a set of behaviours, or an aggregation of the original Framing and Creating Capacity leadership factors. They were in a sense about a whole way of *being* as a leader. Perhaps a change in mindset was also required if leaders' attempts to implement high magnitude change were to be successful?

Testing the Changing Leadership framework

Before we did any further development of the framework, we wanted to find out:

- Were the Changing Leadership practices correlated with greater success in leading change?

- Could we re-validate the original research findings into Shaping, Framing, and Creating Capacity leadership?

To that end, we initiated a second major research and inquiry process to test out the Changing Leadership framework across a wide range of organisations and contexts. We used exactly the same Collaborative Inquiry research method, in other words interviewing practicing change leaders to share their stories of change, and how they were leading them. Our target population was senior leaders from both the private and public sector, and a collection of voluntary and other 'third sector' organisations. We aimed to get global reach in the sample. The common denominator was that all of the leaders we interviewed were leading substantial change in their organisations and communities.

This time we interviewed over 40 leaders and captured 61 stories of high magnitude change. The interviews were all transcribed. We developed a coding framework for the four Changing Leadership practices and used this to code each sample of leader behaviour in the stories. We also coded the transcripts for evidence of the three original leadership factors described in Chapter 3. We kept with the same change contexts in order to understand the nature of the change being implemented, in other words degree of change magnitude (complexity combined with scope), timescales required (short, medium, long term), history of change (static or volatile), whether the drivers were internal or external, and whether the change was primarily led by an individual or team. In order to arrive at the success ratings for each change story we this time adopted an integrated approach that aggregated the success rating of the interviewee, the interviewer, the coder, and then a success rating from an independent rating panel who read all of the 40 transcripts. The independent panel were able to compare all the change stories and assign them into four different tiers of success. The panel looked for evidence such as: did the change achieve its desired outcomes, at the required pace; was there sustainable, irreversible change in how the organisation operated to achieve its outcomes – including the development of its capability to handle future change; how effortless was the change – in other words, what return was generated for what level of input; did the change deliver distinctive competitive advantage (for the private sector) and/or improved service to its customers and beneficiaries; to what extent did the organisation become a more attractive and engaging place to work, enabling the retention of talent and greater employee commitment?

We subjected the data to a rigorous qualitative and quantitative analysis. For the quantitative study we looked at two kinds of analysis: correlations, to find out which of the variables was associated with what; and regressions, to discover what makes the biggest difference in terms of the outcome. For the qualitative analysis we: conducted a content analysis to identify the primary stories, or examples, of the four Changing Leadership practices in action – from this we were able to deduce the specific practices that leaders were engaged in under each of the four practices; undertook a cross-case analysis to compare the top five scoring transcripts according to the success of the change with the lowest five scoring transcripts – and from this were able to identify the differentiating behaviours of the leaders capable of putting all four of the practices together to deliver successful high magnitude change. In investigating the original three leadership factors, we were primarily interested in testing our original finding that Shaping behaviour leads to less successful change.

The big messages coming from this round of research were:

In every context we analysed, the Changing Leadership practices brought successful change, and once again Shaping behaviour was negatively correlated with success

The four leadership practices were significantly correlated with successful change outcomes across the whole sample we studied, and the statistical relationship was extremely significant. Whereas Shaping behaviour was again found to be strongly negatively related to the success of change, and this time across all of the change contexts. The following Shaping behaviours were those most strongly linked to unsuccessful change outcomes: leaders acting as strong personal catalysts for the change; leaders being the movers and shakers; and leaders being personally expressive and persuasive. We did uncover an inverse relationship between Shaping behaviour and seniority, in other words Shaping behaviours were less common at senior leadership levels. This finding has implications for leadership development and progression if one of an organisation's criteria for senior leaders is their ability to lead big change. Our finding would indicate that high potential leaders need to move beyond their own personal style and impact to act more in service of the wider organisation around them, create a sense of collective direction, and then build capability in others to implement.

The Changing Leadership practices – which *were* associated with greater seniority in our sample – scored positively across the board. And this was true even for contexts where the chances of change success might seem less likely. While our original research had found that a Directive change approach was negatively related to change success, this time we found that when Changing Leadership behaviours are used the outcome can be successful. This means that even if you have to do top down programmatic change, a certain style of leadership can be adopted to make this kind of change work. Likewise we had originally found that high Sociability cultures were not in themselves related to the ability to implement significant change. Yet even in these contexts the Changing Leadership practices did lead to successful change.

We also looked at how the combination of the two most successful leadership factors from the first round of research, i.e. Framing and Creating Capacity, were related to successful change, and how this compared to the newly created four Changing Leadership practices. While the two original dimensions were again related to success in this sample, the overall impact of the four Changing Leadership practices added significantly more to the success of change than the combination of Framing and Creating Capacity alone. The development of the Changing Leadership framework therefore seemed to be describing behaviours which had a greater impact than purely the combination of Framing and Creating Capacity. There appeared to be strong evidence that these new factors were adding to our previous understanding.

Using Transforming Space in isolation from the other three practices does not lead to successful change

When we analysed the different Changing Leadership practices in isolation of each other, the Transforming Space practice was not statistically related to success, however *when combined* with the others had a positive, amplifying impact on the change outcome. It gives a boost to the other practices. Yet in and of itself, creating change and movement in the present moment has little consequence. Indeed, without a clear context and intent (Attractor), without stretching goals and insight into the repeating patterns in the culture (Edge and Tension), and without an affirming presence and safe conditions (Container), then Transforming Space leadership can be quite dangerous. We have seen in our own practice how leaders can be labelled 'weird' and self indulgent when their interventions to bring about change are not anchored in what the organisation is trying to deliver – indeed such practice can limit the relevance of change and forever damage its credibility.

The leaders who led the most successful change efforts practiced all four of the Changing Leadership practices

When all four of the Changing Leadership practices were present in the leader's change story, the success rating of the change was consistently higher. Moreover, the most skilful leaders managed to combine all four practices into just one setting, which we started to call 'multi-hit' interventions. The leader need only be doing one thing – like convening a leadership team meeting, engaging with the wider organisation at an event, or making just one contribution to a conversation – yet they manage to use all four of the practices simultaneously. Clearly, these four practices were not separate behaviours but factors that could be woven together and integrated into extremely powerful and transforming leadership interventions. This triggered our interest into exploring the interrelationships between the four different practices. Why did combinations tend to work harder?

In examining the data we found that Edge and Tension was often combined with Container to devastating effect. The two practices seemed to be the 'yin and yang' of energy creation. Edge and Tension creates raw power and disturbance. Container channels this into a powerful force. It reminded us of the Hukka Falls in New Zealand's North Island where a vast flow of water from a lake moves into a river, and then cascades furiously through an extremely narrow and relatively short river bed. This channel – with its fierce and strong rock bed and sides – converts the pounding water into an energy source that enables the supply of electricity to hundreds of thousands of homes. The river without the rock channel would just continue to flow furiously and eventually dissipate. The channel without the enormous flow of water could become a picturesque yet unnecessary rock formation. Both are needed to create energy. And in our sample these two leadership practices were strongly related to success in high magnitude change.

We found other combinations in the data. As balance to the above we found that Attractor and Transforming Space were often inter-related. When leaders combined these two practices there was significant movement in the present moment towards an organisation's purpose or vision. One leader did this by bringing in personalised statements from customers about the organisation into key change events with senior leaders. The messages from the outside helped build a new and compelling sense for where their organisation needed to go to win in the market place. At the meetings themselves the leaders started living this new sense of purpose through simulation exercises and 'socio drama'. The Transforming Space placed them in the future in the here and now. The change became less academic and words driven and more lived and behaviourally driven. The more we played with the framework of four practices the more we saw other connections – a combination of Attractor and Edge and Tension created a sense of excitement for the change, Edge and Tension when combined with Transforming Space created extremely uncomfortable yet paradigm-shifting moments, Attractor when combined with Container anchored people's energy towards the organisation's mission and the process for how to get there.

Leaders often asked us the question, 'do you need to be good at all four of the practices?' Different leadership team members can have quite different styles, backgrounds and strengths in their approach to leading change. In these contexts, the combined and collective capability of the leadership team could be sufficient; it would have the same impact on the change outcome as an individual leader practicing all four. While this might be the case, our research has indicated that if all individuals could master all four then the leadership team would have a significantly better chance of implementing high magnitude change.

The Changing Leadership framework has high face validity – it makes sense to leaders

During our research debriefs – and in our client work both before and after the research – we found that the Changing Leadership framework was accessible and practical. One thing it is not is a competency framework; it's a grouping of leadership practices that we have found can be learnable (though as mentioned above it does require the holding of certain beliefs to avoid the leader slipping into Shaping type behaviour).

In Part II of this book we illustrate each of the practices in detail. In summary, the essence of the Changing Leadership framework as it emerged from the research is outlined below, together with illustrative quotations from leaders we interviewed.

Attractor Leadership is about developing a magnetic energy force in the organisation in order to pull it towards its purpose. The notion of a 'strange attractor' comes from the world of physics. Attractors are invisible forces in the living world that turn otherwise random chaos into identifiable patterns – there is a tug and a pull in the universe, a bit like gravity. When present, they help line things up and keep them in a stable state, just like iron filings in the presence of magnetic force, or how water in valleys will always flow down to the same river. Attractors therefore explain how systems work. In organisations, individuals who practice Attractor leadership instigate processes that create the pulling power energy of an organisation towards its strategic intent, or purpose. The leader's intent is to engage people's ideas, and tap into the collective sense of what's needed. From the collective ideas the leader frames and authors a 'story' for the change that fosters excitement about the future and new meaning for the present, and the story is continually referred to and updated as the change progresses. The 'field' is a living concept. It is continually being created. The leader senses and taps into what is happening in the organisation and convenes conversations about that, such that the collective sense of the endeavour grows. As this progresses people start to interpret day to day reality in a more consistent, energetic and creative way. The story is there to change the present, not paint a picture of a future vision that might happen one day. It moves people today into new directions. Attractor leadership can therefore produce a sense of shared identity, belonging and togetherness. This is not about heroic or 'dazzling' leadership. Leaders who master Attractor practice pull people towards what the organisation is trying to do, not towards themselves.

Here is an excerpt from one of our research transcripts which illustrates how a leader could do this in the space of a few moments at a meeting. The leader involved was project managing the development of a global capability building programme requiring the whole hearted effort of many diverse stakeholders. It was important to her that each and every person could see their place in the effort in order to build excitement for their collective purpose.

I told the story of how we had got to where we had got to, and I started with the guy who had done the leadership work and who was in the room, and I said, 'Bob, will you stand up!' And I said 'so here's how the story started, and Bob did this, and then he gave us the energy for . . . and then such and such happened . . .' And I invited more people to stand up and share their stories, so by the end of the time the entire room was standing up and they could see their place . . . and that created this incredible energy, so that when I got to the senior leadership team meeting the following month they had already been prepped by their HR community that there was something very exciting going on.

Edge and Tension Leadership stokes up the fires of movement. Leaders in our sample who did this found ways to create disturbance in their organisation, because disturbance dislodges stuck-ness and disturbance releases energy, even though it may feel a little uncomfortable. We tend to be most disturbed when we feel we are on an 'edge', when we are tipping between a solid secure and safe place and looking into an unknown and more dangerous place where the world no longer feels secure. When we are on this edge we pay closer attention to what is happening around us. Things heat up. We learn new ways of dealing with the situation. Being on the edge therefore draws forth innovation. When we are on our edge we tremble on the verge of breakthrough, knowing that we might have to break down first. The most frequent way in which leaders practiced Edge and Tension was to talk straight, confront reality, and name things. They dared to raise the awkward subjects, they risked drawing attention to 'ripe issues' that were causing heat and noise in the organisation, yet which were being consciously avoided. They could notice (often when others could not) and challenge unhelpful paradigms and assumptions underlying people's behaviour. They then set stretching, though attainable goals and standards, to change and improve the situation. They were uncompromising on the standards and staying on course. When Edge and Tension leadership is overdone, not used in combination with the other three practices, or done in service of the individual leader, then this practice becomes intimidation and the organisation switches off. People get scared not disturbed.

A seminal excerpt from a research transcript of a leader who successfully accomplished Edge and Tension follows. He was initiating a fundamental turnaround in the performance of his organisation and had gathered his team to find a way through.

I said 'nobody is leaving this room until we've bottomed out an implementation plan'. And it wasn't a discussion point, you know, one member said 'I've got band practice to go to'. I said 'well I'm sorry, that's tough . . . the world has just changed. You're now a senior leader, you've got to commit to sorting this out'. And we stayed in the room until 2 a.m., sorting out an implementation plan, division by division, function by function . . . it got known as the 'thumbscrew meeting'. And that was probably the first point that the team realised that 'act and commitment' meant delivery, as opposed to 'maybe we'll do it sometime'.

Container Leadership holds and channels energy. High magnitude change brings anxiety and turbulence which can result in people becoming 'stuck' and unable to function. Without strong containment Edge and Tension becomes paralysing. The disturbance it creates gets dissipated as anxiety. And yet disturbance becomes a powerful force for change when people feel guided and supported. When we looked up the meaning of the word 'container' in the dictionary we found a definition: 'holds for the purposes of movement'. Container leadership is not about putting a lid on hot things in a protective storage jar. Its purpose is to skilfully move people through important 'thresholds' that take them to a new place – which might include being able to hold people through tough conversations that feel like things are breaking down before they get any better. Leaders in our sample who practiced Container leadership well set boundaries, expectations, and hard rules, and gave affirming signals that channelled the energy of the organisation towards it purpose and direction. Boundaries enable people to know the scope within which they can play – leaders could clearly articulate what was 'in' and what was 'out' for the change work. Expectations clarified what the leader was asking of the organisation, and what they were asking of players within that. They helped set a 'contract' around what was important to achieve. The hard rules tended to be around the behaviour that was expected in the organisation, they shone a light on what was deemed to be important and valued. The rules helped people navigate day to day activity, *and gave them the freedom to act on their own without leader control.* Throughout the often unnerving times in change, the Container leader is calm, confident, and provides affirming signals that allow people to find positive meaning and sense in an anxious situation. If practised in isolation to the other three factors, or done with the intent to control and restrain rather than enable and support, Container leadership can feel suffocating, overly protective, and the organisation becomes either covertly compliant or overtly rebellious.

Here's an excerpt from our research of a leader who set up an organisation where she took a stand for its founding beliefs, clearly contracted its boundaries, and established firm membership expectations.

We say we insist on you being non-violent. We insist on you being non-sectarian and non-party political . . . we made those [points] clear fairly early on and then we made the space . . . and I spent quite a bit of time just saying to people it's okay if there's a bit of friction around, it's okay if there's a bit of controversy, it's healthy, as long as we stay close and decide where we're going.

Transforming Space Leadership creates change in the 'here and now'. It is based on the assumption that the only thing you can change is the present moment. And the present moment contains endless possibilities to shift the attention, amend the organisation's unwritten rules and behaviour, and alter the future course of events. Leaders who practice this well see the possibility of the future emerging in the current situation. Their attention turns away from the planning of change to its enactment. They will see the process of moving from A to B as an opportunity *to live B*. They therefore consciously create both the mental and physical spaces that can transform behaviour. That space can be created in the course of a conversation – by inquiring into the patterns of behaviour they see in front of them that could hold the change back. This can be risky and challenging both for themselves and for those present, however when done with the intent to move the organisation closer towards its purpose, can create extraordinary 'aha' moments. It makes the change feel real and present. The current space becomes an experimental 'laboratory' for testing out new ways of doing things. However Transforming Space leadership does not always have to rely on the leader being present; it also encompasses the design of processes that will live the change. If the goal is to become a more 'commercial' organisation then the means to get there should be commercial; if the goal is to become a more customer-centric organisation then bring customers into the process to get there. Given the close attention to the present moment and the focus on process, Transforming Space leaders also consciously attended to the physical qualities of the environment within which change can occur. Environments create atmospheres and atmospheres have a potent impact on mindset and behaviour. While most of organisational life has to be spent within the constraint of one's office environment, rather than a distinctly different 'off site' venue, nonetheless leaders in our research became creative in how meeting rooms got set up and what was displayed around the place on walls. Their intent was to create physical spaces that felt different and that were more in tune with the change they were trying to create.

It's hard to capture full excerpts of this practice from one transcript quote alone, however what follows is an illustration of a leader who made an intervention in the moment of a conversation. He skilfully inquired into a systemic issue present in the culture in a way that did not leave the other individual in the conversation feeling 'blamed' – the individual was simply manifesting a dynamic that was symptomatic of the wider pattern in the organisation. And in doing the inquiry, the leader was taking a risk by demonstrating a behaviour that was in itself counter-cultural, and thereby shifting things in the moment.

I said 'I am really curious as to why you feel you have to speak on behalf of everybody else. What's happening that you feel like you have to do that?' You know, she kind of almost broke down in tears and said 'Because we've never had anybody before who sat and listened to us as individuals, and this is the first time I feel I'm really being listened to'.

Why does the Changing Leadership framework work?

Both the research data and our direct work with leaders in organisations were telling us that the four Changing Leadership practices worked. There was rigour and there was relevance. To deepen our insights into the nature of these practices we wanted to answer the question 'why do they work?' If we could begin to answer this question, it would help us not just to share them, but also to explain them – they could become more 'teachable'. We therefore explored various theoretical fields that explain why organisations can either get 'stuck', or unable to change, or why they can 'move'. The following summarises the theories we found that shed most light on our understanding of the practices and how they relate to change.

Positive Psychology

Positive Psychology is a rapidly emerging area which has been significantly influenced by Martin Seligman. He has asserted that the 'traditional' psychological focus on dysfunction has neglected a significant area of human experience and that this needs to be balanced with an exploration of, and development, of positive qualities. In its simplest form it is concerned with balancing a deficit focus with a focus on strengths and potential. Two particular strands seemed relevant to an understanding of why the Changing Leadership practices worked.

An embracing of the field of *Appreciative Inquiry*, defined as 'the art and practice of asking questions that strengthen a system's capacity to apprehend, anticipate and heighten positive potential' (Cooperrider and Whitney, 2000). Its underpinning components are: (i) a developmental focus, building on organisational and individual strengths; (ii) vision led conversations and actions; (iii) a 'glass half-full' mind-set; (iv) the use of generative thinking and positive conversations; and (v) releasing the positive energy for change within the organisation. Within this context the leadership practices tend to be facilitative rather than directive, and are engaging rather than 'leader-centric'.

Secondly, there is a growing interest in the role that *positive emotions* play in healthy functioning systems. Researchers have identified that 'situations that promote positive emotions broaden individuals' attention scope, allowing them to see both the forest and the trees' (Fredrikson, 1998). Clearly such research has notable impact and relevance in the context of change. In such a context it is evident that negative emotions lead to: fear; resistance; adherence to established behaviours and ways of working; and lack of openness and flexibility. Positive emotions, on the other hand, will result in; greater appreciation of the 'big picture'; willingness to explore new thinking; willingness to experiment with new behaviours; increased flexibility and innovation; enhanced understanding of, and ability to cope with, complexity. The leader's challenge is to facilitate the creation of a climate which releases such positive emotions. However, *balance* is again important. A group which experiences only positive emotions will find the conditions create a level of comfort which can lead to complacency and dampen growth, change and development.

Reflecting on the above it can be seen that there are some clear underpinnings to our four Changing Leadership practices and the significance of the impact of leaders combining all four practices. Attractor leadership employs principles of Appreciative Inquiry and it engenders the positive emotions associated with belonging and togetherness. Edge and Tension leadership provides balance in terms of emotions and strengths. Critical weaknesses are named and in creating disturbance negative emotions are released. Container leadership provides positive emotional input linked with elements of Appreciative Inquiry in providing a framework for channelling energy and reducing anxiety. The clarity of expectations and boundaries creates a framework within which individual and group strengths may be realised. Transforming Space leadership provides the possibilities for utilising the strengths of individuals and the group, and the basis of Appreciative Inquiry to develop an understanding of vision and the future in an emerging sense.

Paradoxes

Theoretical fields that explore why individuals, groups and organisations can get 'stuck' are those that posit that the presence of seeming paradoxes, or ambiguity in the environment, lead to an inability to function. People can get trapped in the double binds of a paradox and perplexed in the face of ambiguity.

Paradoxes are seemingly contradictory opposites. A frequent one encountered in large complex organisations is the fact that the more senior leaders become, the more power-less they find themselves. This is because they can no longer directly control outcomes but have to rely on the acts of many other people. When people feel power-less they can become stuck. This is just one paradox out of many in organisational life. We began to hypothesise that another reason why the Changing Leadership framework works is because it helps to reconcile organisational paradoxes. Attractor leadership, in its quest to uncover unifying purpose and intent, can help people uncover the common source that underlies paradox. In the above example the paradox gets reconciled when senior leaders understand that the more power they give away in large systems, the more powerful they will actually become, because the giving away of power creates strong 'followership'; and this then authorises their own leadership. Edge and Tension leadership makes visible the opposing forces and tensions inherent in the organisation – be that power and control in matrix structures, complex and systemic team dynamics – which helps make the paradoxes discussable and thereby less disabling. Container leadership, with its emphasis on the holding of tension and anxiety, can safely channel or process paradoxes towards creative resolution.

Complexity theory

Complexity theory is an emerging field of inquiry which seeks to understand the collective behaviour of systems. Systems are defined as 'complex' when they are comprised of many individual components, or agents. They are a 'system' because the agents are connected and can simultaneously interact. Over time these multiple interactions produce startlingly dynamic patterns of behaviour, or emergent outcomes, which cannot be explained by studying the behaviour of the individual agents alone. Such 'adaptive' behaviour is therefore a property of the system and its underlying conditions, and consequently cannot be controlled from any one part. The study of what has come to be known as 'complex adaptive systems' originated as a collective field of inquiry at the Sante Fe Institute in New Mexico in the mid-1980's. It is not our intent to explore this field in this book; however, our own study of complexity theory has shed light on understanding why the Changing Leadership practices work. The main premises of Complexity Theory are as follows:

- The collective behaviour of complex adaptive systems can be explained by the individual agents following certain underlying 'rules'.

- These few underlying rules, which govern behaviour at the micro level of the individual agents, produce patterns of behaviour at the macro systemic level that can be dynamic and ever changing.

- If there are too many rules and not enough connections between the agents then the system becomes frozen and stuck.

- If there are too few rules and too many random connections the system descends into churn, chaos and no repeating patterns.

- The amplification of feedback around 'ripe issues', where there is tension, tips the system into disturbance and novelty.

- Magnetic structures, or 'attractors', maintain the system in a stable state.

- The system can move into self organised, perpetual motion (in other words change without any centralised control), when the system contains an equal balance of order, structure, or stability; and disorder, chaos, or change (the so called 'edge of chaos').

Such findings could explain why Shaping leadership behaviour is ineffective in generating successful change. Its leader-centric style is concerned with pushing and personally directing the behaviour of individuals (or 'agents') rather than working on the conditions of the underlying system. The four Changing Leadership practices, on the other hand, seek to build power in the system, not any individual agent. Leaders who practised all four had visions of the whole system and the dynamics at work that transcended individual components or personalities.

Whilst we were able to see examples of how each individual practice could be explained in terms of complexity theory, the biggest connection we made with the Changing Leadership practices *as a holistic framework* is that the necessary condition to keep a complex system in perpetual motion is the equal co-existence of two states – the forces for order and the forces for disorder. In looking at the four practices it struck us that Attractor and Container leadership contain the forces for order, stability and structure, whereas Edge and Tension and Transforming Space leadership contain the forces for disorder, change and chaos. Could this explain the reason why leaders who could practice all four seemed to be the most able to lead high magnitude change in big complex systems? Had we found the essential leadership practices that can keep an organisation at 'the edge of chaos'? We will explore the holistic nature of the framework later in Chapter 9. The systemic balance between order and disorder is illustrated graphically in Figure 4.1.

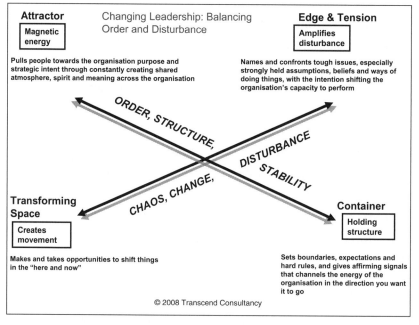

Figure 4.1   Changing Leadership: Balancing Order and Disturbance © 2008 Transcend Consultancy

Summary

In this chapter we continued to explore the precise nature of what it is that leaders do to successfully lead high magnitude change. Our own research was telling us that the *doing of it* did seem to be more important than the *planning of it*. And the doing of it required leaders to be continually aware of their own behaviour in the moment; since every single encounter, every single conversation, every single act, had the potential to change the moment and hence the future course of the change. We also signalled the importance of leaders designing the *change process* to embody the intent of the change. In that way they built the capability of the organisation to step into a new way of thinking and behaving. So at one level the leader needs to be aware of their behaviour and at the system level they need to be aware of the power of process to guide other's behaviour. Both will create movement in the organisation, as distinct from simply launching new activity and initiatives which can keep the organisation busy and stuck in its repeating patterns.

While Framing and Creating Capacity leadership had been proven to be successful practices in creating organisational movement, we pushed further in exploring the precise nature of successful 'changing leadership'. Over the course of our client work we developed four transforming leadership practices which we called Attractor, Edge and Tension, Container, and Transforming Space. Attractor leadership creates a magnetic energy that aligns and propels change, Edge and Tension amplifies disturbance and shakes things up, Container leadership provides a strong and safe structure to channel tension into constructive energy, and Transforming Space leadership seeks to make change happen in the here and now. We named these four practices the Changing Leadership framework, and when tested with leaders they seemed to be able to generate insight and new ways of approaching the leadership of high magnitude change – with improved outcomes.

Our latest round of research put these four practices to a more rigorous test and the findings indicated that they had a strong relationship to successful change. The combinations of the practices generated creative and energetic movement. In particular, leaders who could practice all four stood head and shoulders above the rest in their ability to implement high magnitude change; the practices seemed to enable organisational leaders to create the conditions for moving large systems towards improved performance – without them having to personally shape and control the outcomes.

In exploring theories as to *why* the Changing Leadership framework works, several fields of inquiry shed light on their practice; in particular positive psychology; organisational paradoxes, and complexity theory. These theories provide different lenses yet all highlight the importance of working on the underlying conditions that will generate constructive movement towards change goals. Pushing and prodding the organisation towards change simply doesn't work.

Finally, we offer the insight that the Changing Leadership framework, with its equal balance on creating order (through Attractor and Container), and creating disorder (through Edge and Tension and Transforming Space), can maintain an organisation or any system in a perpetual state of change and movement. Leaders who can practice all four should therefore be able to keep their organisations dynamic and adaptive – without them having to personally direct and carry the load.

Part II

Seeing Changing Leadership

Introduction to Part II

In Part I we have set the stage for defining what we mean by the Changing Leadership practices, and we explored how and why they seem to work in high magnitude change. In this section of the book we aim to richly illustrate *what it is that leaders do* to put the practices into action.

In order to do this we will be drawing extensively both from the research transcripts and our own stories of working with leaders in change. Our intent is to be evidence based. In this way we hope that the illustrations of Changing Leadership offered in Part II *will enable you to see your own leadership*.

To help you become aware of your own practice you might wish to consider the following questions as you read this section.

- To what extent do you see these practices in your own leadership approach?

- Are you more naturally drawn towards the descriptions of some over others? What might that be telling you about yourself?

- Do any of the practices 'trouble' you in some way? What might that be telling you about yourself?

The examples that we illustrate in this section are all positive ones, in other words they are illustrations of leaders who have mastered different elements of the Changing Leadership practices. We have purposefully done this in order to help you visualise what they look like in practice. In Chapter 10, 'Developing Changing Leadership', we will highlight more the struggles we have seen when leaders try to practice them, and what learnings these struggles bring, since it would be misleading to portray that this is all rather easy, and unrealistic to think that we have only ever worked with world class change leaders (if indeed they do exist!).

However in this section we do touch on how unskilled adoption of these practices can lead to unintended consequences. We have noted in previous chapters how easy it is for a leader to adopt Changing Leadership practices while still holding on to certain personal beliefs and ego-driven needs that actually do more harm than help (for example Attractor slipping into 'seduction', Edge and Tension into 'intimidation', Container into 'protection', and Transforming Space into 'manipulation'). In this sense there is a so called 'dark side', or 'shadow', to these practices. A basic natural law in all spiritual systems is that light and dark are complementary forces that cannot be separated. While a leader may be consciously adopting the 'light side' of each Changing Leadership practice their personal intent (e.g. for self promotion and/or control), or unconscious needs (e.g. for affirmation and being omnipotent), could be casting a 'shadow' into the organisation (e.g. of denied vulnerability) such that their behaviour feels to others untrustworthy. The dark side is present in all of us; and it is usually only recognised when somebody feeds it back to us.

We therefore found that leaders who could bring out the light side of the practices were extremely self aware. They sought out, listened to, and *heard* the feedback of those around them. Based on this they would reflect on the (real) intent behind their practice and remodel that if necessary. Had the ego become the all consuming focus of action and behaviour? Was personal reputation being placed before organisational need? Had natural pride tipped into hubris and such belief in one's own invulnerability that the leader had created social distance with others; they now only surrounded themselves with followers who would act on and endorse their actions and suggestions? In such situations Edge and Tension could easily just serve to discourage the dissenting voice as being 'wrong', 'disloyal', or 'unfair', and Attractor to create an idealised, 'charmer' image of the leader expecting blind devotion.

In exploring the 'dark side' there appears to be two broad categories of leaders who can 'derail' in this way. The first category is those who exhibit 'pseudo' leadership behaviours. Such leaders understand the effective dimensions of the Changing Leadership practices yet deliberately employ them to serve their own ego needs and sustain their hubris. One leader we encountered stated his intention to have open dialogue with his team and seek broad based input to developing the organisation's strategy (in the spirit of Attractor practice). However the final strategy failed to take others' views into account and anyone who challenged his strategy were soon found to be 'pursuing their careers elsewhere'. The possibilities of shifting the behaviours of such 'pseudo' leaders are virtually zero.

The second category are those leaders who genuinely believe that their actions are designed to serve the needs of the organisation, yet they have relatively low levels of self awareness, resulting in their unconscious needs getting projected into the organisation. Another leader we encountered genuinely wanted to take the performance of her organisation up to its full potential, yet when she tried to practice Edge and Tension to raise its standards her unconscious desire to continually excel in the eyes of others only created fear and performance pressure in those around her. In such situations (which we have found to be very common) leaders attempting to practice Changing Leadership behaviour could be slipping into Shaping-type practices. Leaders in this category however can learn to switch from their ego controlled practice to a more situational driven practice through greater self awareness and interventions such as coaching.

The following chapters will make reference to the dark sides of the Changing Leadership practices and pin point the beliefs, individual psychological traits, *and* the cultural and systemic contexts that could tip leaders into them; because the dysfunction can be caused by both the personality of the leader *and* the organisational context. While the organisation inevitably does reflect the leader, the leader is also a product of the organisational patterns. For example in closed systems that encourage conformity, Edge and Tension could just seek to screen out the 'wrong sort of person'; in organisations where employees feel wounded, over-enacted Container could become self-absorbed and negotiated protection. As with individual feedback, organisational dysfunction can be denied and those bringing the message may be vilified for exposing it. However if organisational leaders can again *hear* and acknowledge the organisation's shadow helpful lessons can be learned; the organisation and its leaders will become more self aware and thereby able to change its systemic patterns. In reading this section you might therefore also wish to pursue a systemic inquiry.

- How do the Changing Leadership practices sit within the cultural system around you? Does this context influence how they get played out?

Thus the areas which determine the potential for preventing organisations and its leaders acting out of the 'dark side' are those concerned with intent and self awareness. Together these provide the basis for authenticity in leadership behaviour and action. Within our own study of leadership behaviour the greatest potential for dysfunctional tendencies arose within the leader-centric Shaping behaviour. However as pointed out above even the adoption of Changing Leadership practices can provide a leader with 'dark side' opportunities, especially if their intent is to serve themselves before the organisation. Again we emphasise that ego controlled

behaviours are in all of us, and are only natural. The task becomes one of recognising them when they are bubbling up and then consciously choosing to relinquish their hold on us in the situation.

As you read this section you might want to jot down notes about what you reacted to, what you found appealed to you, and what you found troublesome; all of which are indicators into what you both consciously know and what might be stirring in your own unconscious. Most of all, we hope you enjoy the stories and illustrations that follow in our attempt to bring Changing Leadership to life.

5

Attractor – creating magnetic energy

'A leader is a servant first'

Herman Hesse

Attractor leadership: the essence

When leaders serve as Attractors they move their organisations purposefully into new directions. Their primary tool
with which to generate this movement is the creation of
meaning. They stay continually attuned to what's bubbling
up in the organisation around them, and through creating an
unfolding story for the new possibilities that are arising draw
people together and help them move into the unknown. The
collective story is created in ways that generate a magnetic
pull towards the purpose of the organisation (the 'light side'),
not in ways that draw attention to the personality of the
leader (the 'dark side'). Leaders who practice Attractor therefore have the humility to place power in the system, not in

their position. Their presence inspires commitment, not devotion.

What follows is a short story that illustrates the impact of how a leader managed to change the entire meaning that people were ascribing to a change process through the leader facilitating a contextual shift in how people perceived the purpose of the change; and when the story, or sense, of the change moved, so did the energy and commitment behind it. As you read the story notice not just what the leader *did* in this situation, but how she *was* as a leader, since one's presence and use of self is a subtle yet vital element to leaders being able to work with Attractor practice.

Anne had joined an unsettled group of country leaders, gathered for three days to build skills in implementing a new regional organisational structure. She had arrived on day two, and as she entered the room she let herself be led to a wall full of pictures that the leaders had drawn on day one, depicting how they currently viewed the organisation's changes. At the centre of the wall of pictures was a large drawing of an Unidentified Flying Object (UFO) which had captured for participants the essence of how they currently viewed the change. A new Regional Leadership Team (RLT) had been tasked with reorganising the previously autonomous 29 countries into a unified regional business structure. All kinds of dark metaphors, labels, and projections were now being attributed by the country leaders to the new RLT, and a UFO was the image of all images. A bunch of aliens was about to land on their territory and snatch power. It was unknown territory for them, it was scary, and they had better get ready for it: 'let's either challenge this lady [who was from the RLT] or sit back and take cover'. They were in classic 'fight or flight' mode.

As Anne left the pictures and walked to the front of the room she put away her pre-prepared notes. She wanted to respond to what was emerging in the room, not read out what she had come to say. After a few minutes of polite interchange with the group, she moved to a flip chart close to their wall of pictures and turned over the pages to find a blank sheet of paper. The room was expectant and waiting. She asked the group, 'what do you think this new organisation is for?' People shuffled a touch uneasily in their chairs. That seemed like a big question, and it had tuned in to the very essence of their personal journey to discover what their roles as leaders were for in the new structure; the question invited them to consider their purpose. As local leaders they began to voice to Anne (and to each other for the first time) how hard it was seeming to sell the reason for the change to their people, since it all felt like a win:lose situation; the regional 'aliens' were going to take power at the expense of the authority of the local countries.

Anne acknowledged their openness and courage in voicing their fears as precisely the kind of leadership that was needed to help move an organisation into the unknown. She then turned to the flip chart and started to draw her own picture, as if she were joining the flow of the activity they had started on day one. Lines started to appear on the paper; there were a couple of blobs up in the top left hand corner, one bigger than the other, then a larger blob started to appear on the rest of the flip chart, with squiggly edges. She stopped and asked the group what they thought she was drawing, and after a while they correctly identified it as the outline of the map of Europe. She then turned back to the picture and started to draw lines within the perimeter of the continent. People were now warming up, 'that's not how you draw Switzerland!', 'where's Portugal?!' Anne kept drawing. When she had finished she asked the group again; what did they think she was drawing? The group eventually realised this was not a picture of 29 different countries: one person stood up, excited, 'you've drawn the river system of Europe!' 'Yes!' Anne replied; and she continued, 'just imagine Europe as a system of interconnected rivers, not a collection of countries. Where do we make our money in this business? Well, for sure in our distribution activities along the rivers, because that's where we transport our products'. She then put up a few facts and figures around the points in the rivers where their business made and lost money. The potential for greater value creation was starting to become clearer for the group who had now shifted forward in their seats. Several of them came up to the flip chart to draw up further details of the supply chain and its distribution terminals. At this point Anne stepped aside and let whoever was connecting with the new possibilities to create greater value along the river system take the lead with the group. An energetic brainstorm followed.

Anne's planned one and a half hour session with the group lasted for three since the picture and the ensuing exchange had generated a new and vital energy in the room; the sense of the change was now seen as a compelling 'call to arms' to make money by organising around rivers, it was no longer seen as a centralisation of power away from the countries. The 'Region' was no longer viewed as a distinct and 'alien' entity onto which they could conveniently displace their anger. From that moment on the purpose for the new structure became crystal clear. The compass points to navigate through the unknown passage were rivers, not countries. The next day the facilitators responded to this new energy and redesigned the workshop such that tasks got accomplished through people based in river groupings, not in their country groupings. New working relationships and insights were formed as a result of these newly aligned configurations; and this energy got carried out into the organisation after the workshop, as alignment towards the meaning and purpose for the change grew.

The group did not completely transform overnight, and the organisation still had to go through two years of challenging and intense change, however, from that moment on things got dramatically easier. No manner of erudite papers from the strategic planning department or power point slide presentations from the RLT could have accomplished the same task of generating a magnetic pull towards purpose (indeed, such communications had already been conveyed to the organisation, with minimal impact in terms of the intended change but with significant unintended emotional impact – hence the UFO!).

What attractor leadership is (and is not)

Attractor leadership creates a magnetic pull towards an organisation's purpose, and is as much about a leader's presence as it is about their 'intervention'. Anne's presence in the group that day was as equally important as the picture she drew and the dialogue she facilitated. As an RLT member, she could have got quite defensive about being branded as an alien, descending from a UFO. If her own ego driven needs for affirmation and authority had taken precedence in this context, a natural response from her would have been to have started the engagement by describing the RLT's core mission statement, followed by an outline of her new role and accountabilities, what she had done so far to help the organisation, and what she felt she was about as a leader. While her intent in so doing might have been to create greater familiarity and intimacy with the group ('I'm really not an "alien"!') all it might have served would have been a drawing of the attention towards her, and away from their own anxiety.

Alternatively, she could have attempted to 'take on' the group, by justifying all the rational arguments about why the restructure was needed, and how they should 'wake up' as leaders and accept the inevitable. And yet this approach would have only served to have drawn position power towards her, and not created greater power in the group. Indeed it would have *amplified* the split between the local leaders and the RLT, not got them alongside, and in so doing have created a 'double bind' for them: 'if I continue to assert my local power I will feel more in charge though out of favour; if I submit to the power of the region I will lose my local credibility yet become more popular with senior leadership'. And that double bind could have been 'tearing' and disabling for the country leaders, creating 'stuck-ness' and apparent 'resistance to change' in the eyes of regional leadership.

Instead, Anne used her leadership 'self' differently. Rather than pulling the energy towards her she positioned herself 'in the stream' with the group; on entering the room she allowed herself to be led by others first, she put away her pre-prepared notes, her picture joined theirs, and she gave space for the dialogue to flow. And her presence allowed both collective leadership and a unifying story to emerge for the change *which helped the group rise above the double bind since it provided a framework that gave place to both the regional and the local.* When we spoke with Anne after the event she said that the idea of the picture of the river system had come to her in the moment. If she had not seen their pictures she would not have thought of it. While she had known the facts and figures she had never thought of drawing the rivers so explicitly before. She had been open to what had moved her while in the group.

In joining the flow, tuning in to its possibilities, and then seeking to influence it, Anne was unquestionably a 'leader' in the eyes of the group from that moment on. They knew they had been served, listened to, and heard; a story had been generated that clearly placed them as central players in the purpose of the organisation – albeit in a different configuration; and on that basis they now wanted to 'follow' and step into the void, despite its inherent risks and local struggles. Her leadership had in a sense been 'authorised' by her followers. One of the central paradoxes that Attractor leadership acknowledges is that *the more power you give to others the more powerful you become.* If Anne had sought to dazzle she would have got compliance (or competitive 'dazzling'). Instead, she worked to make others feel strong and powerful; her power was derived *through* them, not over them. The greater you can hold this intent to serve what's emerging the greater your ability to practice Attractor leadership.

Attractor leadership: core practices

When we studied the transcripts from our research, we identified certain Attractor practices that were strongly related to successful change outcomes. These were:

- Connects with others at an emotional level, embodies the future intent of the organisation.

- Tunes into the day to day reality of the organisation, sees themes and patterns at local level that connect to a wider story, and from this creates a collective story for the whole organisation.

- Uses the collective story to set the context for the change and weaves the story into the life of the organisation so that every decision and action makes sense.

- Visibly works beyond personal ambition to serve a higher purpose, the organisation, and its community.

- Is consciously aware of one's own leadership and adapts this in order to be able to move the organisation around them.

Below we describe these individual practices with illustrations from the leaders we have engaged with – both within the research and in our practice. As you read through these practices, reflect on your own leadership: are these practices part of how you currently lead change; have you thought about doing them but for some reason avoided them; could your change benefit from this kind of leadership; and therefore would you like to bring more of them into your leadership practice, or practice them with greater awareness and skill?

Connects with others at an emotional level, embodies the future intent of the organisation

Leaders typically appeal primarily to the reason when they take others with them on a change journey. They present facts, show data, explain the logic of how the world is changing. While this might create intellectual understanding of why things have to change, it does not touch hearts or stir souls – and yet its this deeper resonance that can really get people passionate, committed, and 'invested' in the change and its successful outcomes. When the National Health Service Chief Executive said to her staff, 'the [government's] targets are our pathway to freedom', she engaged people's pride and desire to serve local patients without constraint and bureaucracy. It moved them from feeling beaten up to feeling engaged. Leaders who are world class at Attractor practice tune in to their organisations and give voice to the collective in all their communications. One Chief Executive in our study would always run his speeches through a representative sample of the organisation – a 'microcosm' – before he gave the speech in order to test out its resonance with his people.

Leaders who practice Attractor embody the organisation's intent; they don't just talk about mission or vision or purpose as a communication message to be delivered. One leader recounted an observation about his Chief Executive, 'she said, "I stand for the possibility of an organisation that does the following . . ." and that was so visionary in the way that she said it that it became our vision'. Another leader we interviewed who was leading a global humanitarian organisation said, 'my job is to hold the identity . . . you just kind of embody the values'. Another Chief Executive we have worked with took three days out of her busy schedule to be trained with her organisation's truck drivers. Her company was introducing hand held computers into every truck and van that distributed the organisation's products. Her whole change process in the organisation was centred on the hierarchy doing a better job to train and serve the front line staff that served the customer. Word flew around the organisation that she had been at this three day training event (not just shown up to give an opening speech). She did not have to be at any more – the organisation knew she meant what she said about putting the front line first.

The leader will also act to touch each person in the organisation in a way that does not require them to be present. One government department we researched had a mission to eradicate pensioner poverty. The leader put up pictures of pensioners everywhere in his department to have the mission felt at the emotional level every day. It created a tug, 'I said "I want you to deliver a service you would want your granny to get". So make it personal, you know, really engage people at the personal level'. Another organisation we worked with introduced their business vision to the organisation through a metaphor of an orchestra competing with others to be the opening ensemble for the opening ceremony at the Beijing 2008 Olympics. They were a supply chain organisation, needing to operate seamlessly as a team across many interfaces. There were some people in the leadership team who thought this was a crazy way to launch a vision, however 'even' when it was tested with a group of very rationally based, engineering driven managers, there was hardly a dry eye in the house. They too wanted to 'bust their guts' in order to excel and win.

In pulling people towards purpose the Attractor leader, while embodying the organisation's intent, is therefore very careful to avoid either over personalising the messages created for the change, or overly shaping the processes through which the messages get created. Within a lightly held frame set by the leader, the collective meaning emerges from the organisation.

Tunes into the day to day reality of the organisation, sees themes and patterns at local level that connect to a wider story, and from this creates a collective story for the whole organisation

We once read that an author researched his novels not by hiding away in a remote retreat but by getting out and about on London buses. He would spend hours riding around, listening to the conversations that people were having. He would pick up themes, tap into the collective psyche of the moment, and create a compelling story that when read made people feel, 'I'm in this story too, I can see myself, this book's for me'. Leaders who practice Attractor leadership adopt similar tactics in their organisation. They help author a story that is already being told in the organisation. They pay intense attention to what's going on around them, however they don't get sucked into the day to day whirl but retain a detachment that allows them to see the patterns of the system, read its signs, and sense the new possibilities emerging. They then connect these themes to the organisation's ultimate intent and create a story from that. The leader's skill is to spot what's emerging and draw out its possibilities so that it becomes *the story* for the organisation as a whole. One leader in our research was working with an organisation in need of fundamental change, a continuing legacy of two merged organisations where vestiges of their two previously competing worlds were still present. He was encouraged in his early days as Chief Executive to launch a new vision for the organisation, and his communications department were urging him to craft the words and vital statements. In his research transcript he recounted, 'I told the people, "We won't write it [the vision] in advance. We'll do it because we simply are describing who we have become" . . . it sort of emerged from the work'.

Immersion in the day to day reality therefore generates collective stories. One leader of a government department realised that her nation's transport system was in need of radical overhaul. It just wasn't providing a timely, clean, reliable service for its customers. She took her leadership team away for two days on a ride around the capital city's public transport network – buses, trains, boats – and they experienced first hand how bad the situation actually was. Based on this tuning in they built a compelling story for their organisation about what had to change, why, and what they had to change to, a story that consequently felt real and credible to the organisation. It was not a 30 000 feet high vision about 'serve the customer better', it touched their day to day reality, it contained their struggle and it held their hope.

Aside from planned interventions the Attractor practice of 'tuning in to what's emerging' is also about being attentive in the moment. Another leader happened to be visiting one of his factories. He spent some time in a coffee break with a production line worker and noticed that this person was constantly shouting. He wondered why and asked him, not to ask him to lower his voice, but to understand what was going on for this person. The worker said that the noise levels were so high in the factory that, despite ear plugs, the only way the production line could communicate with each other was to shout, and unfortunately they then forgot to lower their voice when outside the factory – it had become the norm. The leader in question used this story at his next leadership team meeting to highlight the need for greater attention to health and safety, which had always been part of their change vision yet had never really got the organisation's attention. This small story became a prototypical story for the rest of the change effort.

It's important to note that the leader's intent in paying close attention to the organisation is not to control it, or to change people's behaviour, it's to draw out the 'meta story' that can inspire the whole organisation to move to a new place.

Uses the collective story to set the context for the change and weaves the story into the life of the organisation so that every decision and action makes sense

Once a collective sense for the change has been created, the 'story' is not simply launched at some engagement event and then left to wither on the vine. Leaders who scored highly on Attractor practice took every opportunity to weave the meaning and purpose for the change into the very fabric of how work got done, creating coherent and stable structures that generated new patterns of behaviour. This entailed not just putting up communication posters around the organisation. The story lived in the business planning and decision making process, it informed how performance was managed, it guided how customers were treated, and it determined where money was spent.

One of the authors used to work for an organisation that implemented a very successful change process called the 'Right Side Up Company' (RSUC). The intent of the change was to become more competitive in the market place by creating greater capability in the front line staff to serve the customer better. RSUC was a metaphor for the inversion of the organisational hierarchy. The upside down triangle showed the customers at the top, served by the front line staff of the organisation, who were served by their team leaders, who were served by the market unit managers, who were served by the business unit managers, who were served by the Executive Leadership Team. The most 'senior' people were therefore at the bottom of the pyramid.

The essential meaning of RSUC was known by everyone in the organisation. It informed how the organisation was restructured, how talent was managed, where training money got spent (diverted away from sending a few choice executives to expensive three week long business school courses to training hundreds of front line staff), and how bonuses got paid (half of an executive's bonus was based on their scores on an organisational 'climate' survey which their staff completed every year – in other words, how effective they were as a leader in creating a positive atmosphere for the people they served determined half of their variable pay). Each year the annual operating plan was disseminated to the organisation via a 'Learning Map' – an interactive and visual process created through the lens of the RSUC which leaders used to educate and align the entire organisation behind the business priorities and agenda. If you are really there to serve front line staff you'd better help them see the line of sight between their day to day roles, and how they contribute to the whole business – you don't keep the annual business plan in documents and presentations that only the senior leaders have access to. Through such activities, the Attractor 'tug' of the inverted pyramid became the organising principle behind everything. It defined the context within which results got produced. And because the leaders had woven it so successfully into the life of the organisation, *it meant that their personal presence as leaders around the organisation to 'mobilise' staff was not necessary.* The organisation *became* the Right Side Up Company, it was not a leadership slogan used in charismatic speeches (a more Shaping leadership approach).

When Attractor leadership creates a compelling organisational story that becomes the way in which work gets accomplished, it can foster not just alignment around strategic intent and priorities, it can also generate excitement, inspiration, and positive emotion. Research in the field of 'positive psychology' shows us that when people feel confident and affirmed, they are more likely to become resilient in changing environments and work more creatively. One of the leaders in our research made it his task to bring affirming stories relating to the organisation's mission to life in the day to day work, 'I encouraged everyone in the organisation to capture the good news stories. So every week we had the good news stories . . . we (the leadership team) just asked people to tell us'.

Visibly works beyond personal ambition to serve a higher purpose, the organisation, and its community

One of the leaders in our research study most able to use the Changing Leadership practices is a very humble lady. As CEO of a publicly listed company she has been courted by many journalists over the years to appear in large editorial features in the Sunday supplements, however has repeatedly turned down their offers in order to 'wait for my task in the organisation to be accomplished'. She does not seek personal publicity, and comes across as a leader who is there to serve the stakeholders who have given her the mandate to lead.

This CEO is representative of many of the leaders in our study who excelled at Attractor practice who believed that their leadership task was merely to 'steward' their organisation towards its purpose for a particular moment in time, and no more than that. It was not 'their' organisation to look after. Once a leader frees themselves from seeing the organisation, or their territory within it, as 'their baby', they seem to be able to enter more wholeheartedly into their leadership task; whereas leaders who too personally identify their egos, needs, and reputation with their organisation somehow feel 'bound' to their role, and wrapped up in their own needs, become unavailable to tune into and serve the organisation around them. Such tendencies severely impede their chances of practicing Attractor leadership, and their followers bestowing them with power.

Drawing from the wonderful short novel by Herman Hesse, *Journey to the East,* Richard Greenleaf has brought the notion of 'servant leadership' to the world of business. In 'Journey to the East' Hesse tells the story about a group of religious sect explorers who travel on a great pilgrimage together into unknown territory to find the 'truth', aided by their loyal servant Leo. Many years later the narrator of the story discovers that the servant Leo is actually the leader of the sect, and that he had been all along. Hesse writes, 'a leader is a servant first'. When leaders see their task as serving a wider purpose that goes beyond their individual needs they are released from their own ambition and can act freely for the community around them, even if that means taking risks that work against self promotion and their own personal reputation.

In our own stories we saw an example of a leader recently appointed as head of the Customer Care Centres (CCCs) for his organisation. Many of the operating processes in the CCCs were essentially broken. 'We had a lot of negative press coverage of customers who went to newspapers and to consumer bodies complaining about their dealings with the company'. He could see that this was not the 'fault' of any individual or single department in his company, however in some way everybody contributed a little something to the poor quality of the process such that at the end 'what the customer felt was really dead'; a situation which made this leader feel 'ashamed' (note the emotional connection to purpose). In this scenario an ego controlled response would have been to protect either themselves ('I'd better sort this out quickly or my new career move might have been a mistake'), or their company ('better issue a PR offensive to say the situation is under control and "we're working on it" '). This leader however chose not to. He was serving a purpose wider than self promotion or company reputation. He made a video that highlighted all the mistakes the company was making and showed it to all his staff in a meeting. This could have made him the most unpopular person ever to have led the CCCs. At this meeting he said, ' "I will not work for a company that does this to customers". And I made it very clear'. Another potentially 'career limiting' move. However he went further, his company took out a full page advertisement in the national press apologising to the community for its poor service. One year on, the CCCs had been turned around. His leadership intervention had created a compelling 'tug' in the organisation – to serve their communities more effectively with their energy supply – at personal risk to himself. And the result of the company getting its act together is that they are now voted number one in the country for their customer service.

We are not saying that leaders should not have ambition, or be void of any personal needs and impulses, what we are saying is that if they become all consuming forces it will be extremely hard for the leader to align people behind a collective endeavour, since they will be unavailable to inspire follower-ship, and be blind to the systemic poss-ibilities of the situation. The organisation becomes their instrument; they no longer become an instrument for their organisation.

Is consciously aware of one's own leadership and adapts this in order to be able to move the organisation around them

In our introduction to Part II we noted the general importance of leaders having high levels of self awareness if they are going to be able to practice Changing Leadership. Without self awareness ego controlled needs will influence how a leader reads and responds to situations which can cast unhelpful 'shadows' into the organisation. This requirement is particu-larly the case for Attractor leadership. It's important because unless a leader can screen out the impulses that spring from their own background 'story', they are unavailable to be attuned to the 'story' that needs to emerge in the wider system around them. The organisation and its players become a pro-jection of their unconscious self, often because it is too painful for them to see and acknowledge their own story. A conse-quence of this lack of conscious leadership is that energy in the organisation ends up gravitating towards the leader, not towards purpose. However when a leader becomes more con-scious of their own story and needs, they can then attend more wisely to the situation around them, and become more mindful in their interventions.

One leader in our study was a Sales Vice President for half of the territories in a region, and he had a colleague who was the Vice President for Sales in the remaining territories. Jointly, they were accountable for the overall regional profit and loss. Their targets were very stretching, and they both realised that they had to lead quite a transformation in order to move the business to a different place. However, they just couldn't seem to get on with each other. The leader in our research was highly frustrated with the other VP. He felt that his colleague was analytical, slow, cautious, and just typical of the wider culture in the organisation. How on earth was this kind of style going to create innovation and change? He tried various 'head on' ways to change his colleague's approach; however it seemed that his colleague's behaviour only got reinforced, if not amplified. During some intensive coaching, he discovered that actually this deadlock was as much about his own background issues as it was about the other person. His relationship to authority and power, and 'not giving in to this', were effectively blocking this leader from changing anything. At one important coaching session he realised that the only way to move things forward was to become more conscious of his own issues when they bubbled up, and stop projecting them onto the other person. He was transferring too many buried issues from his personal history onto his colleague, and this was also casting an unhelpful 'shadow' in the wider organisation who felt unable to co-operate across the different sales territories. From this moment on he became more mindful of his leadership style, tried to see the systemic issues at play in the situation, and learned to inquire more of his colleague, *while still staying on course for doing something radical.* As a consequence the relationship between the two VPs shifted, the organisation around them breathed a sigh of relief, and people entered more wholeheartedly into the business improvement task. And when the shadow of the power struggle was removed, energy gravitated towards purpose, and the change started to accelerate.

A corollary to being mindful that your own impulses could spring from your own issues and not those of the situation, is that sometimes what a leader feels and carries inside *belongs to the situation and not them*. If a leader feels envious, then there could be envy in the organisational system; if they are feeling anxious, then the organisation around them is likely to be feeling anxious too. The quintessential Attractor trait of organisational attunement therefore requires self attunement, and the ability to be able to differentiate in yourself the issues that belong to your story, and the issues that belong to the system. Once leaders can with greater self awareness tune in to the wider systemic issues they hold inside, they can skilfully bring that to the attention of others such that the organisation becomes more conscious and thereby able to shift any repeating patterns that are proving unhelpful. Indeed even a tiny shift in how a leader responds to what they are sensing inside can create significant movement in the organisation around them.

One leader in our study was feeling very isolated in his organisation. At first he thought it might just be because he was new in the role and as Managing Director feelings of isolation come with the territory. However, in paying more attention to what was also happening around him he noticed a real lack of co-operation in his organisation, a consequence of a merger in the business that had never quite been cemented. And this lack of co-operation was keeping the organisation stuck and impeding its ability to provide integrated customer solutions to the market place. The competition were starting to do that and were taking away some of their key accounts. The leader decided to adapt his behaviour in order to move the situation around him; 'I spent a lot of time making sure I was being seen everywhere and sort of even-handedly . . . there was a progression whereby people began to recognise that they could work together . . . that we could make this integration happen for the whole organisation'. The mindful shift in this leader's behaviour had a big impact on the speed of the organisational integration; the magnetic energy created through Attractor leadership need not be about grand heroic interventions.

This Attractor practice is not about changing who you are as a person. It is about becoming more conscious of yourself in relation to the situation around you, being in tune with your feelings, and then being able to differentiate which feelings are about you and your own story and which feelings belong to the situation around you. This self reflective practice differentiates the 'blind' impulsive leaders from those who can more skilfully move their organisation to a different place. Therefore the more conscious you are of your inner world the more able you will be to influence the world about you. They are a connected field.

Attractor leadership practices: putting it all together

We return to Rachel's story from Chapter 2. Rachel was appointed to be the global Vice President for a commercial business operating across more than 50 countries. Her business goals were stretching and challenging; to double net income in two years. To achieve this, the business was to be simplified through the standardisation of global business processes and the reduction in number of customer propositions in the market place. Within this context of globalisation and standardisation, customers were still largely won or lost at the local level. The challenge was how to enable leaders at local country level to still run their businesses, set their prices, and manage their product portfolio as they saw fit. At the same time, Rachel recognised that she could increase value in the business through the informal sharing of ideas across the organisation, not through legislation, but through the fostering of a spirit that could unite the countries around the world. Rachel needed to move her organisation into completely uncharted territory.

How Rachel's new leadership team created alignment behind what this change was going to mean for the organisation is an exemplar of Attractor leadership. The team knew they had to develop a 'storyline' for the change that would create a consistent set of messages for the organisation and a framework within which results would be generated differently. What started as a traditional managerial communication activity however became a living and breathing process of story creation and sense making that three years down the track is still guiding how people run the business. Initially, the leadership team developed a set of power point slides for the storyline that contained the 'what', 'why', and the 'how' of the change. The team then took these slides and messages out to their own leadership teams to get their reaction. Basically, it fell flat. The language was felt to be full of managerial jargon, and the organisation had seen these kinds of words many times before in various iterations of change in the business. When the leadership team assembled over dinner one night after this 'market test' they had to admit to each other that they had done little so far to create a compelling story and sense of new purpose for the organisation.

However, at that leadership team meeting things started to change. Rachel and her team had been tuning in to the organisation and sensed that the emerging story had to contain both the passion of local endeavour and the spirit of global camaraderie. In working through the essence of what this meant the team alighted on a metaphor that was going to give the change its coherence. The metaphor was that of a fleet of over 50 battleships in an armada, all having to fight their own local battles and skirmishes, yet united in an overall war to beat their common enemies around the globe. A set of pictures emerged at this meeting to convey the meaning of the metaphor, which became known as Spirit, Speed, and Stretch. These themes were instrumental in joining up the global organisation behind one identity and conveying what had to happen differently in the business. The Spirit picture showed a map of the globe with the ships sailing on the seas, fighting off local pirates and navigating through choppy waters, yet still connected to each other by a satellite system, and by small supply vessels going between the different regional fleets. The global leadership team were represented by a flag ship that was sailing in the waters alongside the local ships (there was much debate in the team as to whether the leadership team should be the satellite system around the globe, and eventually they decided that the team should be sailing the same waters as their people, and the satellite system be the virtual web of signals and networks they were going to create in the organisation). The Speed picture showed a motley set of boats coming into a 'refit' harbour where support functions on shore supplied the ships with new tools and gave them a 'standardisation make over' such that they all left the harbour looking the same and carrying the same tools and equipment on board. The Stretch picture honed in onto one local boat sailing at full tilt towards 'paradise island' where the local crew were doing all they could to get the boat sailing as fast as it could in the local conditions, aided on board by some business 'levers' that were standard equipment on each ship.

Rachel and her team wanted to make sure that these emerging pictures *were created by the whole organisation.* While some of her leadership team were sceptical ('grown up business people don't work with pictures!'), individual members of the team in the next few weeks brought together groups of local staff to test out the emerging organisational story. Rachel had written a short paper herself about the armada metaphor ('just imagine a fleet that . . .') and this was read out at the start of the local meetings to set the scene. Then the pictures were shared on large posters and the local teams got actively engaged with them, drawing on their suggestions, adding local colour and stories, and correcting bits they thought inaccurate. The conversations around these pictures, at times happening at the same time in different countries around the world, created a ground swell of energy in the organisation. Rachel's leadership team surprised themselves at just how engaged the local teams were with the process, and the conversations created insights for the leadership team as to how they should run this global business, insights that they had never thought of before. The organisation was consulting them. Power had been 'given away'. *And the process that had been used to create the story was in itself working as an Attractor.* Irrespective of the story being produced, the engagement in the act of story creation was creating a magnetic energy and pull in the organisation towards its new purpose.

Six weeks after the leadership team meeting that had generated the metaphor and pictures, Rachel's leadership team hosted a meeting of 100 leaders from across the world. An artist had been commissioned to take all of the comments from the many countries that had participated in the local engagements to produce a revised set of pictures for this meeting. In addition to the final pictures however, Rachel wanted all of the posters that had been generated in the local engagements to be posted on the wall of the conference room. Once more, some people in her leadership team felt this was not entirely necessary, yet it was done, and as 100 people walked into the conference room there was instant animation. Their pictures pulled them to the walls. People were pointing to their own contributions. They could even see their hand writing on the charts . . . their words, their sketches! It was hard for the leadership team to start the conference and move people away from the buzz around the pictures and the sense making process that was occurring.

The rest of the meeting was built around the themes of Spirit, Speed and Stretch, and the *meeting process lived their meaning.* Most telling at this conference was how the global leadership team played their role. They wanted to live the role of the flag ship in the fleet, not a detached command and control satellite system that somehow hovered above the organisation, but as a guiding vessel that sailed alongside the local crews. The majority of the meeting was 'open space', in other words the people in the room, within some guiding questions, could set the agenda and run the process themselves. Rachel 'volunteered' her team member who most preferred structure, control, and predictability to facilitate the most open part of the agenda. She was conscious of how this would represent a systemic shift away from a Shaping leadership culture to a more Framing based one. Rachel's colleague was coached beforehand on how to handle the session, and when he opened the session at the conference he conveyed publicly to the group how uncomfortable he was at that moment – with a smile on his face. The group joined him wholeheartedly in the risk and stepped into the space he had created, and the ideas and contributions generated in this session started to form the global business agenda. During the session debrief, one participant took hold of the microphone and said to the 100 people present, 'thank you for letting me lead'.

The leadership team came away from this conference buzzing. By giving power away they had become more powerful. Their humility to create space for others had established their credibility and respect in the eyes of the organisation they served. They had been authorised to lead. The magnetic energy generated in these initial weeks carried through the change process for several years. The metaphor of the fleet and the three themes guided business priorities and how performance was assessed. They generated organisational attention, alignment, and commitment that did not require the leaders to be present; and based on this spirit, energy and enthusiasm the organisation also delivered on its stretching targets – ahead of time.

Attractor: the dark side

Attractor leadership requires the leader to hold certain beliefs, or intent, and to possess an inner self awareness, without which they cannot act with authenticity. In these situations, Attractor behaviours, while practiced on the surface, can feel a little like 'seduction' to others around them. The leader draws power and people towards them, not towards each other and the collective purpose. The leader becomes the magnet, not the change. In this sense Attractor leadership can fall quite easily into the more leader-centric Shaping behaviour. It becomes all about the leader, not about the wider organisation and its endeavour. And this can either be positively enacted – the leader is 'charismatic', visionary, a celebrated 'guru', engages people easily, draws people to them; or negatively enacted – the leader throws a tantrum, withdraws, asks everyone to ignore them because 'their voice does not count anyway'; and this paradoxically draws even greater attention to them, which they crave, though it sucks energy from others towards their withdrawal. Both can spring from a 'narcissistic' tendency, in other words the leader is self absorbed, longing to be special, and more in love with themselves than with others around them.

This 'dark side' of Attractor is usually called forth when the leader has a strong outer orientation. This means they are concerned about external impressions, how they compare to others, what people might think of them, and indeed can be very worried about the opinion that the world has of them. They will then do everything they can to protect this self image; they create a false 'mask' with which to face the world and which eventually becomes impervious to external criticism as a way of defending against the hollowness inside. They see opportunities for self promotion at every turn. To enact this they will make demands, use their position of authority to influence, and want to get their own way. Paradoxically though, by seeking to control the outer world they in fact end up more power-less to influence this world. Their self protective zeal, and sometimes belief in their own invulnerability, makes them unable to look more deeply into the truth about themselves which gets picked up as insincerity by others. The initial noise, energy, and excitement created around them will start to fizzle and wear out. People will recognise that the leader is serving themselves, not the organisation around them.

This might all sound dark and negative and you may be feeling 'this is not me!', however in presenting the visible signs of the exaggerated tendency you might perhaps recognise a tiny bit in your own character. Since even a tiny tendency could tip your behaviour and its impact on others away from creating a tug towards the collective purpose and *to* an attention onto you; the classic Attractor trap. In Chapter 10 we will share developmental tips on how to increase your ability to practice Attractor leadership. In summary, the following questions can help you begin to reflect on your leadership and in noticing the distinction between the 'dark' and the 'light' side consider your current ability to authentically practice Attractor leadership.

- Are you serving yourself, or the organisation around you?

- Do you give voice to the collective, or your own opinions and demands?

- Striving for personal gain is fine, however do you want personal gain in order to give on to others, or to take for yourself?

- Are you more oriented towards external impressions, or your inner truth?

- Do you emanate self indulgence, or self awareness?

Moving towards the light side of Attractor requires a breakdown of the protective ego. This can be scary when it's only human nature to build this armour in order to be able to survive in a demanding world. However do we want to continue to believe in this 'harsh' world as the reality, or see it as an illusion that we create to make ourselves feel good and whole, and where all the misfortune that befalls us is due to other people? If you hold such beliefs it is nigh on impossible to practice Attractor leadership.

The light side of Attractor *does* require a healthy level of self awareness, a consciousness of the inner self, and the intent to serve the wider system. Outer directed leaders – consumed by self esteem and what others think of them – can easily close down the world around them that they are trying to control. Leaders who are inner directed and more able to tune in to themselves are more concerned about reaching purpose, transforming things, reaching potential, and becoming creative and innovative; and paradoxically by being more inner directed can thereby tune into and move the world around them.

Summary

In Table 5.1 we summarise the essence of Attractor leadership; what it is and what it is not, its core practices, and how

Table 5.1 Attractor Leadership

Essence: creates a magnetic energy in the organisation that moves people into new directions

What It Is (Light Side)	*What It Is Not (Dark Side)*
• A pull towards the organisation's purpose	• A pull towards the person: *seduction*
• The creation of meaning about what is going on and what is emerging	• The promotion of one's own version of the story
• An opening to creativity and movement into the unknown	• Movement into dubious places at the whim of the leader
• The fostering of common spirit and identity	• The creation of personal cult and devotion to the leader
• The placing of power into the whole system, or 'field'; inner directed	• The holding on of power to oneself; outer directed

Core Practices
- Connects with others at an emotional level and embodies the future intent of the organisation
- Tunes into day to day reality, sees themes and patterns, and from this creates a collective story for the whole organisation
- Uses this story to set the context, and weaves it into the life of the organisation so that every decision and action makes sense
- Visibly works beyond personal ambition to serve a higher purpose, the organisation, and its community
- Is consciously aware of one's own leadership and adapts this in order to be able to move the organisation around them

How It Serves Change
- Creates alignment and movement towards new paradigms
- Makes people feel part of an exciting endeavour
- Removes ambiguity and unleashes creativity
- Creates unity, coherence, stable structures, and a sense of belonging
- Stays open to mystery and uncertainty . . .

© 2008 Transcend Consultancy

it serves change. In any fundamental change by definition there is newness, ambiguity, and uncertainty, all of which create anxiety. What will happen to me? Where do I now fit? What will I have to give up? What will I have to take on? Previous identities and affiliations are challenged, new relationships have to emerge. In all of these contexts the 'old story' needs to move to a 'new story'; and a new story the organisation can align around and get excited about, a new story in which people can see their place.

Attractor leadership is about creating meaning for the unfolding organisational story within which people can find their identity and discover their contribution. The leader does this in ways that tap into the reality of the organisation and its environment, they join the flow. They then tune in to the possibilities arising in a situation and sense where the organisation needs to move to within this context. Finally they seek to influence this context and frame a new intent, working with the energy of the organisation to create this new story. Attractor leadership helps the organisation find its new compass points. It brings coherence, a new sense of excitement, and unity.

A leader's presence in this task is as important as their interventions. They have the humility to serve the organisation, not draw power to themselves, which requires them to be aware of their own ego needs and put them to one side. Such self awareness avoids them projecting their own issues and unconscious shadow onto the situation around them. Unless they can do this they will be unable to exercise leadership that serves the wider organisation's intent. When they *are* there conscious and present to serve the organisation, this will be responded to with commitment and passion from those they serve. Their leadership will be 'authorised' by their followers, and by giving away power they will have become more powerful.

Without intent to serve the whole, and without self awareness to tune into what's happening inside them and around them, Attractor leadership can easily slip into its dark side, 'seduction'. When this happens attention is drawn towards the leader, not to the organisation's purpose, even though the 'seduction' might make others temporarily feel special and serve their need to be given attention. However this does not make them powerful, it makes them dependent, and the leaders charm and seduction can take them into risky places. Yet with intent to serve the whole, and with high levels of self awareness, Attractor leadership can bring extraordinary levels of commitment, passion and purpose to the change; it's an igniting force.

6

Edge and tension – amplifies disturbance

'Pure compassion is ruthless'

Edge and tension: the essence

When leaders practice Edge and Tension they shift the system's capacity to perform to its potential. The primary way in which they do this is by drawing people's attention to the tough issues which are getting in the way of movement and performance. To create this awareness they seek out the underlying disturbance in the system and make it visible, which in fact can be a releasing rather than a scary move. The underlying disturbance often springs from strongly held, yet unhelpful assumptions and beliefs, which leaders practicing Edge and Tension are able to see and unafraid to confront. In all the above they take themselves and others to their 'edge' of discomfort; and paradoxically by moving into less 'safe' places, create the freedom for innovative and breakthrough behaviour. While this can create anxiety they maintain the tension. At all times their intention is to take their organisation towards its ambition (the 'light side'), not into unnecessary fear and stress (the 'dark side').

What follows is an illustration of how a leader recognised that break through was only going to come when he took his organisation further into discomfort. Indeed he wanted the disturbance to be so amplified that it would make powerfully visible the mindset shift necessary to move the organisation towards its stated ambition. In reading this, notice how the disturbance, or 'perturbation', was initially catalysed within the small 'cell' of a vital design conversation, and then transmitted out to the larger system. It was as if the leader saw the whole systemic issue being played out in the course of one conversation (which could have gone unnoticed), and by then acting in the moment to change that conversation, he changed something much greater. And yet throughout this pivotal and challenging conversation, he did not leave anyone feeling intimidated or beaten up – the 'cell' stayed healthy and functioning, and in fact became more alive and creative.

Johan was hosting a design team teleconference. The design team were only two weeks away from the major event they had been preparing for over several months. The event was a large gathering of the 100 most senior leaders in their organisation. The stated intent of the event was to move the culture closer towards 'customer passion'. While a retail organisation, the perception in the market place of their organisation was 'clean and clinical' rather than 'warm and inviting'. Market research revealed that when customers entered their stores all the shelves were neatly stacked yet the staff seemed disinterested and unavailable; and based on this perceived lack of emotional engagement their customers were starting to defect to their competitors' stores. The leader of this organisation recognised that the culture was set from the top – if his top 100 leaders felt no passion for the customer, how could they expect their frontline staff to be? Hence the conference to explore the theme.

The call that Johan was hosting was for the design team to review a radical new design for the event. He had been feeling uneasy with the way the previous design had been going. He could have just let that go however he had decided to intervene, even though he knew it could cause upset. The event was about passion; yet the design was going to produce one of the most rationally experienced events you could have imagined. It was characterised by structured assignments with pre-set groupings of people; standardised questions about how to define 'passion' were to be given to different syndicate groups, who had to report back their responses within boxes on neatly designed templates; the 'passionate' outputs were going to get aggregated by the conference design team and then presented back on power point slides; the Executive Leadership Team were going to comment on the outputs and create some statements about what they were going to commit to do. In summary, the design was an elegantly engineered piece of work, yet it felt as cold and clinical as the stores that their customers were currently walking into!

A new design was therefore being proposed along the following lines: when leaders walked into the room at the opening of the conference the Rod Stewart track, 'Passion', was going to be playing; hotel staff were to be stationed by the doors holding out platters of strawberries dipped in chocolate and plates of frosted grapes for participants to pick up and eat as they walked in; the room was to have low lighting, with red lamps stationed around the walls; after participants had sat down two of the VP's from the Executive Leadership Team were going to walk onto the stage and. . . . share stories to the group about what outside of work (sparing blushes) they got most passionate about in their lives; then the rest of the group were going to be invited to do the same thing . . . and so on and so forth.

Johan invited reactions to the new design on the call. There were a few muted comments along the lines of 'this feels very different'. However, one of the design team members in particular, let's call her Andrea, was very vocal in her reaction. 'This will not work. It's a ridiculous design. These are very senior managers. This will feel very awkward and silly. It's juvenile. And what's more, let's not forget we are a very logical and rational culture; we like predictability and control, delegates will walk out of the doors at this kind of "show". And how will they justify this kind of event to their people when they get back home? Furthermore, we only have two weeks to go, it's far too late to get any of this arranged'. She was certainly getting passionate on the call about the 'Customer Passion' conference design. The ensuing silence on the call felt sparkly. Things had heated up.

Johan cleared his throat signalling he was going next; 'Andrea, thanks for your comments. I can clearly hear and feel your discomfort – I feel it myself with this design. And you are rightly sensing the discomfort that will be felt by the 100 leaders coming to the event. Well, do you know what, *this is exactly how I want the 100 leaders to feel next week,* that's the whole point, you've got it in one! Unless our leaders can experience leading with passion and feel how counter-cultural that is, we will not have the self-awareness or insight to change anything in our retail sites!' There was another silence, which this time felt more resonant. Andrea eventually replied; 'but, so, you're saying, like, this is really it?! I've got the whole point?' 'Yes Andrea', Johan replied, 'what we feel right now needs to be amplified in two weeks time'. She replied, 'okay, fine, I see what you mean, wow, this is going to be a good conference, I'm glad I've sussed it! Let's get going on making it happen', and Andrea was heard going out into the corridors after this call telling other people what a great and different conference this was going to be.

What edge and tension is (and is not)

Johan knew he was going to have to take people to the edge of their comfort zone in order to stoke things up and create the insight and capacity to perform differently; and he was doing this within the design teleconference call itself, which was presaging the forthcoming event (in fact we often find that the design team experience of an event 'foretells' what the actual event is going to be like). As the most senior leader though Johan could have adopted different behaviours on the call: he could have defended the design and implicitly put Andrea down, 'Andrea, trust the consultants, they know what they're doing'; he could have bypassed the systemic issue and personalised the situation, 'well Andrea, you're just going to have to feel stress-y through this – if you can't take the heat get out of the kitchen'; he could have pretended that it wasn't really all that scary and even compromised on the discomfort, 'Andrea, don't worry, it's only the first couple of hours at the conference, let's try it out because we can always then go back to what we're used to'; or, he could have protected Andrea, 'you don't have to worry Andrea, you're on the design team, ultimately it's going to be us in the Executive Leadership Team that will front this conference and take any flack'.

However, Johan didn't fall into any of these (natural) traps: instead, he held firm on the design, and the need to process the response it elicited in the conversation; he connected the tension felt during the call to the whole ambition for the event (i.e. to transform the culture); *and he gave the discomfort that Andrea was feeling a place, a systemic context.* This enabled her to move away from (unexpressed personal) fear and defensiveness, to, feeling that she was an important change agent in the system. Skilful leaders who practice Edge and Tension therefore do so with positive intent and systemic insight. They tackle the disturbing issues that are causally unhelpful to the organisation reaching its potential. They don't just create a stir for the sake of it. At times this will mean taking people on, and confronting their behaviour. However, this is done to raise excellence, not to score points. Their interventions serve the organisation's desire to move to a better and different place, not any personal desire to make them look good at the expense of others. Johan didn't need to use his authority on the call to make Andrea feel inadequate in order to push the design through.

Paradoxically, positively intended Edge and Tension leadership demonstrates that *going to a place that you don't want often gets you to where you do want.* When people go towards that which most disturbs them they seem to be released from its negative impact. Parents know that having open conversations about sex with their adolescent children can actually help them behave more responsibly. Leadership teams that can talk about the potential for mistrust in the team actually create more trust – because you need to be able to trust each other to talk about edgy subjects like where you mistrust! An associated paradox is that *the more you try to eliminate tension the more dangerous it becomes.* By surfacing tension you release it: by eliminating tension you create it. If ripe issues cannot come out into the open they will only go underground and get 'riper' until they smell and snarl so much they become overwhelming. Parents who say to their children that they can't talk about death actually make the subject scarier. Team leaders who avoid conversations about team dynamics only make the dynamics worse as they become 'undiscussable'. However, when the dragon gets named, the dragon loses its ability to harm. Leaders may have to risk being projected onto and disliked when they practice Edge and Tension, yet by either avoiding tough issues or protecting people from their consequences, things don't change, people will stay in their 'safe prisons' – and far from helping others the non-confrontation can actually do them a disservice.

Facing up to facts, and/or making others aware of the unhelpful elements in the currently enacted 'story', is therefore essential for the creation of movement: it can develop a sense of urgency, unblock stuck issues, stimulate a desire to improve, and paradoxically release negative emotions. So moving to the edge can be a positive and exciting place – though it does take some courage: it's where things come alive; it gives you a grip on what's really happening; and it can make things move faster (as downhill skiers know when they are full tilt on their edges). When your heart thuds a bit faster in a conversation you know you could be on the edge of a break through. How can leaders create such moments and in so doing move things to a better place?

Edge and tension leadership: core practices

When we studied the transcripts from our research, we identi-fied certain Edge and Tension practices that were strongly related to successful change outcomes. These were:

- Tells it as it is – describes reality with respect yet without compromise.

- Stays constant when the going gets tough; does not with-draw from the difficulty; keeps people's 'hands in the fire'.

- Spots and challenges assumptions – creates discomfort by challenging existing paradigms and disrupting habitual ways of doing things.

- Sets high standards for others and keeps the standards up there – stretches the goals and limits of what's possible.

- Does not compromise on talent – pays attention to getting and keeping 'A players'.

Below we describe these individual practices with illustrations from the leaders we have engaged with – both within the research and in our practice. As you read through these practices, reflect on your own leadership: are these practices part of how you currently lead change; have you thought about doing them but for some reason avoided them; could your change benefit from this kind of leadership; and therefore would you like to bring more of them into your practice, or practice them with greater awareness and skill?

Tells it as it is – describes reality with respect yet without compromise

Talking straight is not always easy. It's natural not to want to cause pain, make someone angry or upset, or cause embarrassment. While this is often rationalised as a desire to protect others, it often springs from an unexpressed desire to protect ourselves from the flak we might get back in return; since by not talking straight we protect ourselves from the emotional consequences of drawing attention to that which others find painful and would rather not hear about; 'you're just out to get me!', 'why do you need to stir things up?', 'leave me alone, I thought I was empowered?', 'it's not true, you've got it wrong!', 'you're really pushy aren't you?!'.

Moreover *organisations* can conspire to avoid the truthful telling of reality. In closed and protective cultures it could be 'unsafe' to voice disquiet; it's not that there are overt lies, it's just that it sometimes serves cultures to leave things up in the air, woolly, or ambiguous, leading to often heard statements such as; 'if the senior management's memos are always vague, it means we don't have to do anything about them!', 'I think the CEO was trying to encourage us to change, yet all the graphs he showed looked like our results were pretty much OK, so what's the story?', 'if we only tell our staff what we can say at the moment, and leave all the tricky subjects like cost cutting to later when we know more detail, then we'll avoid unnecessary de-motivation (*and us having to handle awkward conversations!*)'.

In our research leaders who practiced Edge and Tension well got things out on the table, one leader recounted; 'so I said, do you want to treat people as children, or do you want them to know what the next two to three years are going to look like?' *And they do this not through them having to do all of the confronting and straight talk,* they sought to change how conversations happened more generally in their organisations so that people around them became more capable of 'telling it as it is'.

One leader in our study entered an organisation which seemed chronically unable to talk about its poor performance. And the anxiety that this caused led them to displace their feelings of inadequacy *about being unable to talk about it rather than the poor performance itself,* onto intense speculation about who was up to what in the organisation. The leader told us in her interview;

'I was dead up front with them about I didn't expect to find politics, "I'm going to ask some very direct questions and I'm going to be open and direct . . . we're going to be open about things and I expect you to have your views . . . and I'm going to be open back and feedback what you've said and tell you what I'm going to do and establish a completely different pattern of behaviour" '.

As soon as a more open and direct communication style entered the organisation the underperformance was able to be confronted. And once that happened, it was like a release valve, and movement was made towards addressing the situation. Another leader instigated a practice at the end of every management team meeting in which he would get up from the table and move to two different flip charts. On one he wrote at the top, 'what I heard in this meeting', under which he would summarise the agreed decisions and actions. On the other flip chart he wrote up the question, 'what have I *not* heard in this meeting?', and at this point he would put the pen down and invite his team to talk about the things they had been thinking about or feeling in the meeting but had been unable to say. The team often commented that this part of the meeting felt the most 'real and alive'. When they talked about that which they found most disturbing, or hard to talk about, they were able to confront the deeper business issues that were keeping them or the organisation stuck. And when they explored *why* they had been unable to talk about those issues openly in the meeting itself, they became more aware of the team dynamics which might need adjusting.

The power of disclosure and talking straight does not just relate to the unearthing of previously hidden yet vital subjects, *the process itself builds safety and creates movement.*

We once worked with a team who felt that their meetings were scary and unsafe places to talk openly about risky subjects, and because of this they were not generating new and creative ideas about how to improve their organisation's performance. The development intervention adopted was a paradoxical one; the team were asked to talk about *'what could we do to make this team the scariest place it could be?'* A more straightforward intervention would have been to have asked them to identify what they could do to become more open as a team. However, by having them move into the very place they wanted to avoid, it actually made them feel a whole lot safer, because they had to take risks in order to be able to talk about how to make it a more risky place. If they had had a nice polite conversation about the team becoming a safer place, *the conversation in the room would not have changed,* and indeed it could have become even less safe than when they had started. This example reinforces another of our central themes in Changing Leadership; that it is the *process* that leaders adopt, as much as what they say or physically do, that carries the change.

In summary, this element of Edge and Tension leadership encourages the accurate description of reality, having people tell things as they are, *and in the process of so doing* build greater trust and openness. When this happens, people become less defensive, fearful and stuck, thereby enabling new patterns of behaviour to emerge.

Stays constant when the going gets tough; does not withdraw from the difficulty; keeps people's 'hands in the fire'

Edge and Tension leadership does not rest with the acknowledgement and confronting of today's reality; while this can stir things up and bring things out into the open, constancy and resolve are then required to stay on course to improve the situation. When things have been brought out into the open they can easily get re-buried, and avoided, since it becomes too painful to contemplate that *something has to be done about it*. Once again our survival instinct is engaged and we stay stuck in the same pattern – talking brave but not acting brave, keeping things where they are. Edge and Tension however keeps us moving into the fire.

Escaping our 'safe prisons' takes courage: while we might feel trapped in unhelpful repeating patterns at least we are used to them, they are serving a purpose, they look after us, and this makes us feel okay. Breaking out of them can require a significant amount of emotional and psychological courage; and it means sticking to what we say is important to do. One of the leaders in our research recounted; 'some of our staff were very unhappy, but you just keep answering and telling it to them straight', 'I said "right, we're going to sort this supply chain out, we're going to get proper forecasts", and it took me years, but I just kept going at it all the time'. Holding people's hands in the fire requires the skilful maintenance of tension; 'I went back to that again and again to an extent that the team was getting really angry with me, but I just insisted that we look into it in more detail . . . I gave them no wriggle room, it was really driving the line that the business goals mattered'.

Sometimes staying with the disturbance is a necessary journey, since living through it and uncovering its source can create the awareness to move to a different place. We can be in some small way 'in love' with our unhelpful behaviour. While it might look dysfunctional to those around us, we can be caught up in some kind of 'commitment' to staying stuck, because it is serving a need. Leaders who practiced Edge and Tension could spot this so called 'competing commitment' and help walk people through their own resistance to change. In Chapter 4 we shared the illustration of a leader who was tasked with instigating a radical restructuring of his business. He sensed that the competing commitment in his leadership team was towards the avoidance of any activity that would make them individually accountable, in other words their unexpressed commitment was towards personal security – they needed to keep their heads beneath the parapet. This dynamic had sprung from the previous CEO's leadership style which had been to keep his organisation in a state of dependency on him to figure out what had to be done. If the new leader had simply come in and replaced some of this team to try and remove the dysfunction, it might not have solved the problem, since the systemic pattern of dependency could still be there – the pain might just pop up again elsewhere. The new leader therefore tried to address the competing commitment head on by saying 'you're now a senior leader, you've got to commit to sorting this out', and by staying with them, together in the room, working out all their plans until two in the morning, he helped them move into that which they found most troublesome – i.e. creating individually account-able plans of action. He kept their hands in the fire.

A related practice we observed in the leaders from our study was their ability to spot when people were 'explaining away' the reasons for underperformance. People can do this to avoid experiencing the pain of seeing their own responsibility for contributing to the underperformance, and hence them having to do something about it. Underperformance can always be explained away; 'I was told to do it', 'I never wanted to take this on in the first place', 'it was a lousy idea in the first place'. One of the leaders in our study said, 'I was trying to keep us honest; because there is always a tendency to interpret facts . . . I always tried to keep us straight'. Keeping constant on what matters and not getting distracted by defensive expla-nations about the situation helps manage organisational avoidance mechanisms; 'I kept concentrating on products and customers – "OK that's fine, I can see that we've got all these other things, but what are we doing for X (a customer)? How are we going to make it a better offer?" And this got some energy behind it. I let the team know "here are the basics that you've all forgotten you need to do meaningfully"'.

Spots and challenges assumptions – creates discomfort by challenging existing paradigms and disrupting habitual ways of doing things

We have found in our own consulting work that one of the most powerful ways to create movement is to see and name the assumptions that people hold about a given situation. We take action based on our assumptions. However, if the assumptions remain untested or unexamined then our interpretation of the situation and ensuing actions could be misguided. The type of assumption the leaders in our study were most able to detect is what is known as a 'limiting assumption'; our explanation of the situation effectively removes us from having to take a risk, to engage differently in a relationship, and/or to reach a different level of performance.

Some assumptions of course are well founded, and based on extensive, reliable and consistent data; however the skilled leader spots when the limiting assumption could just be a convenient way to avoid taking a risk, or to give up pushing for doing something new; as one leader in our study recounted, 'I learnt about the nonsense we had in our processes. And afterwards they said "do we really have to do it like that?" And I said "well, why do we do it like that?" And actually, it was something we could change. It was our part of the process, it was not the legislation, so we could change it you know'. At times the limiting assumptions we hold relates to how we see our leadership role. One leader in our study challenged his leadership team's assumption that, due to their fixed terms of office, their task as leaders was just to launch a series of 'quick wins' into the organisation. This leader pushed back, and he challenged their assumptions; 'I said to them "this is a 40 year job. Don't kid yourselves. So the challenge is, not that we won't achieve anything as we go, but that it is a long job. Each of us have got to understand that if we don't pass on the baton to our successors. . . . unless we're prepared to ensure that the company can carry on with the support, we can't do it. There has to be longevity" '.

In addition to being able to spot and challenge people's limiting assumptions, Edge and Tension leadership also seeks to work on the deeper structures and processes that could be causing unhelpful behaviour and underperformance. Sometimes this can be making changes to the formal organisational structure and roles; it can also be about making changes to the informal structures and how people work together. One leader realised that the problems his supply chain organisation was having were caused by people not co-operating across the departments. So he set up the performance improvement team in one location. This led to some tension but also quite different patterns of behaviour, and not just in the team, but between the organisational departments they represented in the supply chain. The savvy leader therefore knows where to go to create the disturbance; they do not wreak havoc and change across the organisation in a random fashion, *it's about creating discomfort and disruption in the areas that hold the most potential for moving the rest of the organisation.*

One of the highest leverage areas that can change the organisational system at large is the senior leadership team. Following the 'as above, so below' principle, a tiny shift in behaviour in this part of the system can have an amplifying affect on what happens elsewhere in the organisation. One leader in our study was tasked with turning around a manufacturing site which needed to be run more as a 'business', rather than a function. This was going to require a fundamental shift in mindset and behaviour. She firmly expected her leadership team to be able to rise above their technical manufacturing disciplines and lead the business jointly for the whole of the site, which was going to require them pushing responsibility for operational issues out of their leadership team meetings and down into the organisation. So she decided to change how the leadership team meetings were structured and run. This happened not without discomfort; her team had been used to meeting every Monday morning and listening to a report from each individual team member about what was going on in their part of the plant, which felt very safe and easy.

'I changed it [the Leadership Team meeting] to every other week, and I reduced it from half a day to two hours. *So my intent here was to be consciously different, and to make it clear to people that how you use your time is important.* We also changed the agenda from presentations and information and operation, to policy, strategy, talent management and capability building. We moved away from the short term to a long term focus'.

As she held this change on course, people reporting to the leadership team also started to change their behaviour. They had been used to coming to these meetings with operational updates to present, and lists of decisions they needed the top team to make; now, they started to take on their own responsibility for deciding and acting, since their leaders no longer sought operational updates, or needed to rubber stamp decisions, and as a consequence the organisation beneath them started to take initiative to improve performance. This devolution of ownership and accountability enabled the senior leadership team to feel more confident and relaxed at tackling the more complex, unstructured and strategic issues; in effect they had stopped doing the work of the people beneath them. So simply by changing how her top leadership team spent their time, this leader shifted the paradigm around accountability and this transformed how the whole site performed.

Sets high standards for others and keeps the standards up there – stretches the goals and limits of what's possible

Edge and Tension leadership is very specific and non-compromising about standards of excellence, and when there is any indication that the standards are not being upheld, then the leader acts, as vividly illustrated in this research excerpt;

I said to my boss . . . 'I need to speak to you'. . . . and I said 'this is a disaster. I need to tell you professionally that this is not up to standard'. He said 'I'm no technical expert so I can't comment'. And I said 'you have to take my professional opinion. We have a problem here. This team in this configuration cannot deliver it. So something radical must change'.

We found that there were three ways in which leaders catalysed a new sense of performance ambition in their organisation: setting goals and aspirations to do the unthinkable; challenging people to move into situations of discomfort; and enabling people to see the same situation through a very different lens.

Leaders set goals and aspirations by being very clear about what had to be done, by when, and to what standard; and they recognised that to achieve this standard their people would have to start changing the way they operated, so they would stay alongside their people to help make it happen. One leader in our study was running a regional division of a pharmaceutical company, where getting the timing of product launches soon after drug approval can make or lose a lot of money. She was determined that this drug would be launched on the day of approval, 'so, I just said, "what would it take to launch this on the same day as we got the approval?" and there was a large sucking in of breath. . . . But they worked it and we shipped the product on the day of approval and all sorts of things happened differently, country by country, as people recognised "we can do this!"'.

Good coaches know that it's hard to help people lift their performance when they either stay stuck in their 'comfort zone' or move at the other extreme into their 'panic zone'. In between these extremes is the 'discomfort zone'; the edgy place where your heart beats faster yet you can still function. Sometimes leaders create discomfort by asking people to step up to the plate; 'I collected all my people together in one location, told them I could not accept failure and that the company must meet its target – but that I didn't have the answer as to how we could do that'. Another leader called upon people's ingenuity; 'the goals were very aggressive . . . we spent $20 million in China and the goal was to reduce it to $11 million. The first time the team came back they said they had ideas to give one million back. I told them we had these benchmarks, said that this was not good enough, and asked them to go away and come back with the right answer'. Other leaders kept the standards high through the persistent use of questions; 'I just kept asking all the questions . . . I tended to challenge around "why did you not consider?", and "where was the debate?", and "what would it take to go faster?"'.

The third way in which leaders helped to lift organisational ambition was through interventions that helped people see the world through a new lens. In particular they invited them to imagine or live in a world *where the performance was already different.* We saw this being done by leaders taking their teams out to other organisations which they considered to be already 'world class'. Sometimes it was done through the use of 'just imagine' scenarios. One leader recounted; 'I came up with the idea of having two press releases that we confronted the guys with at the opening of the conference – in the first five minutes. One said we had sold the business off and the other said we had just acquired one of the leading banks in x (country). You could have cut the atmosphere this created with a knife . . .'

In all the above illustrations the leader set high standards of excellence yet engaged others in figuring out how to reach them; they stayed available, supportive, and consistent, projecting a feeling of joint ownership and responsibility. In the absence of such leadership presence the raising of ambition can turn into intimidation and stress.

Does not compromise on talent – pays attention to getting and keeping 'A players'

Two recent books (*From Good to Great*, Jim Collins, 2001; *Execution*, Larry Bossidy & Ram Charan, 2002) have highlighted the importance of leaders' selectivity and retaining key talent. In our own experience of working in change, we have found that companies who recruit what we call 'A players' into the 'mission critical' roles are those that can create sustainable performance improvement. These kinds of leaders take organisations to different places. By 'A players' we don't mean career minded, aggressive, and super confident leaders. We mean people who can set a new direction, take others with them, and do it in a way that is transforming and which can build the capability to do things differently again and again. By 'mission critical' roles we mean those posts in the organisation without which the change would fail. They are the pivotal leadership positions which can unlock most value in the organisation. This is well illustrated by a quotation from one of the leaders in our research study.

In the restructuring we created new roles. We decided from the very beginning that we would go feverishly after the best possible talent available. So I've still got some scars from this but I took the decision. I agreed with the team and held the line that we would not let everyone off and do their own recruitment. We head hunted them. We identified a hundred and sixteen possible people . . . and we went forensically, pathologically, after those people . . .

Beyond recruiting from the outside, sometimes the talent you need to help change the organisation is right there in front of you. Leaders in our study looked beyond the professional, technical, or general managerial skills required for the roles, they also hunted out people with an appetite for change; 'I made sure that the people were not change stoppers . . . they were people who had a passion for the business . . . and they really wanted to excel'. Sometimes this entailed leaders looking in unconventional places; 'I took a risk because this woman I wanted to promote there was a belief that she wasn't ready. But there's a spark there, and so I took the risk'. At other times this meant having to make tough calls on people; 'I had some really tough discussions, they were close to "if this happens again you're fired, you're no longer in my team"'.

Given what we know overall about the vital importance that leader behaviour has on successful change outcomes, it follows that acquiring, developing, and retaining top leadership talent has to be one of the highest leverage areas at any organisation's disposal. Talent attracts talent; and moreover key appointments give out strong signals to the organisation about what kind of performance is really valued.

Edge and tension practices: putting it all together

Patrick had been tasked with turning around the operational performance of a 2500 people strong Customer Call Centre (CCC) organisation that had been repeatedly failing its customers (when he joined 10000 customers were still waiting for their bills). There had been several crises in the years prior to Patrick taking the position and several changes of leadership all of whom had tried to solve the crisis. There had been much frenzied activity to solve the problem and reduce the back log, yet still the organisation seemed 'stuck' in ever decreasing circles of service quality. What was going to be different for Patrick? How could he irreversibly transform the service without creating further fear of reprisals and reorganisations that would aggravate the already anxious workforce?

The first thing Patrick did was to have his organisation come up with a completely accurate and holistic description of the current situation. The problem was that there were many different departments involved in servicing the customer, all of whom were individually delivering a 90 % good enough task, however when these '90%-ers' got multiplied at the end of the chain only two out of ten customers got the service they needed, and eight out of ten did not. Patrick visibly confronted his organisation with this reality; given they had been working separately in their different parts of the service chain, they had not realised just how bad the overall picture was. Patrick's intent was to hold up the mirror so that they could see the scale and extent of the problem; however he made a conscious choice as a leader not to 'act out of fear'; instead, he wanted his people to see him acting out of 'discipline, listening and diagnosing, and going for the root causes.... I needed to convince all these people that I was serious about addressing the issues that had been buried or ignored or not listened to for many years'. He wanted them engaged with performance, not disabled in fear.

Patrick was feeling the edge himself: new to the job and the organisation he had only been given six weeks by his boss to diagnose the situation and establish a complete picture of 'current reality'. When this had been accomplished through engaging all the departments in his organisation, he called a meeting of the Crisis Team. He set them a very challenging goal; 'I have a dream, and my dream is that the frontline people I visited last week can actually serve the customer in one go, first time right'. This stretch goal was going to require a fundamental change in how the organisation functioned. He gave his team just two weeks to go away and find out *how* this goal could be achieved. This use of a cross departmental Crisis Team in itself challenged some deep cultural paradigms. The organisation had become conditioned to its leaders going away, working in a dark room with consultants, and then coming out to announce the solution; 'my in-tray was just unbelievable on my first day in the office, and I refused to take all these decisions, I said "it's your role to make these decisions not mine"'.

The Crisis Team went away and came back with three options for how to reach the new performance standard. The first two Patrick discounted immediately – more people and new systems, and he went for option three, the 'radical one'. This caused some consternation; 'I think the fact that I decided on the spot was probably the biggest culture shock that they'd had for months in that process'. *He kept his eye constantly on changing the process of how people did things.* Just by getting to the root cause of the crisis, and setting priorities based on this diagnosis, was again in itself a new behaviour in a culture used to crisis management and fire fighting. In order to create the conditions for this more sustainable change to happen, Patrick even gave his staff permission *not* to serve the customer; 'at one stage we kept the telephones ringing because picking it up and spending time explaining to the customer that we didn't know the answer was not going to help that much. I don't think anybody else would have had the courage or mandate to do that'. Patrick commented how 'disquieting' for the organisation this new style was, and also 'dangerous for my credibility', and yet he kept the tension there. He was going for performance, not for self promotion.

Once his Crisis Team had figured out the issue and identified how to get out of it, Patrick called a meeting of 70 people from across the CCC. He knew he needed their whole hearted commitment if they were to deliver the challenging 'first time right' service target. In the weeks before this meeting Patrick had read a press article from an angry customer of his company, who had been so frustrated that his letters of complaint to the company had not been responded to, he had needed to voice his frustration in public. Patrick felt bad and ashamed about this, and wanted 'other people to feel bad inside'. He wanted 'the urgency to come from the customer, I wanted to show how customers feel about our collective performance'. He had a video made that told the story of the angry customer, and showed that to the assembled staff. Note how Patrick's intent and action was not about exposing the poor performance of any individual or department, it was about pulling the edge and tension back from the customer right into people's insides. He walked them into what was most troubling and disturbing, without having to personally beat them over the heads.

After this meeting, Patrick gave the group just four weeks to figure out how to implement the radical option three that the Crisis Team had identified. During this time he watched the organisation closely. In the absence of rolling out a big 'change programme' or restructuring, he quietly got the organisation continually standing in a line together, getting to the bottom of the end to end process, and figuring out for themselves how to change things. He pushed hard on the process being different, and this was challenging for people not used to taking responsibility; 'of course there were some people or teams who proved unwilling, and I have no time for that. I try to understand where they are coming from but if we can't find common ground then unfortunately I had to leave them behind because we cannot be held up by what is left behind us. . . . I try to deal with that with respect . . . but there's no time for the unwilling'. Our quiet leader certainly had teeth.

If we forward the story to its outcomes, after just 18 months Patrick's company had the best performance in the market place in terms of customer service – as voted by customers, and as benchmarked on certain operational measures. When he was speaking recently at a conference someone asked him how he managed his own learning process to be able to pull off such a big change, and he replied; 'I've learned how it takes a lot for me not to project who I am, or what I need, into a situation – but to really try to understand what is needed in the situation. And I've found that the most difficult, because I was often confronted with my own unrest, my own pressure, and the judgements I make as a person – which is not always productive'.

Note in Patrick's response another recurring theme running through our inquiry into Changing Leadership; without self awareness into one's own issues a leader cannot accurately and objectively tune in to what is happening and needed in the situation around them, instead their background story could be being re-enacted, over and over again, which leads them to only see what's in front of them through their own unconscious projection. However when a leader is keenly self aware, and able to detach themselves from their own impulses and needs, they can see with greater clarity what they are looking at, and from that diagnosis intervene without prejudice.

Edge and tension: the dark side

Edge and Tension leadership is about moving people towards performance, not towards fear. *It's a fine line to walk between being challenging and confronting on the task and being intimidating, even bullying, with people.* Once again it's the leader's intent and levels of self awareness in the situation that enables them to walk the line between ambition and 'abuse', and indeed for some it can be questionable whether the line can be walked at all. If the leader's intent is to serve oneself at the expense of the purpose around them, then Edge and Tension can easily tip into self promotion – making the leader look good at the expense of others. The organisational 'shadow' of the leader that gets projected feels to others as if the leader does not see their own responsibility for creating the situation – all the attribution for poor performance or the difficulty is put onto others.

Sometimes leaders carry a background story from their past in which they felt they were never good enough in the eyes of those people they most wanted to feel acknowledged by, or they had to fight off others for the attention of those people from whom they most wanted recognition. If the leader is unaware of their story and how it gets played out in today's world, when they now 'confront reality' it can unconsciously be about trying to prove how inadequate someone else's performance or behaviour is. The 'dark side' of Edge and Tension can therefore intentionally put other people down; 'I'm right you're wrong', or, 'my facts are more truthful than yours'; or in unintended ways it can still get played out by ignoring people on their team who they either believe to be incompetent, or indeed competent and therefore threatening to their own needed sense of superiority. When the 'dark side' of Edge and Tension is active the edge of the leader can feel cutting, rather than energising; the tension they create feels dangerous, rather than transforming; the atmosphere crackles around them and people are scared to say something in case it's taken the wrong way, or they are drawn into an argument to ostensibly bring 'edge and tension' into the situation when it's actually all about the other person needing to look good and feel invincible.

If the leader's primary experiences have been in competitive environments or cultures, and they are unaware of the potential win:lose mentality that this might have fostered, they can project their need to look good or win in the eyes of others, into the setting of impossibly high standards of performance. And when they keep up the pressure to perform people around them can collapse in exhaustion. Or they might expect such perfection that people will always be unable to reach this standard and as a consequence feel rather small and helpless. The performance edge then becomes a dangerous and scary place, 'what, you're wanting me to go that far, that quickly?!' When Edge and Tension is not practiced with an ability to tune in to where the other person is coming from, or with the humility to understand that sometimes you can only go so far so soon, then it can feel like the over zealous 'sergeant-major' putting people through unattainable exercises at an army boot camp.

Leaders who have a strong outer orientation (in other words concern to protect the self, and desire for positive reputation in the eyes of others) could even distort Edge and Tension such that the real issues to be confronted are kept hidden and they wreak havoc on things that don't really matter. They 'sweat the small stuff', not the things that count. And they do this because they want to protect their reputation and not let on as to just how bad the situation might be. They fail to listen to those who are trying to raise the edge on important matters and they go aggressively fire fighting and turning over stones where it's not necessary. This misdirected Edge and Tension again comes from the underlying intent to sustain one's self image and control others. It amplifies disturbance in the places that will have no discernible impact on the overall performance of the organisation.

Edge and Tension without positive intent to serve others becomes cutting and controlling; without self awareness to see one's own background story and how that might be being played out into the situation it can become intimidating, misdirected and overly threatening. Once again we have presented the exaggerated tendency of the dark side so that you might recognise even some tiny elements of it in your own behaviour. To help you determine the kind of shadow you may be projecting as a leader, you might find it helpful to reflect on the following questions.

- Are you serving yourself, or the organisation around you?

- Are you causing unnecessary ripples, or amplifying necessary disturbance?

- Do you talk straight to win an argument, or to uncover the truth?

- Do you compete with the inside, or the outside of your organisation?

- Do you set high performance standards to draw attention to yourself, or to raise the excellence of others?

- Do you challenge reality through the force of your own argument, or through creating situations in which people can see for themselves just what has to change?

Summary

In Table 6.1 we summarise the essence of Edge and Tension leadership; what it is and what it is not, its core practices, and how it serves change. Leaders who can take organisations into what they find most disturbing create the conditions ripe for movement. Since where there is discomfort there can be learning, and where there is learning there is energy for doing something new, which opens up possibilities to move to a different place.

Discomfort is a sign that habitual routines or comfortable patterns of behaviour are being challenged; it can be created by talking straight, uncovering reality, challenging existing paradigms and staying firm and non-compromising on standards. This can be risky and scary – both for the individual leader practicing Edge and Tension and those around them; however in alleviating the pressure or discomfort the organisation will only be released back to where it was before. And that's not change, that's relief.

Edge and Tension leadership therefore overcomes the natural tendency we have to avoid the pain of doing something about a situation which is currently unhelpful for us yet which we find hard to do anything about. We prefer to stay in our 'safe prisons'. It's hard to disturb the repeating unhelpful patterns, because deep down inside we might be a little in love with

Table 6.1 Edge and Tension Leadership

Essence: amplifies disturbance in order to shift the organisation's capacity to perform to its potential

What It Is (Light Side)	*What It Is Not (Dark Side)*
• Catalysing ambition	• Generating fear and stress: *intimidation*
• Amplification of disturbance around 'ripe issues'	• Pointing out what people are doing 'wrong'
• Owning of responsibility for difficult situations	• Projecting responsibility onto others
• Challenging and confronting the issues and the task	• Avoiding, undermining and humiliating people
• Holding firm to preserve excellence	• Obstinate to score points

Core Practices
- Tells it as it is; describes reality with respect yet without compromise
- Stays constant when the going gets tough; does not withdraw from difficulty; holds people's hands 'in the fire'
- Spots and challenges assumptions; creates discomfort by challenging existing paradigms and disrupts habitual ways of doing things
- Sets high standards for others and keeps the standards there; stretches the goals and limits of what's possible
- Does not compromise on talent; pays attention to getting and keeping 'A players'

How It Serves Change
- Creates urgency and momentum to address current issues that are threatening 'survival of the system'
- Enables people to break out of limiting assumptions and become more innovative
- Straight talking develops trust and more courage to tackle the real issues
- Excites people towards excellence
- Keeps people moving forward in tough times, when it would be easy to step back and release tension

© 2008 Transcend Consultancy

them, they are serving an unconscious need. Going to the source of the disturbance is therefore important because people could be resisting change due to this 'competing commitment' to staying put.

If leaders try to protect people from the discomfort of self awareness, they could be doing the organisation they serve a disservice. Edge and Tension leadership puts the responsibility for change firmly with the people who need to break through and carry the change themselves. However, they help the process by holding up mirrors to the organisation about its performance, the issues that need resolving, and the behaviours that are currently unhelpful. And they do this with intent to raise the performance of the organisation around them, not to score points or make themselves look good at the expense of others.

7

Container – provides holding structure

'How can I be sure, in a world that's constantly changing,

*How can I be sure, where I stand with you?'**

David Cassidy

Container leadership: the essence

Leaders who serve as Containers take the fire and excitement
that Edge and Tension creates and channel it towards the
organisation's purpose. They are able to process and make
bearable anxiety, difficult emotions, and tension, in ways that
unblock energy and help people through turbulence with confidence and courage. They do this at multiple levels: through
their personal presence, which is non-anxious, affirming and
resolute, while still being able to acknowledge their own
issues and anxiety to others; through processes and structures
that create safety and boundaries, provide clarity on what's

---

*How can I Be Sure" Words and Music by Eddie Brigati Jr and Felix
Cavaliere © 1967, Reproduced by permission of EMI Music Publishing
Ltd, London W8 5SW

expected, and hold firm on how things need to be done; and through networks and connections that channel energy and give space for people to develop independent voice. Container leadership can work through anxiety and fiercely support people through change (the 'light side'), it is not there to absorb anxiety, control behaviour, and protect the organisation against difficulty (the 'dark side').

What follows is an illustration of how a leader managed to hold some very difficult and volatile emotions in an unsettled situation and in so doing move people towards constructive engagement on the source of the anxiety, in this case a change process that was not going fast enough. In seeking to face the difficulty, the situation actually became a whole lot safer. This is contrasted to an earlier leadership style that was 'over contained' in its avoidance of danger and reluctance to open the lid on tricky subjects. In thus seeking to protect, the situation actually became a whole lot less safe.

Hans's organisation was one year into a major change process that had been initiated by market deregulation. Their national government had set an aggressive timetable to move towards a free market in which players slow to act would be acquired. His organisation had a long and proud history. They didn't want to be swallowed up. In the past year Hans and his leadership team had got the organisation's attention behind the required change. Task forces had been established to create a more commercial culture, and reduce unnecessary bureaucracy. However, despite much effort it seemed that one year on things were still essentially the same. Operational service measures had not improved. The only thing that had changed was that people were more tired and less productive. There was much frustration, and time was running out. A major meeting of the top leadership group had been called. Everything had to be 'put onto the table'.

In the morning Hans and his leadership team had given a series of presentations on the lack of progress. The 90 leaders faced them seated in rows facing the stage. The lights had been dimmed. It was hard to see anyone but the senior leaders. A roving microphone was handed out at the end of each presentation for questions and answers. The conversation was largely about interpretation of facts. Timings started to drift. By the later than scheduled coffee break the 90 leaders were getting a bit riled – they already knew all these facts and figures! Didn't the top leadership know they had been trying their hardest over the year?! During the coffee break it was suggested to the leadership team that they change the process to get more interaction and open voicing of the difficulty. Hans pricked up his ears, however the rest of his team wanted to stay on track. After the coffee break they were going to revisit the vision and positive aspects of the change, so that would change the atmosphere! And that's what they did. However by lunchtime there was positive anger in the room. All those slides were full of nice words and jargon – can't they treat us like grown ups!

The room now felt unsettled and unsafe, even dangerous. The leadership team faced their difficulty over the lunch break. In a huddle at the centre of the room we worked with Hans to help his team name their anxiety (not preserve their false 'bravado' displayed earlier in the day), and then process it.

Hans's inquiries helped them to voice and acknowledge that both the process in the room that morning and their own leadership presence had been too constraining and in a sense 'false', which had led to a situation where there was not a strong enough 'container' to process the anxiety around the underperformance. Despite the strong emotions felt by the 90 leaders in the room there was no outlet for these to be expressed. The team eventually acknowledged that this was a reflection of their own fear of letting their anxieties about the situation 'rip'. Their desire to put a lid on strong emotions had actually made the whole system more unsettled. Once the team's anxiety had been named, and its sources understood, Hans helped open his team to redesign the afternoon's session and adjust how they were going to approach it.

With people now seated in small circles, facing each other, the first session was going to be an open and unrehearsed dialogue about where the group 'were at'. Hans would lead its facilitation, starting by expressing his own frustration about the morning and how this had made him anxious. He was to do this in a way that was calm, not accusing, intent on getting out the learning, not judging what had happened. Thereafter the meeting would move into an open space format in which any of the leaders present could identify a critical change barrier, volunteer to host circles of discussion in the room about how to address that, and identify suggestions on how to adjust the change plan. It was to be a structured process with clear rules and timings. Hans and the team were up for this. The more clearly bounded, yet open, design felt risky. However, the processing of their anxiety over lunch had helped them to restrain their own impulses to control what was happening in the room.

By the tea break there were pockets of energy all over the room. People were animatedly discussing ways to accelerate the change. Chairs had been pushed aside; the meeting room looked chaotic, yet at the same time it seemed to have a deeper order. In the debrief after tea the leadership team made it clear that they were open to all ideas, that challenge was invited, *as long as the intent and goals for the change stayed the same.* The meeting closed with an adjusted change plan, and new energy. More people had volunteered to get engaged on task forces that had seemed stuck. The task force leaders themselves felt more confident and back on track with what they had to do. The leadership team felt that they could now share a lot of the responsibility they had been carrying with the leadership group around them. They had started to accept their dependency on the skills of others, and had allowed their followers to develop an independent voice. By authorising others to lead the leadership team now had far more command than when they had tried to control.

What container leadership is (and is not)

In psychodynamics 'containment' is defined as the ability to restrain your own impulses by developing an awareness of your own anxiety and its source, and from that awareness create the safe space for others to process their issues and anxiety. When you become more mindful of your own issues, and recognise them when they arise, you can then somehow 'sidestep' them in order to be more fully present and available for what is happening in the situation around you. Unless you are able to do this you can only stay acting out of your own anxiety, or story, which does not make you available to hear and work with the anxiety, or story, of others. In the above illustration, it was not until Hans's leadership team were able to put their own issues out onto the table at lunchtime that they could more clearly read the situation and be able to deal with the challenging conditions differently in the afternoon.

Furthermore, by Hans publicly sharing the anxiety that he and his leadership team had worked through after the lunch break, he gave a place for the emotions that the whole group had been feeling but had been unable to express. Once that happened, the difficult emotions were able to be processed, the anxiety of the whole group no longer became disabling, and it released energy onto the task at hand. The Edge and Tension created by confronting the reality of lack of change progress could now be more safely channelled. Hans had also publicly shared his anxiety while *remaining non-anxious himself.* His calm presence made the processing of emotions bearable for others.

In high magnitude change anxiety is inevitable. Good Container leadership provides a firm yet supportive presence to help people process the anxiety in order to develop the awareness, courage, and responsibility to move through tough times together. It is not about protecting the organisation against its difficulties or taking on the anxiety for the whole system. We have seen leaders become emotionally subsumed when they take on strong personal responsibility to 'parent' the organisation (more on the 'dark side' later).

A more structural definition of the verb, 'to contain', is 'to hold for the purpose of movement', just as container ships safely carry their cargo. At another level Container leadership is about the creation and implementation of structures that can hold and move along the organisation. In the core practices described below we illustrate how this is primarily done through the leader contracting the boundaries, expectations, and 'rules' for the organisation which in some way define the playing field, the game people need to play, and the code of conduct in which it should be played. Once these have been established, people can be authorised to go and play the game. At Hans's meeting the afternoon's design had strong process structure (the 'open space' format and rules) within which people had complete freedom to become fully contributing leaders. This change in structure changed the emotional charge in the room – it created responsibility, positive energy, and movement. And the change plan came out a whole lot better as a consequence.

Container leadership therefore channels rather than constrains. It provides structures and rules to move and release others, not to hold on to them and in so doing preserve one's own power. We confront here the paradox of rules and freedom: the stronger the rules the greater the freedom. If organisational rules are vague or not upheld, it actually becomes more constraining because people are unsure how to act and can therefore become 'stuck' in the non-clarity. In the illustration above, Hans was as rigorous in his demands that his leaders take responsibility in the afternoon for the difficulty, as he was open to what would emerge. Container leadership therefore sets up strong conditions; it does not exert microscopic control. Through the clear setting of expectations and boundaries, it helps people navigate through the uncertainty of high magnitude change. And its calm, affirming, and constant presence builds confidence and commitment when people feel most insecure.

Container leadership practices: provides holding structure

When we studied the transcripts from our research, we identified certain Container practices that were strongly related to successful change outcomes. These were:

- Is self assured, confident, and takes a stand for one's beliefs – is non-anxious in challenging conditions.

- Provides affirming and encouraging signals: builds ownership, trust and confidence.

- Makes it safe to say risky things and have the 'hard to have' conversations through empathy and high quality dialogue skills.

- Sets and contracts boundaries, clear expectations and hard rules so that people know what to operate on and how to operate.

- Creates alignment at the top and builds networks of relationships that stay in tune with the system and can channel the change.

Below we describe these individual practices with illustrations from the leaders we have engaged with – both within the research and in our practice. As you read through these practices, reflect on your own leadership: are these practices part of how you currently lead change; have you thought about doing them but for some reason avoided them; could your change benefit from this kind of leadership; and therefore would you like to bring more of them into your practice, or practice them with greater awareness and skill?

Is self assured, confident, and takes a stand for one's beliefs – is non-anxious in challenging conditions

A 'container' can be created at multiple levels in the organisation; however the personal presence of the leader is pivotal. How they come across to others sets the atmosphere within which people can either feel supported, challenged, and affirmed, or confused, uncertain, and anxious. Leaders we have worked with who practice Container well hold the balance of being extremely firm and extremely fair, which requires a deep sense of inner strength in order to uphold the boundaries and rules. It can feel much easier to negotiate, compromise, or protect. Container leadership can therefore feel very fierce, and its strength will be tested by others. One leader in our research study in anticipation of this commented,

'I made this [change] a very important part of my management agenda. Change was in every management team's meeting agenda. I just insisted we put this on an equal footing as everything else'. *The fierceness is not there to get one over people, or to act out of one's own ego needs; it is there to serve what needs to happen in the organisation,* as another leader recounted, 'I was absolutely straight down the line and said "no". I don't waiver at all anymore with them . . . the situation needed more clarity, a stronger voice, longer term thinking and that's what I gave them'.

The greater the anxiety in the situation, the stronger the requirement is for containing leadership. From our own facilitation experience we know that Container leadership is needed most when the team or group starts to heat up and the emotions or dynamics are at risk of becoming dysfunctional. *In these situations Container leadership is not about taking on the anxiety oneself, or trying to smooth things over or rescue people, it is about making the anxiety visible and becoming as open as you can be about what is happening.* This makes the environment much safer than if things are being avoided. When leaders practice this it can take great courage *and* service to what is present. And it requires them to restrain their own impulses or personal anxieties that might have been triggered by the situation. This challenge is acute when the leader has been the instigator of the system's anxiety, in other words they have generated the Edge and Tension as a necessary move to improve the organisation's performance. In these situations the leader has to make bearable the anxiety they have themselves generated without feeling 'guilty' or protective about its consequence. Here's an excerpt from a leader who had instigated turbulence (job losses) yet in the face of extreme anxiety (in front of 60 people) was honest, self assured, and managed to restrain his own impulses to be protective in the situation.

'One person said to me, "do you know how many jobs are going to be affected by this?" And while we didn't know what the final detailed impact was the assessment we had done at that point said that there would be 175 jobs affected . . . so I had to make a decision on the spot and I hesitated for a second and I thought gee, do I give them a number which is what they want even though the number is fluid . . . or do I tell them we really don't know for sure yet and we'll get back to you? I actually made the decision to tell them and I said, "Look, I'm going to give you all the caveats around this number . . . but the best number I have right now is 175". And I got feedback from people that said they really appreciated the honesty . . . they felt we answered the questions directly and did not skirt the issue'.

Leaders who practise Container create environments that are purposeful, focused, and calm, and thereby able to bear the anxiety created by Edge and Tension. *A key risk however is that the leader soaks up too much of the anxiety in the organisation which then limits their processing ability to move things forward.* Good Container leadership requires detachment; unless you stay slightly on the edge of the system by definition you can't hold it or contain it. You become it. This risk can be avoided by keeping a sense of detachment from what is happening in the moment in front of you (by processing your own impulses and issues) and it can simply mean taking time out every now and then to pause and look after yourself.

Provides affirming and encouraging signals: builds ownership, trust and confidence

Container leadership affirms and enables people to adapt and grow. It affirms others by helping people find their place in the change and acknowledging their contribution. We once worked with a leader who was holding a kick off meeting for his new leadership team. They were about to have to go through some tough times together in an organisation which was looking to their HR leadership to implement a major restructuring. As they assembled together for the first time, the team leader spent the first two hours expressing to each individual on the team why he had hired them (ending with why he thought he had been hired to this role by his boss). It was a transforming moment. While each individual implicitly knew why they were on the team they had not heard it said with such clarity before, and in front of other members of their team. It made them feel they could walk on water together. One team member at the end of the two days commented how those two hours had been the most memorable of the meeting, and in particular she noticed how the team leader had spent care and attention over the task – he had arrived with sheets of prepared notes as to what he wanted to say to each individual.

Affirming others is also about being absolutely straight with people – it's not about being nice to everybody in order to have an easy life. One of the authors used to work with a boss who continually said 'you're a star'. In the beginning, this made the author feel great and committed to doing anything that was needed. However after a while the author discovered that this person said the same thing to everybody on the team which eventually devalued the statement and de-motivated the author. Strong affirming leadership is clear about the 'deal' that is being made. One of the leaders in our study, who was the Chief Executive of a public sector organisation, struck a clear deal with the leader of one of his key stakeholder groups that while he himself was going to bring money and resources to the party, he expected the other leader (who had been opposing him) to make a go of it and improve the service. He said to this leader, ' "in all that we do we will never usurp your authority . . . you can depend on us, and if it goes right you take the credit, and if it goes wrong we'll take the flak, you will never see us wanting to stamp our name on successful projects". We shook hands on that and over the years became great friends'.

In this excerpt the leader was practicing both affirming and authorising behaviour. Good containment is when leaders are clear about the mandate and authority they will give to others. Far from taking on the responsibility and work of the organisation around them, they will place the responsibility for decision making and action where it needs to be. In this way they create a container that is active and purposeful, not stuck on waiting for somebody else to take charge. Another leader in our study was very clear about this. He was working in a public sector organisation that seemed frozen in its inability to take decisions. His leadership style built confidence and leadership around him, and as a consequence the change process which had been stuck for several months became dislodged and movement happened.

I have a representative there who has my delegated authority and that means that any decision she takes I will support her . . . and I never went to those meetings . . . it started a trend, and I never had to unpick decisions. . . . I reassured them and said, 'look, I'm not doing this for any macho reasons I just need to spend my time on other things. I don't need to be at this meeting, this person has my full confidence, why would I need to be there?'.

Once the leader's affirming presence is felt, and clarity and confidence in authority is established, then trust can flow through the system. And once trust is present, the container is at its safest and strongest; it can enable quite fundamental change and transformation to occur, which might even require regression before the system can break through. In situations requiring a 'rebirth' into a new state, such as the integration of an acquisition, or the merger of previously autonomous units, this kind of containing leadership is essential. Indeed the commitment to any collective change effort requires it.

Makes it safe to say risky things and have the 'hard to have' conversations through empathy and high quality dialogue skills

Influenced by complexity theory, which emphasises the importance of changing local interactions in order to be able to influence the whole system, there is a growing awareness that by changing the quality of dialogue, leaders can change the whole culture. Indeed, conversations hold the potential for both intervention and diagnosis *at the same time*; in conversations you can see the whole system (if you are attuned to noticing how things get said, not just what's being said), so, if you can influence the way in which conversations are held, then you can influence the system. Container leadership can foster positive interactions in many ways; it can bring more authenticity to conversations so that the whole change process gets more credible; it can engender more openness, disclosure and risk such that the whole change process moves more courageously; and it can promote greater trust such that the change process achieves full commitment.

Given that the essence of Container leadership is about the channelling of anxiety and turbulence towards purposeful energy, its role in promoting effective conversations is about the engendering of safety to have more risky and authentic dialogue. It therefore acts as a complement to the Edge and Tension practice of 'telling it as it is'. Talking straight can get you so far however people need to feel confident that such disclosure is going to be okay, that their voice will be heard, and that any turbulent consequences will be skilfully managed. Container leadership is therefore concerned with the setting up of the conditions within which better conversations can happen.

One of the primary ways in which we saw leaders doing this in our study was through the use of inquiry, the asking of powerful questions. *Inquiry in itself provides a container; it lifts up what is deemed to be important,* it creates boundaries and sets expectations. One leader recounted, 'I was the one who would just be listening very calmly and asking questions . . . stopping and thinking before I spoke'. Inquiry sets agendas in a way that is non-directive and empowering of others. In this research excerpt the leader was implementing a major safety process in his manufacturing sites and he had to reconcile this imperative with the need to keep focus on production targets. He held an important meeting with his leadership team.

So I asked the question, 'How do we balance the two? If safety means slowing down are we really going to do it?' . . . and at the end I asked 'what are we committing to out of this room?' And we got the management and the operating guys to agree the next week's production targets . . . the key is actually allowing those conversations to happen, or creating an environment where people don't feel they're going to get their heads bitten off.

Skilful inquiry therefore generates openness and an atmosphere in which dangerous subjects can get talked about. It sets up a container that enables people to voice. Another leader stated, 'I wanted a real sense of openness where there were no taboos, if people thought something was stupid they could say so, so all I did was ask lots of questions'.

An obvious consequence of using inquiry and enabling people to voice what's on their mind, is that the dialogue might produce topics and/or bring out emotions that the leader would rather not have to deal with. Container leadership is therefore also about the ability to hear and bear the message that comes back, without taking on the anxiety that might be being projected into the situation (and onto the leader). It's only human nature that the messages get taken personally. However, when this happens the leader can respond in ways that appear hurt and painful to others, who then take on guilty feelings about voicing things in the first place, which then makes it no longer 'safe' to have the hard to have conversations. Skilful containment takes the dialogue, hears what is trying to be said, puts to one side the interference of more ego-driven impulses, and then processes the conversation such that responsibility for moving through the risky subjects is held in the group, not in the individual leader.

Sets and contracts boundaries, clear expectations and hard rules so that people know what to operate on and how to operate

The practices above have been centred on the presence and skill of the individual leader doing the 'containing'. However effective Container leadership moves beyond that to create the system's capability to do its own containing, and manage independent action. A key way in which leaders do that is through the setting and contracting of boundaries and 'rules' for the organisation. Boundaries focus the attention; they define what's in and out of play. And the field of play requires rules. Otherwise no one knows how to play the game, activity becomes random, and no one can referee. Container leadership makes these rules clear. Together boundaries and rules provide an enabling structure that gives people 'hand rails' with which to navigate their way through the uncertainty of change.

The boundaries that Containing leadership set are around expectations of performance and definitions of success, as illustrated by the following quotes from our research: 'we were absolutely clear on our deliverables from this session', 'I set the three goals which we still have – profitable business, sustainable growth, and a company to be proud of', 'I set some firm expectations of what I thought a leadership team was'. The rules determine the values, behaviours and practices that are going to be important to deliver the change, as illustrated; 'and whoever sits around the table on my leadership team has to wear two hats', 'we [the HR Director with their business team] made a decision that one of the rules we'd work to is that this work would not be led by HR'.

This setting of boundaries, rules, and expectations *helps leaders channel the day to day behaviour of their organisation without them having to be personally present* to control and monitor activity. And complexity theory tells us that *these rules have to be set at the level of the micro behaviour of the 'agents' in a system.* It's hard to influence the behaviour of the whole system by only setting high level statements such as 'generate more margin'. Given that the macro level behaviour of the system is produced from all the tiny interactions at the local level, it's at this local level that leaders need to set the rules. You don't tell birds to 'fly in formation', but you do tell them to 'move in the same direction as your neighbour'. Once these micro level rules are generated you can then let people get on with purposeful activity. One leader in our research study recalled, 'we made the calculation and we gave them [sales people] some very simple rules so you could actually see whether this or that customer would deliver a return on the money . . . they then negotiated under their own authority and it gave them a completely different way of looking at the customer'. The implementation of these rules enabled this organisation to radically transform the composition and profitability of their customer base – through the intelligent activity of their front line sales people. All previous attempts to do this from analyses and directives of a central sales planning department had consistently failed to deliver any performance improvement.

The magic of having a few hard rules is that they can produce an endless variety of behaviour, which can be liberating, not constraining. And the prescribing of constraints, or what people should *not* do, is sometimes more liberating than setting out what people *should* do. Because once you know what you should not do, everything else you can do! *The trick is not to have too few rules – when the container becomes loose and behaviour tips into randomness and chaos, or too many – when the container becomes too tight and behaviour becomes stuck, constrained and frozen in inactivity.* One leader we worked with, who was implementing a significant restructuring, realised that 'governance', or who was now going to have the power to take decisions about what, was going to be a major issue. There had been various iterations of 'manuals of authorities', worked through in several task forces, and after four months of being communicated to the organisation had still not produced any new forms of decision making behaviour. The new structure was there only as boxes on a power point slide. This leader decided to do something different, and in a creative containing intervention created a metaphor of what became known as the 'Noddy book'. It was a book that had been cut horizontally across each page to produce three strips on each page (just as some children's books are). The book contained the rules of how the new structure was going to operate. However when you leafed through the book you could put these rules together in an endless variety of ways to produce the necessary 'story' about what you could do in your local operation. From that moment on the rules became liberating, not constraining.

Once the rules and boundaries are set they need to be upheld. Container leadership is non-compromising and resolute, otherwise it seems that the organisation no longer upholds what it believes to be important and fundamental, the boundaries and rules lose credibility, the climate is no longer secure, and the unity of the system collapses. One leader in our study commented 'my role is to hold a focus, to hold the values and to hold the ring. You make agreements about what the ring is and then you hold it. You get consensual agreement but then someone needs to hold it and not get caught up in anything else. So that was very often my job'. We would contest that the leader also needs to build a system that is able to do its own containing, however unless the leader can do so then it becomes harder for those around them. It also helps if the rules and boundaries are established early on in a change process. The initial conditions can be fateful for the behaviour and outcomes that will follow. One leader commented, 'I talked to them very early on about my expectations, what they could expect of me and what I in turn expected of them. Because I decided that if I did not lay that foundation early on, we'd have a real problem'.

Creates alignment at the top and builds networks of relationships that stay in tune with the system and can channel the change

Beyond the establishment of boundaries, expectations and rules, another way in which leaders can enable the organisation to do its own containing is through the social fabric of relationships in the system. An important part of this 'human' container is the top leadership team. When the top team is aligned the whole organisation can join up. When it is fragmented, the organisation splits. The dynamics that get played out in the top team will be felt and enacted elsewhere in the system. When this team feels secure, the organisation feels held. When it has cracks the organisation feels dangerous. Part of the container work is therefore consciously managing the processes and anxieties that inevitably surface in top teams leading big change in order to help the organisation move through its change. One leader in the study recounted, 'the organisation watches how the top team is working together. I therefore spent a lot of time and effort getting everybody in the room into discussions that built this relationship of trust and respect'.

Creating alignment in the top team does not mean that they have to agree on everything and show no sense of healthy internal challenge. In fact when organisations can witness their top team having a good dialogue, in which differences are aired, permission is then given to the culture at large to bring up alternative view points, which is vital in high magnitude change where no person or group can have the 'answer'. However, the top team do need to demonstrate that they are together on the direction of the change, that they understand what's important to get accomplished, and how that needs to be done. Such alignment builds a strong and effective containing presence for the rest of the organisation, which can then act with clarity and confidence.

Another way in which collective containment can be created is through the establishment of critical leadership groups and change networks across the organisation. It cannot be left to the most senior leader or their leadership team alone, since the rest of the organisation could be effectively disabled if the senior leader is away on holiday, or the top team holed away in strategic planning processes. Moreover, building a broader collective container across the system can 'insure' the change against the potential dysfunction of the top team or leader, since the organisation can then become a touch more immune to their foibles.

We have experienced the power of 'extended leadership teams' being established – usually the layer of leaders beneath the top team – to collectively guide a change effort. Networks of 'change agents' can also perform this collective containing role. One of the authors once worked on a global restructuring process that created significant upheaval. A task force was created from across the various regions and business units, and for six weeks they worked intensively on their mandate to redesign the entire organisation. When the team gathered it became clear that they could not progress their overt task, i.e. the organisational redesign, unless they also tackled the deeper dynamics they were bringing. Their local organisations were all very fearful of the pending restructure, and whenever the task force members left them to go to the global design meetings they were asked to take all the local issues and demands with them, and when they returned to their local organisations they were inundated with questions about the future shape of the organisation. Within this 'swirl' it became very important for the global task force to stay in tune with *and at the same time detached from* the local dynamics. The conscious effort to work through their own processes enabled them to do that and they became a very strong, calm, and confident change presence in the restructuring (one of their ground rules was 'team together, team apart'). The senior leadership team could not have successfully pulled off the change without them.

Container leadership practices: putting it all together

Nicola is one of the calmest and most assured leaders we have worked with. She is very clear on what's important, holds firm on this, and guides people very skilfully through change. She can connect with the organisation without becoming absorbed in it. She allows space for difficult conversations without them taking her off course. She can process emotions without getting emotional. She listens without siding. She reassures without protecting. She asserts without alienating. Not surprisingly, given this skill set, her leadership roles have often been those in which the situation required big change to happen in a very sensitive way. The way in which Nicola brings all of the components of Container together is illustrated by a story of a specific challenge she faced.

This story is about Nicola's leadership of a consumer goods organisation that had been formed out of a merger of two previously competing companies. She was appointed as Managing Director one year after the merger had occurred, and on arrival quickly realised that it was practically a merger in name only, and as a consequence, none of the synergy benefits were being realised. The organisations had never been truly integrated. Due to this the company's customers were getting a confusing picture and soon after Nicola arrived, their most important customer de-listed their products from their stores in frustration. Nicola realised that change was needed at many levels – not least of which was a concerted effort to streamline and integrate several parts of the organisation. However she also sensed that such a push would not succeed without a clearer context for people as to why this was needed, a stronger leadership team mandate to the organisation on what had to happen, and critically the processing of angry, fearful and frustrated emotions that had lain repressed in the organisation. She got to work on setting up the 'container'.

Her leadership team were not aligned, in any sense, around a change pathway. This was not a team of incompetent leaders, it's just that until this point in time they had not had the deep conversations together about what had to change and how. As Nicola inquired she also sensed that this was partly attributable to the fact that they were still carrying a sense of loss from their former companies into the team. Nicola invested time in working with her team to create a safer place for their frustrations of the past and their hopes for the future to come out. She herself is an open and no-nonsense leader, so the team quickly realised they had to shape up and get real. Together they started to articulate the boundaries and hard rules for the organisation. These became known as 'the grid'. The grid was going to define for the organisation the essential performance expectations and behaviours that were necessary to get the merged entity humming as one unit. The team also identified a 'call to arms' statement for the change which became known as 'fixing our way forward', the very words and tone of which conveyed a secure and affirming container message.

Nicola also established an extended leadership group (the ELG) for the change process, a broader coalition of around 40 leaders from the senior management levels. They were as confused as anyone about what had to happen. They were getting anger and complaints from the front line staff about how lousy everything had become since the merger, and they were feeling the anxiety from the top leadership team about the poor performance. Nicola realised she had to build confidence amongst members of the ELG, help them establish their leadership role, and work with them to bring greater clarity about how the change was to move forward. In the early days of her leadership as she went round the organisation she would keep repeating some basic statements of what was required – 'customers, products, and getting the basics right'. In order to reach the front line of the organisation she had a video made of a representative sample of staff talking to camera frankly and openly about the situation. She wanted to encourage candid dialogue and make it okay to raise risky subjects. Up till then the senior management had hidden behind opinion surveys to read the pulse of their staff, she wanted to build greater trust by having more earthy and direct dialogue.

With her leadership team, she then set up a series of meetings for the coming months that were going to be pivotal in the organisation's navigation of the change. Aside from fortnightly management meetings, every quarter her team were going to meet at a facilitated offsite meeting to conduct deeper inquiry into the change process and help steer its progress. She also planned out a schedule of meetings for the ELG to build a broader collective container. The schedule of meetings was communicated to the organisation and the venue booked. These meetings were always going to take place at the same offsite venue, and they became known as the 'Warwick meetings'. The rhythm of these meetings performed an important container function for the organisation; it established a beat, a repeating pattern that gave structure to the uncertainty.

The first gathering of the ELG was a vital intervention which set the tone and agenda for the next 12 months. Nicola wanted the meeting to be both skilfully structured and sufficiently open to allow everyone to step in and lead. Its design was intended to take people along an emotional journey. It began with the showing of the video of front line staff talking frankly to camera which generated a dialogue in which emotions such as shame, guilt, anger, and sadness were expressed by the leaders present. Nicola role-modelled becoming a non-anxious presence in the midst of these emotions; she encouraged the group to speak openly, and it was a cathartic moment. At the appropriate time she enabled the group to move to a different place by stating that, given the now open acceptance that they the leaders had created this situation, they were also the leadership group who could move the organisation to a different place. This affirmation generated hopeful energy.

The 'grid' was shared with the group and the rest of the day was spent getting to grips with what it meant. The leaders developed a set of 'from–to' statements to guide where they needed to move the organisation, and to set tangible measures upon which the change progress became tracked. As work was created in the room Nicola and her team had its outputs posted visibly around the meeting room walls, so that people could see their thinking and their contributions made visible. This helped develop further openness and confidence. Throughout the day, during the breaks, the facilitators were taking informal 'temperature checks' by having conversations with participants about how the day was progressing. These were captured on camera and periodically shown back to the group. This helped to create safety – given that the comments were extremely open about where people were coming from, and it charted the group's emotional movement which gave them a sense of progress. The day closed with Nicola taking just a few minutes to express what the day had meant for her. She congratulated the group on the work done that day, reminded everyone very clearly as to what was now expected in terms of deliverables and accountabilities, and concluded with her sense of what had to be done. The group left the room highly charged and energetic.

Following this meeting the 'grid' became the mechanism against which progress was monitored. It was road tested and conveyed to the whole organisation so that every employee knew what had to happen to get their company back on track. If tasks were not completed or timings slipped, Nicola never picked up the slack and took things on herself. She made sure she kept the accountability and responsibility where it should be. The regular 'Warwick' gatherings of the ELG kept attention in the organisation on what had to happen. Nicola did not launch new initiatives along the way. Throughout this period Nicola invested in regular coaching time for herself. As Managing Director she needed some space to go talk in confidence to a coach about what was going on, how she was feeling about progress, and how she could keep her own leadership sure, steady, and on track. It helped create detachment from the process. It gave her perspective.

After one year of 'fixing our way forward' the organisation felt a different place. There was more cooperation, openness, and commitment to making things work. It had become rare for people to talk about which company they had originally come from prior to the merger. The top leadership team were less anxious and more in charge. The ELG felt clear and accountable. The organisation hit plan. And the customer that had de-listed them now brought their products back onto their shelves. Shortly after this they presented Nicola's company with an award for 'best supplier of the year'.

Container: the dark side

If Container leadership is practiced without certain beliefs, intent, and self awareness, it can tip over into unhelpful behaviour. Emotional management control is particularly important for this practice, since containers are not safe when the leader's own issues and anxieties spill out into the situation. When this happens they become unavailable to deal with the realities of the situation around them. Indeed, this leads to situations where there is no container at all and the atmosphere can become extremely unsettling around the leader, so much so that people become fearful of taking independent action. They end up trying to protect the leader from their anxiety, which can lead to dysfunctional behaviour that avoids the real performance difficulty in the situation. Instead, it becomes all about the leader.

On the other hand, *over* containment happens when the leader takes on *too* much responsibility for the anxiety in the situation around them. This might arise from a personal story that has the leader acting out the need to be wanted, affirmed, or omnipotent. Whatever the origin of the impulse, if the leader is unaware of the need, or aware yet unable to restrain the personal anxiety, they can seek to 'rescue' difficult situations around them (by trying to take charge of the conversation, by withholding any further difficult messages from the organisation, by saying 'don't worry, leave it to me') and in so doing disallow the organisation from being able to process its own anxiety. While the rescuing behaviour might leave the leader feeling 'heroic' and needed, others around them are left feeling paradoxically *unattended* to; and the lack of collective processing of the difficulty disables the organisation's ability to become more resilient to face the tough stuff together. In these situations, the dark side of Container leadership becomes overly *protective*, and their affirming presence starts to feel smothering and disquietingly false (since people around them can sense the difficulty that is being hidden).

In addition to the justification of self worth another unconscious desire underpinning this protective 'dark side' could be that, in return for the leader looking after people, the leader will get devotion and loyalty in return. Their overly affirming presence however creates an unhealthy dependency – it can be profoundly disempowering for others and keeps their organisation in a child-like state. The container has become so thick and protective that there is no longer space to move inside. Any taking of independent action could be seen as disloyalty.

Another dark side to Container leadership is over control on behalf of the leader. If they become too strict and non-compromising on the rules and boundaries then the container ends up feeling like *constraint*, it is too firm, too constricting. The containing structure, far from being liberating, feels like a prison to others. While the leader's behaviour might initially feel helpful and welcoming for the organisation, 'at last some one is getting a grip on things for us!', if not practised in service of the organisation, but to serve one's own need for control, people can feel caught and trapped, 'I play by the rules to appear loyal and devoted, yet I really want to rebel and do something different or get out!' This dynamic can put the organisation in a double bind, 'If I follow the rules I'll be seen as a good employee and my leader will feel affirmed, yet I end up feeling somehow small and compromised. If I try to take charge and assert myself then I'll feel a whole lot better and resourceful yet my leader might think I'm being disloyal and it won't make them happy!' In double binds, the inevitable outcome is stuck-ness, not movement. If a leader is unaware of this control tendency their overly containing leadership can therefore undermine change.

What might also draw forth the dark side of Container leadership, however, is a *conscious* desire to serve oneself and one's own needs. When the need is to feel powerful, important and in charge, then Container leadership can feel like an *abuse* of authority to others. The boundaries, expectations and hard rules are used for the leader's advantage. They help them get what they want. They might be deliberately deploying skilful Container leadership skills – for example encouraging people to be open, staying calm themselves, building confidence in others, clarifying what has to be done – and yet it ends up feeling that the only person who's going to gain from the situation is them. Once this sincerity cover is blown trust collapses. At its extreme people start to see them as a touch despotic.

Here are some pointers to help you distinguish the 'dark' and 'light' side of Container leadership. Again we present the questions as opposite extremes in order to stimulate your reflection. It's only human to slip into the dark side; however what is vital for leadership is having an awareness of what mode you might (really) be in at any one time, the ability to stop yourself and pause if you feel these unhelpful tendencies might be bubbling up, and then taking mindful action to switch to the light side – *in order to be more available to serve the situation you are responsible for leading.*

- Are you serving yourself, or the organisation around you?

- Are the rules you create there to get what you want, or to get what the situation needs?

- When contracting outcomes with people is your intent to build reputation for yourself, or success for the organisation?

- Do you affirm others to keep them loyal and make you feel wanted, or to make them feel independent and powerful?

- Do you take a stand for your beliefs to promote yourself, or to safeguard the 'truth'?

- Do you bear and face difficult emotions with others to protect your own needs to rescue, or to promote break through learning in the situation?

Summary

In Table 7.1 we summarise the features of Container leadership. While Attractor and Edge and Tension can generate

Table 7.1 Container Leadership

Essence: channels anxiety and turbulence into purposeful energy

What It Is (Light Side)	*What It Is Not (Dark Side)*
• Setting up of safe conditions to go to risky places	• Fending the organisation against difficulty; *protection*
• Helping people bear and face difficult emotions	• Taking on and absorbing other people's anxiety
• Fierce contracting and upholding of rules	• Providing constraining managerial checks and controls
• Authorisation of independent action	• Bargaining and negotiating what has to be done
• Fostering of positive interaction	• Building a 'happy commune' that loses sight of the difficulties
• Calm and confident presence	• Smothering looking after

Core Practices
- Is self assured, confident, and takes a stand for one's beliefs – is non-anxious in challenging conditions
- Provides affirming and encouraging signals: builds ownership, trust and confidence
- Makes it safe to say risky things and have the 'hard to have' conversations through empathy and high quality dialogue skills
- Sets and contracts boundaries, clear expectations and hard rules so that people know what to operate on and how to operate
- Creates alignment at the top and builds networks of relationships that stay in tune with the system and can channel the change

How It Serves Change
- Allows buried and difficult emotions to be visibly processed so they no longer become disabling
- Creates courage and confidence to go through tough times
- Clear rules bring freedom; guides consistent behaviour without need for centralised control
- Aligns an organisation behind what's important
- Promotes webs of interactions that build resilience and spread change

© 2008 Transcend Consultancy

feelings of purpose and excitement, this needs to be channelled into productive energy. This is the primary purpose of Container leadership. Without Container leadership excitement and tension go nowhere. They create fire but not heat. Container leadership generates purposeful and confident activity. It can make bearable the anxiety stirred up by Edge and Tension, and it makes actionable the purpose created by Attractor.

Container leadership is enacted in several ways. First, the leader's own personal presence is self assured, confident, and unwavering. They deal with difficult emotions in the organisation without absorbing these emotions – since this would then render them unable to act with detached perspective. They do not hide their own anxiety about the situation, and can openly share how they are processing it, however at all times their presence is non-anxious. In so doing they create trust and confidence in others. They provide encouragement and promote high quality dialogue to help people bear and face difficult emotions and situations.

Secondly, Container leadership involves the setting of clear boundaries, priorities and rules for the organisation that help people know what is expected of them and how things should be done. This structural element of the container helps the leader influence the activity of the organisation without them having to be personally present. It also paradoxically creates more freedom and space for people since once they know what the 'givens', or constraints, are, they can then be left and trusted to get on with things – they are authorised to act, a vital requirement in high magnitude change.

Finally, this leadership practice is about creating 'human' containers; pivotally through alignment in the top team yet also with self sustaining networks deeper in the organisation. These webs of interactions provide the organisation with the strength and cohesion to bring about self organised and collective change. The social networks set up the organisation's ability to do its own containing and make the organisation more resilient to go through the choppy waters of high magnitude change.

Without the leader having a healthy awareness of one's own personal story about being needed, or in control, Container leadership can come across as overly protective and constraining. In these situations leaders seek to rescue the organisation and take the anxiety away from others so that they feel they have a role and a place. The protection can be felt by others as if loyalty should be given back in return. This becomes a disempowering situation and it creates stuck-ness. Likewise if the leader's conscious intent is to get power and control for themselves, Container leadership can also feel constraining and if consciously intended unfair and self serving.

Without Container leadership the organisation can feel a rudderless and scary place, unable to productively move through tough times. With well practiced and well intended Container leadership, it can be safely and confidently steered into new directions.

8

Transforming Space – creates movement

'The future won't change unless we look thoughtfully at the present'

Margaret Wheatley

Transforming Space leadership: the essence

Leaders who work with Transforming Space are able to break established patterns of thinking and behaviour in the 'here and now' moment, based on an assumption that the only thing that can be changed *is* the present. They break patterns by setting up transforming physical or mental spaces that hold the potential for learning and acting differently. Within such space they pay acute attention to what is happening, both within them and around them (observation), process the possibilities and actions occurring in the present moment (inquiry and reflection), and then take courageous action to change what they and others are paying attention to in order for change to be enacted there and then (transforming intervention). In creating Transforming Spaces they are sufficiently confident to make themselves vulnerable; they pick their timing to intervene extremely well; and what happens in the space can irreversibly change everything that flows from that moment. People will now say 'I get it!'

What follows is a short story that illustrates the transforming power of a leader paying close attention to the deeper processes that were occurring in a situation.

Erik was completely present and engaged with his leadership team. They had flown in the night before from various locations across Asia. Erik always held these monthly meetings in team members' markets to be closer to their customer base, not the corporate hierarchy. Indeed their entire change process was centred on serving and equipping their front line staff to provide a more distinctive service to their customers. In order to understand how to do this, and shift their style from directive control to coaching their organisation, the leadership team went out on 'bus tours' to the markets, inviting anyone from their organisation's local offices to come with them, and visit the customers. These tours had been enthusiastically received to date and had created a lot of energy in the organisation.

The meeting that day had opened with the Territory leaders sharing the first half year results. Despite a lot of investment in training local staff they were still losing customers to their

competitors. Erik closed this session by restating the fundamental principles behind the change: reducing the costs of
back office operations, de-layering the hierarchy, getting more
investment to the front line sale operation, all underpinned
by a significant change in mindset. For years the unwritten
rules in the culture had been to please the senior leaders and
serve the hierarchy. People were rewarded for keeping their
noses clean and doing what they were told. For this change
to succeed these norms had to be transformed to a culture in
which the senior leaders were serving and enabling the organisation beneath them to take resourceful action to improve
performance.

The next item on the agenda was planning the forthcoming
schedule of market 'bus tours', seen to be a straightforward
item and just scheduled for thirty minutes. The VP responsible started to run through the planned schedule and the
conversation flowed. However, at one point there was a
bit of a ripple. One person commented that one of the planned
days was a local national holiday, so was the date correct?
The VP responsible for that market said that it was, and moreover 'isn't it great that these bus tours are creating such
energy and commitment that our local staff are prepared
to take this time out!' Other team members nodded in
assent. He continued '. . . and it would be very hard to
change the date because it would have a knock on effect with
the rest of our schedule'. They agreed to continue with the
dates.

However Eric felt an uneasy feeling inside him (observation).
He tuned in to that. What was it that was making him feel
uncomfortable? Was it just his discomfort or could he sense

there was also something not quite right in the room (reflection)? He had noticed that the team all looked away from each other during that conversation. There were a few nervous laughs. He noticed the poster of change principles on the meeting room wall, 'the leader's task is to serve the front line staff to serve the customer better'. How did this context help him process the source of his discomfort? His attention turned from seeing this moment as a schedule confirmation time to one that was far more fundamental. He had heard some beliefs and mindsets present in his team that he felt needed naming and checking out. He wasn't quite sure where this would end up but he sensed he had to do something (risky intervention).

First, he asked the team to move their chairs to sit round in a circle where they could face each other. He then inquired, 'can we just go back a bit to this tour in the country where it's a national holiday? I noticed we felt this was a positive sign of commitment, yet I also saw we were shuffling around a bit during that moment. What was going on?' His team hesitantly started to talk, 'well, it all seemed a bit too difficult to change', 'it's only a small country so it's not really affecting too many of our staff', and, 'why don't we pay them a special bonus for working overtime that day?' Erik asked another question, 'if we are the leaders of this region can we not take responsibility for figuring out a different way through this?' At that point one team member asked 'whose idea was it to go to that country on that day?!' There was a heated exchange in the group, 'it was Chong! Chong sent out an email to us last week'. Chong was not physically in the room, yet he was being conveniently brought in to the room.

Erik brought it back to the people present, 'let's explore this a little more. How is it that we could say we were comfortable while looking distinctly uncomfortable?' The straightforward thirty minute schedule planning session turned into a deep two hour reflective dialogue. During this time, and through Erik's courageous inquiry, the leadership team realised that while they had stated that the change was about the senior leaders serving the frontline staff, they were enacting the complete opposite – expecting the local staff to serve them and their needs. And if this could happen on a relatively small item such as schedule planning, how was this unwritten rule still getting played out by them in the entire organisation? Erik handled the dialogue in a way that held a space for self awareness and significant learning in the team. Once this had been processed, Erick called 'time out' and suggested an extended lunch break during which his team could reflect on what had just happened, and return with ideas for how to move forward differently.

When they returned the Territory VP said that he had just called Chong to suggest a time when they could talk to re-fix the date for the country. The two hours had been a transforming moment for the team. It happened several years ago; however, the leaders then present still recall it to this day. It was a turning point for them in the change. They were far more conscious from that moment forward of their *leadership intent* in any situation. Was it to have their needs or the frontline needs served? This greater mindfulness helped them to adjust behaviour, and the organisation over the coming months sensed a very different presence from the leadership team as a consequence of this single two hour conversation.

What Transforming Space leadership is (and is not)

Erik had changed the focus of his attention in the moment (from diary planning to rules getting played out in the culture), and that switch in attention transformed the space in front of him. The team meeting became a 'changing' moment; it was no longer about planning for change. When leaders pay attention to what they are noticing, and how they are noticing it, then the present moment changes. It's as if it has to. Awareness *becomes* action.

Imagine you are with a group of staff during a market tour; you might pay attention to the market data they are sharing and reflect on how the results here compare to the market you visited yesterday. You sit thinking about how this can help you write the report you need to send to head office at the end of the week. You see the people in front of you as sales professionals needing to be on top of their game. However, what if you switched your attention, *away* from the task and its outcome, and *to* the present moment and its process? You might then start paying attention to not just what they are telling you, but how they are telling you things. You let go of your sense of the outcomes and work with what is happening in front of you – how do they respond to your questions? What is it that they are wanting from the conversation with you and are they able to make that explicit? Have the ground conditions and context been set up clearly enough? How are they relating to you and you to them? And how, through observation and inquiry, can you bring your attention to their attention and in so doing promote some learning about the current moment? *The moment you start to focus your attention on the present encounter you can then take a chance to change the unwritten rules that are being presented in it.* The question is, how attuned are leaders to the moment in front of them? Is it just seen as a means to an end, or an opportunity to change what is happening now?

Leaders who practice Transforming Space take their chances, and in so doing can de-stabilise and change things in the moment. They create the mental and physical spaces to name and shift the potentially limiting aspects of people's assumptions and ways of working. The physical space was changed when Erik moved his team to sit in a circle of chairs, and when he suggested they go for an extended lunch break. He created the mental space through the quality of his attention (to his own source of discomfort and then to that which was around him), and his questioning and inquiry – which brought forth a heightened awareness of what was happening in the present moment. He had been observing *how* the conversation was being conducted, he did not just tune in to what was being said. And then he made an in the moment intervention to bring his attention and process to the awareness of others, and in so doing he created a Transforming Space. Change happened within the space and between the individuals within that space.

Yet Erik's attention was intentional. Without an organisational frame or context, you can't practice Transforming

Space. *Our research showed us that leaders who only practiced Transforming Space did not deliver successful change outcomes.* The practice in and of itself can take you nowhere. Indeed it moves leaders close to the 'dark side' and can feel self serving, indulgent, and even manipulative to others; its de-stabilising quality can become 'weird and spooky'. Transforming Space leadership requires the intentional pull of Attractor so that people know what the intervention is for. It requires the fire and disturbance of Edge and Tension to justify why things still require changing. And it needs the safety and structure of Container to keep people engaged with the process. *When leaders put Transforming Space together with these three other practices it had a positively amplifying impact on the success of the change.*

Leaders who can therefore create Transforming Spaces speed up change (it's a bit like the turbo charge on a three cylinder engine, the three cylinders being the other Changing Leadership practices); they take advantage of the continually available opportunities for movement. They know that every action in the system holds the potential to move the system. Even activities such as planning and diagnosis can be designed as interventions that break established patterns, as long as close attention is paid to process, or how things are done, and awareness is created for the present moment, not just its outcomes. When done with conscious intent and a commitment to the system that goes beyond personal ambition, Transforming Space leadership creates lasting change (its 'light side'), if done purely to stir things up or serve ego-driven needs, it can only build mesmerising cults around the individual leader (its 'dark side').

Transforming Space leadership practices: creates movement

When we studied the transcripts from our research, we identified certain Transforming Space practices that were strongly related to successful change outcomes. These were:

- Demonstrates a commitment that engenders trust, enabling the system to go to new places, learn about itself, and act differently.

- Frees people to new possibilities through making oneself vulnerable and open.

- Understands what is happening in the moment and breaks established patterns and structures in ways that create movement in the 'here and now'.

- Powerfully inquires into ripe systemic issues to enable deep change to happen.

- Creates time and space (including attending to its physical quality) for transforming encounters.

Below we describe these individual practices with illustrations from the leaders we have engaged with – both within the research and in our practice. As you read through these practices, reflect on your own leadership: are these practices part of how you currently lead change; have you thought about doing them but for some reason avoided them; could your change benefit from this kind of leadership; and therefore would you like to bring more of them into your practice, or practice them with more awareness and skill?

Demonstrates a commitment that engenders trust, enabling the system to go to new places, learn about itself, and act differently

Leaders who practice Transforming Space take active personal responsibility for the present moment. They see every encounter, every call, and every email response as an opportunity to consciously exercise leadership. They therefore focus their attention on what is happening in front of them, right there right then, and 'put themselves out and about' in the organisation since they know that every moment could be a 'changing one'. Their intent is not to be the charismatic mover and shaker (tipping into Shaping leadership), rather, they go out into the organisation to pay attention to its pulse, help the organisation learn about itself, and in so doing act differently.

One leader in our study practiced a technique called 'Be Here Now'. He tried consciously to shut out from his mind any distracting thoughts that would prevent him from attending to what was happening in front of him. He was fully committed to the present moment. This enabled him to notice what was going on, how he was responding in a situation, run through the choices he had to act in any situation, and then consciously act with intent. Quantum physics shows us that space is never empty; it is full with potential, and what you do within the space can irreversibly change it. Another leader in our study was integrating an acquisition into his company. He wanted to make sure that learning from the acquired company was going to be given a place in the new organisation. He recalls, 'I personally intervened in the retail business and the manufacturing sites. I personally intervened to make sure there was space for the "X" guys and their ways of working'. He was doing this with intent to build trust through the integration and enable the whole organisation to learn from each other.

Leaders who practice Transforming Space recognise that every moment can be a changing moment. In every interaction you can either change what is happening or reinforce established patterns. One leader from our study got her team to change their factory visits away from being some form of presidential tour into an opportunity to make change happen in the moment, 'our factory visits are no longer going to be regimented tours . . . let's now go on to the factory floors and see the routine, and let's sort the problem out here and now, let's not wait until the next health and safety review'. Once leaders are seen to be helping make change happen in the moment it builds trust that they are leaders who 'mean what they say', and it builds credibility for the overall change process. Leaders who practice Transforming Space therefore consciously choose how they want to act in the flow of the present moment. For example one manufacturing general manager invested in hosting 'town hall meetings' at her sites. These are opportunities for the organisation to meet with senior leaders and engage with them in unrehearsed ways with the issues of the moment. 'I would spend the time allocated whether one hundred people showed up or three people. Probably the best thing I ever did was when three guys showed up at a night shift meeting . . . and I stayed for four hours with these three guys . . . and it got out over the whole plant that I had done that and the people in the plant decided that I really cared about what they were doing'.

Every moment *is*, and every moment has its purpose – if you are attuned to it. A commitment to the present moment engenders trust in others and a willingness to work with its unfolding potential. Transforming Space leadership acknowledges that each and every interaction in the organisation could impact the future flow of events, and is akin to the major theory of Edmond Locard's in forensic science, which holds that: 'every contact leaves a trace'.

Frees people to new possibilities through making oneself vulnerable and open

When leaders show their vulnerability to others it can create transforming moments; it becomes an invitation for others to come out and join them where they are at in their struggle, and in so doing levels the playing field. In these moments people engage with what is presently happening differently, since in the release of the struggle they are set free. Being more relationally present transforms the situation *because you can work with what is happening now 'between us', rather than act out of pre-ordained assumptions and rules,* and it's the 'here and now moment' that holds the most available opportunity for making change happen. However, it does require a continual awareness of and openness to how others might be relating to you, and an insight into how your own behaviour as leader – what you say and do – has the potential to transform the situation, which requires a high level of self awareness. This particular practice works well when combined with Container, since without the leader being confident, affirming, calm, and clear on what needs to get done, the act of exposing vulnerability could just create panic in others.

One of the most frequent 'levellers' we saw leaders in our study using was the acknowledgement that they didn't have the answer: 'I said "I don't know this stuff either"'; 'I was really honest with them and said at the very first team meeting that "I'm no retail expert"'; 'you have to be sincere about the fact that you don't know the answers'; 'I show that I'm learning and feeling vulnerable so that encourages other people to do likewise'. Asking for help can create extraordinary followership for the leader, since people will respond and step up to figuring out what has to happen. Clearly it has to be counter balanced by the leader showing command of certain aspects of the situation; otherwise they would lose all credibility. However if this swings to becoming all knowing on all matters it can effectively disempower the taking of responsibility in the organisation around the leader; which does not free the system to be open to new possibilities.

In addition to asking for help, a leader's acceptance of feeling lost or being stuck can be an even more powerfully transforming moment. It creates a fertile void of 'not knowing', a preparedness to go on new journeys, without which nothing new or transforming can emerge. This has become to be known as 'negative capability' – the ability to not know, to stay in inquiry, and thereby explore new potential. The human ego is such that we don't naturally tend to say 'I'm losing the plot', particularly in our professional working life where we wish to promote our sense of coping and being on top of things, indeed one leader in our study said 'being prepared to expose my insecurities and weaknesses was the biggest challenge for me'. However, it is very normal to feel stuck in the face of high magnitude change, and when the leader can share this with others it makes it 'okay' for others to confess to their sense of feeling lost, and that mutual acceptance of 'lostness' generates a rich inquiry into its source. When this occurs, the reasons why the change is not going fast enough, or seems too difficult to implement, become clear. *The leader therefore holds and exposes the vulnerability of the whole system, not just their own.*

One dramatic example of this, which we experienced, was with a leader who, to the organisation, seemed infallible. She had a reputation of being way ahead of everyone else in their ability to know what was needed in a situation; she never seemed lost. Moreover, there was a strong unconscious projection into the organisation that this leader *didn't want to be seen to be lost*. At an engagement event for this leader's top 100 she made a conscious intervention to reveal a side of her that she knew about yet others did not. She did this through the sharing of a story (Attractor) which enabled the full meaning of her message to come alive to the group. In front of the assembled 100 she told the story of how she had once taken her transformation team away on an outdoor physical orienteering event in order to develop their skills in taking risks and stepping into the unknown. At one point in the story she found herself standing on the top of a pole four metres off the ground onto which she had proudly managed to haul herself up. The next action for her was to wait for a trapeze swing to come round onto which she had to jump to be taken to the ground. She described how, when the swing came round for the first time, she found herself unable to jump; and this happened for the second time . . . and the third . . . she was literally frozen to the top of the pole, unable to jump, even though her brain was telling her, 'it's only four metres down, you have a safety harness on, and you've just seen other people do it'. When recounting the story she even described and re-enacted physically the bodily sensation at the time – of having tingles going all the way up her 'stuck' arms. The moment at this event was mesmerising, her leaders were on the edge of their seats; 'she gets stuck too!' She had created a transforming space. It opened up the leaders present to being able to speak about what they were currently finding hard in the change, where they were feeling unable to act, and in so doing it created movement.

Understands what is happening in the moment and breaks established patterns and structures in ways that create movement in the 'here and now'

Transforming Space leadership takes action in the moment to enable people to see the usefulness or otherwise of the patterns of behaviour *that they are playing out right there in the present moment.* By promoting open feedback about behaviour this practice is therefore closely akin to Edge and Tension. What Transforming Space leadership adds is that the feedback happens in a very live way, and it is also processed very experientially to enable movement to a new mindset and behaviour there and then. This can feel extremely destabilising and confronting for people, and needs to be practiced with skill. Yet leaders who can do this well enable people to *walk* into new ways of being and doing rather than talk their way into them, which creates deeper learning and faster change.

The first step is for the leader to recognise the behaviour being played out, and identify its impact in the context of its purpose. It may be that the impact of the behaviour currently evident will not achieve the change's intended outcome – as Erik saw in his team at the start of this chapter, they were talking service yet living entitlement. The next step is to bring your awareness of the situation to the attention of others present in ways that do not elicit their defensive behaviour. Key to achieving this is the leader expressing the intent of their intervention – for example Erik was acting in service of moving the culture to becoming more market competitive; and it also requires the setting up of 'safety' in the room, for example Erik asked his team to draw their chairs into a circle so that they could see each other, and he used inquiry, not judgemental statements. Once the behaviour has been named and acknowledged the next step is to inquire into what this behaviour is serving in the current context, in other words the behaviour is not labelled as helpful or unhelpful until it is identified. The inquiry in the transformed space then attributes meaning. People are generally not being deliberately unhelpful! It might be that the behaviour is seeking to serve something that is important in the current context, and unless this is unravelled the purpose of the behaviour will not be understood. If this doesn't happen then learning will not take place, people will be unable to reframe the situation, and no change can occur. Finally, the leader invites those present to try starting now with any new mindset or behaviour, based on their new understanding; he or she invites them into the void.

In accomplishing the above the leader's intervention can be creative. One leader in our study was the Chief Executive of a troubled and underperforming City Council. He noticed that one of the real issues in the culture of the organisation was the split between the elected politicians and the appointed managers. They were intruding into each other's role which was causing duplication of effort and much frustration. At one meeting he wanted to bring this to the attention of the team (comprising elected members and executives) and facilitate their moving to a new place. Completely un-premeditated he got up and drew a line down the middle of the room. He asked the executive managers to stand on one side and the politicians on the other;

. . . so we stood facing each other and I said 'right, let's just change over' . . . so we swapped sides. And I said 'right, now the politicians are going to be the executive directors and the executive directors are going to be the councillors, and I want you to ape the behaviour of the other!' We physically role played, standing there, doing this, and confronting the behaviours that actually were the core of the problem. And it was fascinating to see the dynamic and the dawning realisation that we have to give the other a whole lot more space here, and support them in exercising their particular roles. We wrote some new commitments on boards and we used them from that moment on in the meeting. And that was one of the best bits of learning – changing the dynamic of the relationship – which we ever did.

In this intervention the leader, while being catalytic, acted in such a way that the awareness of the mindset and behaviour, its attached meaning, and therefore the desire to change, sat clearly within the Council.

Transforming Space leadership therefore creates change in the 'here and now'. It is based on the assumption that the only thing you can change *is* what is happening in the present. And if you can design and create spaces in which people start to think and act differently now, then the change becomes real, not just a bolt on slogan or an organisational programme. *Transforming Space leaders design the change as if it is already happening.*

Powerfully inquires into ripe systemic issues to enable deep change to happen

The most skilful way in which to expose any potentially limiting aspects of an organisation's norms and behaviours is through the use of inquiry that goes to the heart of the issues that require transforming. Inquiry helps others do their own thinking, it changes perceptions, and it enables deeper learning. The first move is to detect the systemic issue; the second to know what it is you are interested in helping others see through your inquiry; and the third move is to formulate and conduct the inquiry in a way that elicits a transforming response. 'Why did you?' questions only serve to create defensive behaviour and more stuck-ness in the situation, since people tense up in justification and thereby become unavailable for self awareness and learning. On the other hand, 'what was it that led to?', or, 'how is it that?' questions are more helpful. Such kinds of questions have more 'containing' qualities, making it safer for people to respond, while still staying true to Edge and Tension – confronting what is really going on. The leader's intent in these transforming inquiries is always to help others understand and make meaning of what is going on through their own process of inquiring and responding, it's not down to the leader to be making expert or biased interpretations.

Two of the easiest ways to detect a systemic issue 'ripe' for inquiry are: being closely attentive to moments in which what is being said in the situation and what is being done is completely different; or, noticing those moments when people are attributing unhelpful behaviours to others which behaviours they themselves are blindly following. In both situations people are unconsciously *acting out* systemic impulses while being consciously conversant as to what *should* be happening in the situation. Their intention and their behaviour are somehow 'out of synch'. These are perfect situations for creating a transforming space.

An example of the first dynamic occurred at a meeting where a group of leaders were planning the restructuring of their business into one region. Participants had gathered from several countries. At one point in the meeting a participant was presenting the output from their breakout group which had been tasked with identifying the new ways of working imperative to make the new structure function effectively. One of the most important behaviours the presenter was sharing was the need to 'collaborate and draw on all ideas'. However, when he invited the whole group to respond to his proposals he shut them down and did not listen. What was being *said* in the room and what was being *done* was the complete opposite. The group could sense this incongruity and yet did nothing to intervene. When the presenter had sat down the leader present invited the group to talk not just about the content of what had been proposed, but what they had been noticing happening in the room *in relation to the intent of the change being presented.* The inquiry enabled the surfacing of the current dynamics in ways that did not leave the individual presenter feeling criticised, he was helped to see how he was simply 'carrying the current culture' in his behaviour, and the rest of the group were helped to see how their very own inaction in the moment had also served to keep the culture where it currently was – by not raising the issue they were also stuck in its repeating pattern.

An example of the second dynamic occurred with a leader of a professional services firm who was planning with her team how to change the 'partnership culture' in their organisation. To reach the firm's strategic goals the culture had to become more risk taking and action oriented. The leader's team were attributing to the partners a behavioural tendency that they called '80:20'; partners spent 80 % of their time planning change and crafting elegant papers and only 20 % of their time in implementation. At one meeting with her team the leader sensed that her own team were at risk of doing exactly the same thing – the behavioural tendency was systemic, not just one exhibited by the partners. They had already spent one day of a two day meeting planning the change and writing up the unhelpful behaviours they felt needed transforming in the partner community. When the leader inquired into how this (Human Resources) group could influence the partners to change their behaviour, they cautiously replied that they wanted to write a paper about it. The 'unhelpful behaviours' they had listed on the walls in this meeting were being enacted in their very own behaviour – they mimicked everything they felt was unhelpful behaviour in a group elsewhere in the system, *and they were blind to this*. Through skilful inquiry into what was being noticed about their own behaviour in the room the group came to quite an 'aha' moment of self awareness and realisation. *And the most significant shift came when they were encouraged to approach the partners in a way that would enact the behaviours they were expecting to see in the new culture* – in this instance taking immediate action to get some partners engaged in leading the organisation differently, not crafting the perfect paper to them. One of the HR team members present when this was suggested said, 'that's a huge risk, and sounds like the craziest idea in the world, and it makes me feel really uncomfortable. So maybe that's why we need to do it!'

Through the use of powerful inquiry leaders can turn unaware, and taken for granted behaviour, into aware and conscious behaviour. Once there is awareness people can make choices about what has to change and how this can be achieved, and leaders can enable deep change to happen. Inquiry shines a torch on how the organisation is acting. It's hard to change things you cannot see.

Creates time and space (including attending to its physical quality) for transforming encounters

While Transforming Space leadership is about facilitating 'live' change in the moment, its practice also requires a heightened sensitivity to and awareness of process design, and the physical time and space within which the change occurs. In that respect leaders in our study paid as much attention to where things would happen, how, and among whom, as they did to what was happening in the moment. Their intent was to create the conditions that would facilitate the live enactment of change. If the purpose of change is to create collective responsibility for performance improvement, you don't set up a meeting room with rows of chairs facing a stage on which the senior leadership team sit behind a table. The spoken messages might communicate active responsibility while the unspoken message communicates passive dependency. Being diligent in the design of encounters and the setting up of the physical space can therefore have a big impact on the outcome. One leader from our study recounted, 'the key thing was to get these guys together and exorcise the past and get all sorts of unmentionable stuff out on the table . . . we therefore sat in the room in an unstructured and informal way, and some people were then brave enough to tell stories'.

The format and design of the encounter can also create transforming moments, as leaders in the study observed, 'we don't have team meetings, we just have gatherings, we'll just gather and talk about whatever we want', 'I now have quick buzz meetings in the open space area that generates all kinds of ideas', 'I now plan "random encounter" moments into my engagement events since that's where all the new ideas seem to come from'. One leader changed their team's meeting experience from conducting formal factory tours after presentations and in its place;

. . .

. . . flipped this on its head, and I said 'the first thing we'll do is visit the factory', and we went and did something called a team talk over breakfast, early in the morning with the night shift coming off and the new shift happening, and take a section of people off the factory floor, and actually spent some time listening to how they saw things.

The point to note is that *you can't transform what is happening in the moment unless you create an authentic snap shot of what is actually happening in the moment.* Transforming Space leadership is therefore like setting up a 'laboratory', or a live practice field, within which reality is played out. And when reality can be played out then it can be changed. Otherwise, you are working on something that is abstract and 'not in the room'.

One way of replicating reality is to ensure that a representative sample of the organisation is present within the transforming space. If a cross section of the system is not present by definition you can't change things in the moment that represents the wider systemic issues. One leader in our study was leading a change process to reduce a very hierarchical and paternalistic culture into one in which people at all levels in the organisation felt they could take decisions to better serve their customers. Rather than get the top leadership group together to plan how this could happen, he set up a live one day 'hot house' at which a cross section of the organisation was present. This had never been done before. A bank teller was in the same room as the Chief Executive. And the day was designed to enact the new culture such that the change was happening as it was being planned, 'we put them in a laboratory and let them get on with it and that's what we did'. The space was not about the change. *The space became the change.*

Another way of bringing reality into the room is through the use of arts based interventions. Even when the physical setting might be transforming and you have the 'right' people in the room, it can still be hard to enact what is truly happening. People can stay sitting around talking about changing things while still enacting current mindsets and behaviours, either because they are unaware of what they are doing or because it can be just too awkward and threatening to confront current mindsets and behaviour. We have found that leaders who are prepared to work with creative interventions such as 'socio-drama' create greater authenticity in the present moment, and when that happens the space holds the potential to become a transforming one.

Transforming Space leadership practices: putting it all together

We have noted in this chapter that leaders who practice Trans-forming Space alone are unlikely to bring about successful change, and indeed it can have a negative impact on out-comes. It is therefore inappropriate to share a successful story that just illustrates Transforming Space practices. In addition, given that this practice is about enacting change in the moment, it is hard to share a story that encapsulates move-ment over an extended period of time. However, what follows is a short story that is primarily about Transforming Space leadership, and it is a story that kaleidoscopes just one day in the life of a leadership team. And it is a day which brought about some profound change, not just in the team, but as a consequence the organisation around them.

The day had been set up to make a breakthrough in how this leadership team functioned. Mark the Chief Operating Officer (COO) was the team leader. His team had been established to transform the operational excellence of the company. The team was nine months into its existence, and yet was still acting in a very dysfunctional way; there was little trust and cooperation in the team, which got played out as non-listening and competitive behaviour at team meetings. Mark's own leadership style was very direct, action oriented and results driven, and yet this tipped into a pace setting and sometimes coercive managerial style. Based on the low trust in the team it had been hard up to this point for its members to talk openly and courageously about their behaviour. This was not helping them move forward. Despite the pain and frustration they felt during the weekly team meetings, the reason such behaviour persisted had to be serving a need they were most likely unaware of (such as preserving their sense of autonomy, stature, and authority over their own part of the organisation).

Mark's leadership was instrumental to the creative and potentially risky design of the day. A magical venue had been found in the middle of nowhere in some beautiful countryside. It was a small cottage style restaurant, with a roaring log fire, wooden beams, and tranquil garden. It felt special and inviting, and ripe for Transforming Space. The main restaurant area had been cleared for the meeting. As team members showed up on that frosty December morning Mark helped people to their steaming mugs of coffee. Once the team had taken their chairs in the circle Mark opened by stating how important the day was for him and how he hoped it was going to lead to something positive happening. This he felt had to happen in order for their organisational change process to succeed, 'if this team can't be aligned and operationally excellent how can we expect the organisation beneath us to join up and improve performance?' His opening messages contained both Attractor and Edge and Tension leadership. He continued by saying that he wasn't too sure about how the design would work and yet he had every confidence that what would happen was what was meant to happen. The Container had been set.

The two facilitators then started to have a conversation live in front of the leadership team; they reflected on how the design process had gone, how they were feeling coming into this day, and how they thought the team might respond to the process. The team listened curiously . . . this was a different kind of opening . . . the facilitators were talking about them as if they weren't in the room! The facilitators were committed to being present and 'in the moment', talking live and unprompted; and they introduced into their conversation the notion that often in play, or drama, people can speak more truthfully than when they are just asked to talk about a situation. Somehow people can find it easier to bring out awkward subjects when they transpose them into an enacted story. They then turned to the team and briefed them on the task. The entire morning was an invitation to create and act out a drama, or play, about the story of this team up to that point in time. It was to be done in three acts. Mark asked the team to define what those three acts should be: Act One became the moment he joined the organisation and set up this team; Act Two the time when they as a leadership team had held a big engagement event with the organisation; and Act Three was going to be a recreation of their team meeting the previous week. The team broke up into three corresponding groups to develop the script and prepare how they were going to act it out in front of their colleagues.

After an hour the 'actors' moved onto the stage and the play about the life of this team commenced. At the end of each act Mark invited the 'audience' to respond to what they had seen being acted out in front of them. The whole play was very real and gritty; it felt like a hard hitting 'docu-drama'. Subjects that had been too painful to talk about within the team were getting named and acknowledged in the play. In particular, Mark's own leadership style became apparent as different members of his team chose to play him in their acts. The perceptions of his behaviour were strong and consistent. And yet it also became clear that the team had been 'colluding' to keep his behaviour where it was, since if he *had* stepped back to coach and empower more, that would have meant them having to take greater responsibility! Each and every individual in some way had to confront the fact that they had been systemically responsible for the poor behaviour and performance of the team. The structure of the play and its three acts served as the Container, and within this secure space Edge and Tension burned brightly.

The processing of the play became the Transforming Space. Mark inquired throughout the debrief times, which in itself enacted a move away from his repeating pace setter style; he was curious and non-defensive. His vulnerability opened up the potential for greater honesty in the team, who said they had felt 'ashamed' when witnessing the acts of the play. The mutual acceptance of 'lostness' enabled the team to speak openly and frankly to each other for the first time. During those moments no one looked outside to see the weather, no one got up to get some more coffee, and no one looked at their watches; they were totally present to the awareness of what was happening in the moment. When it felt like people had said what they needed to, Mark suggested the team break for lunch. Despite the chilly air the team chose to walk outside around the tranquil garden to simply take time out and mark the moment.

When they returned Mark had decided to take the transformation another step forward. He realised that his own behaviour had been a big feature in the play, and therefore invited the team to sit down on their return and to talk more specifically about his behaviour and what changes they felt were needed in his style in order to help them all win. It was a request from the team leader to be coached, yet also an offer to improve the team's ability to function. The team responded, hesitatingly at first. However, they became more confident during the conversation in helping Mark to see what he could do differently. At one moment in time, a team member then asked that Mark give *them* feedback on what he would like to see different in their behaviour. The team had become fully responsible for its own effectiveness, and it felt a direct, open, and equal space. The team had never been in that space together before. And it felt good. *The act of conversing about making the team a better place had in itself made the team a better place to be.* Mark's close paying of attention to the play in the morning, the invitation for all to become more aware of their current processes, and then Mark's courage to open up the reflections on his own leadership, had all changed the ground upon which the team operated. It could never be the same again. While the next session of the day was about

'Act Four', during which the team identified concrete behaviours and measures of success for the team going forward, the change had already occurred. It had become a Transforming Space.

Transforming Space: the dark side

There are several ways in which leaders practicing Transforming Space can have dysfunctional impact, and once again the degrees of this are dependent on the leader's level of self awareness and personal intent in the situation. If unaware of their own impulses leaders could inadvertently cast an egotistical and self indulgent shadow into the organisation; and the desire to bring about change in the 'here and now' moment will feel like *manipulation*. Their attempts at creating transforming spaces, despite good intentions, can appear as weird, tangential and at times downright irrelevant to those around them, leading to responses such as, 'I thought I was here to do a job rather than get drawn into all kinds of fantastical games!' In such situations any containing qualities are lost, the space can feel fragile, energy is dissipated as anxiety, and the leader loses the attention of the organisation. People will tend to switch off, either overtly, 'I'm not going to do that!', or covertly, 'well, I'll just play along with this attempt at changing me and wait till it blows over'.

At its most extreme a leader consciously uses Transforming Space type interventions to pursue their own ends. If left unchallenged by the organisation its practice can build up mesmerising cults centred on the individual leader. Attempts at exposing vulnerability are actually self serving and arrogant attempts to prove that one is invincible, rather than invitations to open up sources of discomfort in the organisation. Leaders who are able to make change happen in the moment can be very mesmerising, and can take on almost magical properties in the eyes of others. They seem to be able to see things other ordinary mortals can't. And when they transform the mindsets and behaviours of others it can become hypnotic and addictive, 'I really want to be with that leader, all kinds of weird and wonderful things happen around them, I'm a changed person!'

Clearly if the leader's self interest borders on the unethical, then Transforming Space leadership becomes extremely dangerous for an organisation. Mostly, though, this dysfunction is a product of a leader's low humility and an organisational context that promotes idealisation of the leader. In these systems childhood longings for an all powerful parent can get projected onto the leader, and the leader's attempts to bring self serving transforming encounters into the organisation go unchallenged.

Here are some pointers to help you recognise the 'light side' of Transforming Space leadership and its potential to tip into the 'dark side'. Again monitor your response to the questions below while remembering that any recognition of the dark side does not make you a 'dysfunctional' leader. We all have these tendencies within us, yet the quality and impact of our shadow in the organisation, and thereby our chances of facilitating fundamental and systemic change, will be determined by the extent to which we can recognise them and in so doing adjust our leadership stance in the situation.

- Are you serving yourself, or the organisation around you?

- Do you notice systemic issues as 'loop holes' that you can take advantage of, or as opportunities for learning and change in the organisation?

- Do you observe things around you to pick up short falls, or to be curious about why things are as they are?

- Do you inquire into what's going on to assert your superiority over someone, or to help change the nature of your relationship with them?

- Do you make yourself vulnerable to draw attention to you, or to help others talk about how they might be lost?

- Do you create the time and space for transforming encounters to distract from the main agenda, or to act in its service?

Summary

In this chapter we have described how Transforming Space leadership can make change happen in real time. In Table 8.1 we summarise its key features. When combined with Attractor it can make the organisation's essential purpose come alive in the moment. When combined with Edge and Tension it can take disturbance and adjust paradigms as the conversation is happening. When combined with Container it provides

Table 8.1 Transforming Space Leadership

Essence: makes change happen in the 'here and now' moment

What It Is (Light Side)	*What It Is Not (Dark Side)*
• A focus and attention on and in the present moment	• Changing the present moment without good intention; *manipulation*
• Building awareness about sources of behaviour	• Self indulgent learning
• Courageous interventions that break deep patterns in the system	• Mesmerising interventions that build cults around the individual leader
• Designing of processes that live the change	• Unnecessary experiments with people's heads
• A practice that serves the other three Changing Leadership practices in moving the organisation towards its purpose	• A tangential and potentially damaging practice that serves the leader's own needs

Core Practices
- Demonstrates a commitment that engenders trust, enabling the system to go to new places, learn about itself, and act differently
- Frees people to new possibilities by making themselves vulnerable and open
- Understands what is happening in the moment and breaks established patterns in ways that create movement in the 'here and now'
- Powerfully inquires into ripe systemic issues to enable deep change to happen in the present moment
- Creates times and space (including attending to its physical quality) for transforming encounters

How It Serves Change
- Speeds up movement by taking advantage of the continually available opportunities to change things here and now
- Increases the impact of the other three Changing Leadership practices
- By enacting change it makes it real and present and forever changes the future flow
- Helps the organisation to learn about itself and act differently, keeps it alert and 'on its toes'
- Can shift deep paradigms and thereby transform behaviour sustainably
- Creates more systemic and holistic insight about the organization

a safe space to boldly experiment with a new mindset and a new voice. When practiced in isolation from these other three Changing Leadership practices it leads to weird and wonderful transformational processes that are unable to connect with people's day to day reality and in so doing becomes self indulgent.

Transforming Space leadership requires a committed focus and attention on the present moment. Its practices relate to the ability to be completely in tune with what is happening to you and around you and then consciously and responsibly acting in the moment to change what is happening around you *in order to take the organisation closer to its purpose*. Leaders see the emerging potential of the current moment. They stay attentive and observant. And they step in to alter the flow of what is happening since they realise that the only thing you can really change is the present moment, and this can be changed by focussing attention upon the here and now. If the chance is not taken to change the present, they have lost the opportunity to change its future. When the organisation enacts change in the present rather than talks about it for the future it becomes real and tangible. The change is not bolted in to the organisation; the organisation lives it and breathes it.

To change what is happening in the moment Transforming Space leaders make themselves vulnerable and human in order to be able to release others from their stuckness. When the playing field is levelled people become more open and honest about their own struggles and this then allows the situation to be remedied through a shift in awareness of the present. Observing, acting in the moment, and admitting one's own limitations are combined with close attention to the time and space within which transforming encounters can occur. This includes attending to the physical space, design, and format of the encounters. Transforming Space leaders work with process to enable live change to happen.

If practiced to serve ones own needs, either consciously or unconsciously, it can become manipulative, cult-like, tangential and dangerous. When practiced with high levels of self awareness and intent to create movement towards the organisation's purpose, Transforming Space leadership accelerates change, produces profound learning, and enables special moments to happen.

Part III
Working with Changing Leadership

Introduction to Part III

In Part II we aimed to illustrate *what it is that leaders do* to put the Changing Leadership practices into action. We drew extensively from the research transcripts to provide short examples of each of the behaviours, and we drew from our own organisational and consulting practice to illustrate the stories and cases at the opening and close of each chapter. When we had completed Part II we had to take a pause and a bit of a 'time out' to reflect on what we had discovered in writing it. The Changing Leadership practices in total cover 20 different individual behaviours, which while inter-related still offer quite specific and distinct elements for consideration. It's a full landscape, potentially daunting to absorb in one go, and having travelled its territory we felt it would be worthwhile to now pause and reflect on what has been covered before heading off into an exploration of *how to work with the Changing Leadership practices.*

This brief introduction to Part III therefore invites you to pause, breathe, reflect and notice. To aid your reflection you may wish to consider the following questions.

At which points in the landscape did you stop most to notice what you were seeing?

It pays to notice what you most notice. Perhaps there were some particular passages, descriptions, or stories that most caught your attention. Which points were you drawn to, and what was it that led you to pause and reflect on them? Did they seem relevant to the change challenges you are currently facing? Had they provided you with a new insight into your own leadership? Did you wish to challenge their assumptions? Were they confronting any of your assumptions and beliefs? Any other reasons why you stopped to pause?

Where in the landscape did you most want to keep going and move through quickly?

At some points you might have just skimmed through the passages – what was that about? Perhaps you were already familiar with the concepts and practices being presented, they seemed less relevant to your challenges, or they simply held no appeal to you. On the other hand, did you at times move on quickly because they were asking you to notice something about yourself or the situation around you that you maybe unconsciously wanted to avoid staying with and exploring? Was the subject matter a bit too tricky or too complex to handle? Can you go to the source of that difficulty?

Which parts of the landscape seemed most familiar to you?

It's always comforting to see landscape that you recognise. Familiarity provides affirmation and a sense of security. It gives you a sense of connection to what you know and recognise. It validates what you know to be true. Which aspects of the practices did you most recognise – and where do you recognise them from? Your own leadership approach, the leadership you see around you, or other concepts and frameworks that you have encountered? What did you take away from these 'yes, that's it', encounters?

Where did you seem to be going into 'foreign places'?

When we enter unfamiliar territory there is the potential to either discover something new or to see what you already know about in a new light. Which points in the landscape presented you with this opportunity? Did any of the practices or concepts help you expand your thinking as to what's important in how to lead high magnitude change? If you did not recognise any of the practices either in your own behaviour or that of the organisational system around you, what is that saying in terms of your own approach to leading change or indeed what gets valued in the culture around you? Did any parts of the unfamiliar territory disturb you in some way? What might that be saying?

Without coming to any conclusions, since the purpose of this pause and reflect is not to wrap things up in any way, can you now identify a few big questions that you hold about the Changing Leadership framework that you would like to take forward into this next section on working with its practices?

When we stopped to pause and survey the total landscape covered, from both Parts I and II, we identified the following sign posts that had led us to this stage of the journey:

- Successful and sustainable change implementation needs to assume that organisations are complex systems that cannot be simply controlled or directed from any one source.

- The beliefs and practices that leaders adopt when implementing change are fundamental in determining its outcome.

- An overly leader-centric Shaping leadership style does not lead to successful change because the change becomes all about the leader, not about creating the total capability of the organisation to move to a new place.

- The four Changing Leadership practices, which combine equal forces for creating order and disorder, seem to be able to create the conditions within which high magnitude change can readily occur and capability be built for the organisation to do its 'own changing'.

- All of these practices are driven by an intent to create power, purpose, and capability in the system around them; when driven by an intent to build power over others in order to serve and promote oneself, the leader's behaviour can lead to extreme organisational dysfunction.

- A leader needs to combine positive intent with high levels of self awareness in order to accurately read the organisational situation around them and not see what gets presented as a projection of their unconscious ego-controlled needs. Unless they become more conscious their well intended leadership can still cast an unhelpful shadow into the organisation under which people find it hard to engage whole heartedly with the change and its leadership.

- Working 'in the moment' seems to be a recurring theme across all four of the practices. When the leader can spot wider systemic issues getting played out in the conversation and behaviour around them they can intervene to change its patterns and in so doing be able to change the wider organisational patterns and routines.

Overall, our reflections led us to see how Changing Leadership is in its essence a *mindful* activity; becoming present, becoming aware, and becoming available for what might be unfolding. This deeper consciousness opens one up to be able to see and work with paradoxes – tighter rules bring greater freedom, acknowledging vulnerability draws forth strength, eliminating tension creates more danger, giving away power builds power – which can guide leaders into what can feel like quite counter-intuitive interventions. And yet the risk involved in going towards the opposite of what you think you should do, can bring forth that which you most wished for. Changing Leadership can be a surprising and rewarding practice!

In this section we aim to draw together all of the research findings, concepts and definitions of the Changing Leadership framework shared so far and show how its four practices can be practically integrated, applied, and developed. While this is primarily focussed on how you as an individual leader can learn to work with the practices, we will also cover how collective leadership capability can be built in the leadership team. We hope that the territory covered in this final part of the landscape will draw forth insights for the 'big questions' you still hold for the framework, and provide some practical pointers for where you wish to take your own leadership practice.

9

Linking Changing Leadership

'The success of any intervention is dependent on the inner condition of the interviewer'

William O'Brien, former CEO of the Hanover Insurance Company
quoted by Otto Sharmer in Theory U:
Leading from the Emerging Future (2005)

Having explored the four leadership practices individually in Part II, we now turn in this chapter to considering how they work together. For in reality they do not exist as 'real' and separate entities. The activity of leadership is more complex than that. As we began to integrate the four practices into our organisational work, it became apparent that we needed to see the four practices as an interdependent and connected whole. When leaders tackle real life change situations, the texture, balance, and impact of all four seemed necessary. It's not enough to draw people magnetically towards purpose (Attractor) without clarifying its boundaries (Container) and making it come to life (Transforming Space). It's not helpful to confront today's unhelpful patterns (Edge and Tension) without channelling the resultant anxiety (Container) and making the discomfort meaningful (Attractor). On the other hand, leaders who *could* creatively link and work with all four practices tended to get their organisations moving towards performance improvement at a faster pace.

We also had independent validation from our research findings that leaders who used all four practices produced more successful change – especially high magnitude change. When exploring why this might be the case we alighted on the insight from Complexity Theory that systems able to stay in perpetual motion and change contain an equal amount of the forces for structure, patterning, or order (Attractor and Container), and, the forces for chaos, disruption, or disorder (Edge and Tension and Transforming Space). If a leader had strengths or preferences along only one of these axes they could risk either over stabilising or destabilising their organisations. Both tendencies only led to stuck systems – the first in complacency the second in anxiety. Yet a leader's attention across both of these axes seemed to get things moving. Moreover, when we coded the research transcripts we were uncovering what we called 'multi-hit interventions'; i.e. single instances in a story when the leader linked combinations of the four different Changing Leadership practices, and as a consequence was able to generate significant movement.

Based on these insights from our practice and our research we pursued three further lines of inquiry:

• What characterised those leaders able to link all four of the Changing Leadership practices?

- How can leaders learn to hold the balance of all four and know which practice, or combinations of practices, are needed when?

- What can leaders do to combine the four practices to get maximum impact?

In this chapter we will share the outcomes of this further inquiry. We hope its findings will provide you with deeper insight into how you can work at a holistic level with the Changing Leadership framework. The Tables and Figures in this chapter are designed to offer you practical aids to both assess the current way in which the practices are deployed (in combination or not?) and to guide you in how to better link them.

What characterised those leaders able to link all four of the Changing Leadership practices?

To help answer this question in a rigorous way we took the 'top five' transcripts from our research (stories which had successful change outcomes, and in which leaders repeatedly combined all four practices), and the 'bottom five' transcripts (unsuccessful change where the leader did not demonstrate the practices with any frequency, and when they did only used one or two of them), and undertook a 'cross case analysis'. Two researchers independently read through all 10 of these transcripts to identify what made the difference between the top five and the bottom five in terms of leader orientation, behaviour, and intervention.

The differences between the leaders who could combine the practices, and those who could not, were very striking. What follows is a summary of these factors. As you read them you might recognise themes you have already noticed from the leaders' stories and illustrations in Part II.

Leaders who could work with all four of the Changing Leadership practices were:

- extremely self aware and conscious of how to use their presence in a change process;

- able to work in the moment, staying attentive, expectant, and available to work with what arises;

- still in tune with the bigger picture, and almost demanding of the organisation around them to see and lead for the whole.

Extremely self aware and conscious of how to use their presence in a change process

Already we have extensively noted the importance of self awareness. Leaders who could work with all four of the Changing Leadership practices visibly demonstrated this self awareness. This included in their research interviews with us a continual tendency to reflect on their practice as they recounted their change stories. They noticed their impulses, they were aware of their struggles, and they reflected on what they could have done differently. This self reflection on practice was also evident in the stories themselves. They regularly sought out feedback, often engaged the services of a coach, and they put themselves into other people's shoes to be able to see how their leadership came across, and learn how it could be adapted to better serve the needs of the situation. By seeking out feedback about their impact in the organisation their so called 'unconscious self' could become more 'conscious'. This strong orientation towards becoming more self aware was not driven by some ego trip or self interest, but by a genuine desire to learn and improve how to take the organisation to a different place. In contrast, leaders in the low performing stories seemed woefully un-self aware, they were stuck in their own interests and needs, and as a consequence were unavailable to steward their organisations with any degree of disinterested and systemic insight. In their research interviews any reflection present was focussed solely on the outcome of the intervention, they did not demonstrate reflective practice on the process of the change and how they had led it.

Thus the leaders able to combine all four practices seemed able to develop a level of self awareness that was not driven by the ego. It meant instead becoming inwardly aware of all the contradictions and compromises that made up the ego. That part in us with which we can accept these facts about ourselves is the seed from which we can develop into our authentic self. It can be more comfortable to ignore the symptoms of our dysfunction in the organisation, since it is hard for us to be able to see how we could be working against ourselves, how through our own behaviour we are getting the opposite of what we most wish for. However, if we can give a place to the painful acceptance of our shadow then we can turn towards truth and sincerity and in so doing develop our ability to serve. *This is why self awareness is so vital for a leader being able to master all four of the Changing Leadership practices.* Detachment from (not elimination of!) the self-protective, self-promoting impulses of the ego frees us to take risks with others (essential for Edge and Tension), opens us to serve a purpose wider than self (without which Attractor becomes self promotion), releases us to stay non-anxious in challenging conditions (the vital Container presence), and gives us the wisdom and courage to make catalytic 'in the moment' interventions (without which Transforming Space is either avoided or falls flat).

Once a leader is self aware, they can then use their presence in the organisation in mindful, not impulsive, ways. The 'top five' leaders from the cross case analysis frequently spent time becoming available to enter into strong informal engagements with their organisations, often collectively with their leadership teams, *and these provided ripe opportunities to combine all four practices.* They were also very explicit with the organisation about the processes they were deploying, in other words, they shared with others the intent behind what they were doing – their own mindfulness became collective mindfulness. Once leaders can explain their process to others it builds trust (Container), conveys to the organisation the conscious shift required in mindset or ways of working (Edge and Tension), and it also builds broader collective capability for others to change their ways (Transforming Space).

Importantly, the egoless sharing of both process and intent invites inquiry and learning into what is happening in the moment. One of the 'top five' leaders called this 'evidencing leadership', and he made a crucial distinction between this and 'role modelling'. Evidencing leadership entailed being 'very clear about what I was doing and why', whereas role modelling leadership can just end up in a more Shaping style that only *implicitly* enacts new behaviour. The former is mindful, the latter impulsive. In the former approach a leader's presence becomes educative and collectively transforming, in the latter it remains individually led and pace setting. People might blindly follow the new practice without really knowing why, or, in the case of some of the 'bottom five' stories, chose to follow because this is the accepted practice and found themselves in a position where they did not believe they could challenge.

Able to work in the moment, staying attentive, expectant, and available to work with what arises

A very striking feature of the leaders who combined all four of the Changing Leadership practices was their intense ability to put aside their own impulses and 'tune in' to their organisation, a capability known as 'disinterested attention'. People around the leader feel safe and listened to, since they do not detect any whiff of personal agenda or self interest in the leader. Once a leader holds a disinterested attention, they can notice patterns around them, through inquiry understand what these patterns are serving, and then work in the moment to disturb any of the repeating patterns that are proving unhelpful to improving the organisation's performance. The 'top five' leaders were continually available and attentive to what was happening in the present as an opportunity to exercise Changing Leadership.

Why is this capability so important for linking all the practices? Unless a leader gets interested in the day to day and tunes into the system it becomes hard to lead the organisation along paths of new possibilities (Attractor); without the curiosity and courage to work on the deeper forces a leader is unable to disturb the repeating patterns that most require the organisation's attention (Edge and Tension); unless the leader can put their ego to one side and stay present and patient with what is arising, and not judge what is happening at face value, then their detached, purposeful, and affirming Container presence gets compromised; and finally, if they don't attempt to set up spaces that bring people's attention to the processes at play in the current culture, and they remain focussed just on outcomes rather than observing the present, they will miss opportunities to make visible the current systemic patterns and in so doing miss the chance to make change happen in the 'here and now' (Transforming Space).

We saw the leaders most able to combine the practices continually working on the underlying system that produced and supported the performance outcomes of their organisation. One leader described this activity as working with the 'system's sound'. They listened to the noise, echoes, language, and style of conversation in the organisation and almost detective like sought to uncover from this the truth of its current workings. They did not seek to make immediate judgements as to what was happening, or simply take things at face value, *instead they tried to perceive and make visible for collective sense making the forces that were giving rise to the present.*

Making visible the forces that give rise to the present requires the leader to be able to spot the 'vital signs' that are not just about the current situation but manifestations of the deeper system being either dysfunctional or disturbed. At times these vital signs can be picked up in recurring patterns of behaviour. The leader in our study who was the Chief Executive of the underperforming City Council noticed that his pest control department categorised all customer incidents of vermin in their premises as mice. Even when customers insisted that they were rats, the pest control department (without any inspection of the premises) still claimed on interviewing the poor city inhabitant over the phone that they had to be mice. At one significant meeting the leader of the council inquired into the system that was getting played out in this somewhat surreal behaviour and he learned that time targets for responding to mice was far longer than that required for responding to rats, so by continuing to categorise the vermin as mice the pest control department could avoid the performance improvement changes needed to increase urgency, efficiency, and customer service. The people in the pest control department were not 'bad people', they were simply caught up in the taken for granted assumptions around what good performance looked like. By making these forces present visible, this leader opened up the wider culture to acknowledge how each and every department in the Council was in some way caught up in its pattern.

At other times staying attentive and responsive to 'system sound' can be done within the fleeting moment of a single conversation. We were once facilitating a 'fish bowl' dialogue with a leadership group; a process in which volunteers sit in a small circle at the centre of the rest of the group who are seated in concentric circles fanning out from this inner circle. The small circle of participants seated in the middle conduct a dialogue in front of the group about a subject of vital importance to those present. There is always an empty 'hot seat' available for anyone in the wider group to enter the small inner circle and temporarily join the dialogue that is being observed by others – usually to inquire or challenge what is being said or noticed. The purpose of this so called 'fish bowl' is to enable the wider group to not just tune in to what is being said in the circle, but from their detached perspective be also able to read the signs in the culture that are getting played out in its process (for example if no one steps into the 'hot seat', what is that saying about risk and ability to confront in the culture?).

During the debrief of this fishbowl one of the participants in the outer ring said that he had felt 'excluded' from the dialogue (despite the hot seat available) and that this had been unhelpful for him. He was processing his own issues, not those of the system that had given rise to his discomfort in the first place. As quick as a flash however one of the leaders present connected his feeling of discomfort to the wider change that was being introduced to the organisation. They were moving away from consensual and collective decision making to a more executive style – involving smaller groups of people. In a sense she said, courageously voicing to the whole group, the discomfort of exclusion that people were feeling seated in the outer circle of the fishbowl was precisely the discomfort that would have to be gone through in order to shift their culture. Rather than judging the fishbowl process at face value, she inquired into the way in which people's experience of it had given them insights into the deeper forces at play, which unless changed, would always keep their organisation in its current state.

How easy it was for people present at this gathering to 'get' this leader's point was questionable, because our natural tendency is to just read the situation through our own needs, rather than tuning into the systemic forces at play. Even if we have experienced a potentially transforming encounter, we can remain immune to interpreting it other than from our own (often unaware) interests. *Yet if we cannot see and understand what arises in the present differently, we will forever be unable to change it.* In some respects, therefore, this particular aspect of Changing Leadership can be the most challenging to pull off. However, without the will, belief, and temperament to stay attentive to the moment and work with what is arising in a systemic way, it is hard to bring all four practices to play.

Our cross case analysis therefore saw the tuning into, and the working on, the systemic dynamics at play as a clear differentiator between those who could combine the four Changing Leadership practices, and those who could not. For those leaders who could, they seemed to see their organisation as a multidimensional, living force, which they could influence through the setting up of new conditions within which the organisation could learn about itself and act differently. Those leaders in our study who did not combine the four practices seemed more likely to enter the organisation, do their own diagnosis, launch some initiatives into the system, and then either sit back and wait for things to happen or push and prod for things to move faster. They were safely wrapped up in the immediate task and their own interests in it, and had not consciously freed themselves to risk disturbing the wider forces at play.

Still in tune with the bigger picture, and almost demanding of the organisation around them to see and lead for the whole

Those leaders most able to practice Changing Leadership not only paid an intense attention to the present moment that was arising, they could also step back and stay in tune with the wider context within which the change was being enacted. *Indeed, without this ability to see the bigger picture they would have been unable to have seen the whole system getting played out in the present moment – they would have only got swamped in its detail, not its inherent structure.* Leaders who could link all four practices understood and incorporated the wider context into their change process, they opened up the organisation to be able to 'know how to win' in this wider context, and they built the collective capability of their leadership teams to be able to lead for the whole. When leaders made this wider context known and visible, they enabled their organisations to learn when and how to make meaningful change happen in the day to day.

Examples of this included leaders educating the organisation about how city analysts rated their company; bringing in customers to talk about their changing requirements and how they compared the organisation either unfavourably or favourably to its competitors; more directly and tangibly it could involve the leader comparing their own organisation's performance to others – the City Council Chief Executive could say to his staff that their Council demanded the highest council tax in the land, while at the same time providing the worst service to its citizens. Bringing in the wider context therefore helps supply leaders with the mandate upon which they can start to construct meaning for the internal change required. It provides contextual insights and systemic connections without which the attention on the present moment and day to day activity becomes tactical and random.

An ever present feature in the leaders who were able to combine all four of the Changing Leadership practices together was an expectation, indeed, requirement, that their leadership teams should likewise step up and lead from this wider context. They selected, developed, managed, and appraised their teams on their ability to think and act for the whole. While they also expected their individual team members to be on top of their own particular area of responsibility, they made it clear that, unless they could also 'wear two hats' on their leadership team (i.e. have equal responsibility for leading the wider systemic change as for managing the performance of their own unit), then they would not have a place on that team. This was a very striking feature in the 'top five' leaders, and it manifested itself in two ways.

Firstly, the leader would often select or reconfigure their team to create the capability to lead as one unit, not as a group of individuals. Having the leadership team work as one unit was about creating a collective systemic force that could change the way in which their organisation functioned. One of the leaders recounted;

I wanted to rethink how we managed and moved the organisation, from a silo based approach to a more collaborative team approach . . . I therefore hired in managers who were about running the business as a whole, as opposed to running separate departments . . . and in doing this I halved the team in size . . . they started to work together on each other's portfolios . . . the house line was, when you talk to one of us you talk to all of us . . . and we said to the organisation we were now going to run this as one piece, as opposed to silos . . . and the change in that team was one of the most seismic points of the change agenda.

The second feature of creating the leadership team's capability to lead for the whole was how the leaders went about clarifying the essential work of the team, and on this basis focussing how they spent their time together. The primary agenda of the team became the strategic, systemic work in the organisation for which they were all mutually accountable. In all of the 'top five' stories leaders practically put a halt to the team giving each other reports and updates on activities arising in their own part of the organisation. Operational tension not fundamental to the wider change effort was pushed down and away from the team and in its place the leader would hold the team accountable for moving forward those activities and interventions designed to transform the place from which the organisation operated (for example in one story increasing speed of product innovation, development, and launch across the organisation). Leadership team meetings and processes therefore became quite challenging and intense activities, and in that sense held and represented the wider struggle for the whole change effort; for if a leadership team cannot learn to shift the ground from which they operate, they will find it hard to develop the wisdom and capability to shift the ground of the organisation around them.

Understanding and incorporating the wider context, and building the capability of their leadership teams to do likewise, was therefore the third characteristic of leaders who could link the Changing Leadership practices together. They held a broader systemic frame and connection, within and through which they challenged their leadership team and their organisation at large to learn about itself and act differently. This is why it is so important to being able to practice Changing Leadership: an attention to and connection with the wider context expands a leader's ability to create a meaningful and inspiring purpose for their organisation that enables people to venture into the unknown (Attractor); insight into the organisation's position within a wider context can stoke up ambition and draw attention to where and how it might be 'failing' (Edge and Tension); creating integrated and united leadership teams that act as one in the system provides a firm yet guiding steer to the organisation (Container); and seeing and holding the wider systemic dynamics enables leaders to intervene to change things in the moment with precision and relevance (Transforming Space).

How can leaders learn to hold the balance of all four and know which practice, or combinations of practices, are needed when?

Leaders often ask us, 'which practice should I start with first?', and focus their attention on moving ahead with just one of the four. While their change process might indeed require a 'boost' from just one, as we said at the start of the chapter deploying one in the absence of the others can get you into tricky places. In addition to becoming self aware, working in the moment, and leading from a wider context, the leaders most able to deliver high magnitude change were able to creatively integrate all four of the Changing Leadership practices and to know what kind of combination was needed when. Given that each of the practices serves different, yet complementary purposes, in combination, they can be used to devastating effect.

In Figure 9.1, Linking Changing Leadership, we share our synthesis of how all combinations of the four practices can be brought to bear in change. Not only are there axes mentioned earlier in this book between Attractor and Container (serving patterning, order, structure), and between Edge and Tension and Transforming Space (serving disruption, disorder, chaos), there are also axes that combine the practices

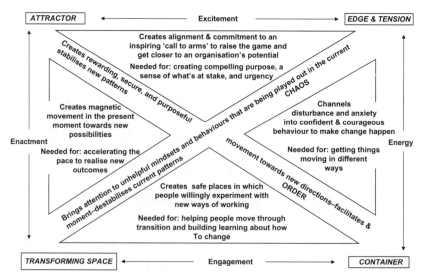

Figure 9.1 Linking Changing Leadership © 2008 Transcend Consultancy

around the perimeter of the framework. Each practice therefore has its own unique purpose, described in Chapters' 5 to 8, *and*, an essential connecting energy with each of the other three. Successful Changing Leadership is about working with all of these energies in unison. Reflect a while on this Table: given where your change process is at right now, which combinations of practices might now be needed, and where and in what context could they be applied? Can you begin to map these requirements onto some important organisational interventions you have planned for your change process in the coming months? We suggest you also do this reflection with your leadership team: what does successful change look like for you, where do you need to target your collective leadership impact, and how might you use combinations of the Changing Leadership practices to successfully accomplish that?

To help you plan what combinations are needed, it is also helpful to recognise the visible signs of where there is currently a deficit of any of the Changing Leadership practices. When the practices are not combined a leader sub-optimises their ability to bring about change. In Table 9.1, Changing Leadership Imbalances, we provide a summary of how to recognise the signs that indicate how each particular practice might either be over played (and lacking the complementary energy of the other practices), or missing from your change process. There are risks inherent in either over playing, or under playing, any one of the four.

What follows are some classic traps we saw leaders falling into who struggled to balance all four, along with reference to where increased linkage of the different practices can maximise the ability to more successfully intervene.

Table 9.1   Changing Leadership Imbalances

Attractor	*Edge and Tension*
Overdone:	*Overdone:*
• People feel they are moving in dubious directions	• Fear and panic are becoming evident
• The unknown feels risky not exciting	• Anxiety is creating pressure which stifles risk taking and creativity
• Over zealous behaviour is becoming off putting to others	• Real issues are getting buried; people comply just to avoid taking the blame
• Stories and missions lack substance and connection to reality	• People only seem able to talk about good news
• People were inspired and focussed yet now starting to drift away	• Stress is creating dysfunction, corrosive politics, and withdrawal
• People start to question the leader's motives	• Increased development of sub groups who chatter among themselves
Underdone:	*Underdone:*
• There is a sense of aimlessness to the change	• People are fiddling with the bricks while Rome is burning
• People feel no sense of an inspiring purpose, and remain caught in today's anxiety and/or uncertainty	• Inward focus vs outward 'customer' mindset
• People are moving in different directions and the change lacks a consistent and coherent story	• Good performance equals poor result and a good excuse
• Lack of excitement and commitment to staying the course	• People can be left to go off track with no consequences
• People start to question the capability of the leader	• Slow execution of key projects – cost overruns, missed budgets etc
	• Organisation can appear to be drifting

Table 9.1 *Continued*

Transforming Space	*Container*
Overdone:	*Overdone:*
• 'Change' is becoming tangential to the 'work'; leaders focus on transformation as if it is separate to 'the business' • Interventions are seen as spooky and they cross into personal boundaries without reference to the overall change purpose • Cults are being built up; over indulgence in 'off sites' • People are feeling controlled and manipulated • People start to feel powerless and disconnect from the change	• Structure and process dominate over movement, lack of urgency • People feel protected and looked after, creating an irrational sense of invulnerability • Reflective dialogues become indulgent introspection • Control and rules are understood yet not enacted • Complacency – nothing seems 'at stake'
Underdone:	*Underdone:*
• Change is talked not walked • Repeating patterns of unhelpful behaviour stay stuck • Change seems to take for ever, the pace is not going fast enough, and no one says they know why • Lack of comprehension about what the change really means in practice, people lack systemic insight • Conversations go round in circles with little breakthrough in thinking; boring and stuck meetings • People avoid discomfort and changing how they and others operate	• The atmosphere no longer feels safe • People lack confidence and conviction – they do not know where they stand – role and personal ambiguity • Inefficient working and duplication of activity; no one knows what they are authorised to do and not do • Leaders seem to have to run around shouldering the effort • Lack of creativity and innovation – stepping out gets no recognition • People do what they want without connecting the use of precious resource to the overall purpose

Creating Edge and Tension without Containment and sufficient Attractor

Leaders who regularly confront reality without creating sufficient safety and context can spread fear, panic or compliance in their organisations. They seek out ripe issues and bring them to the attention of their organisation without giving careful enough attention to the setting up of appropriate channels of communication through which the issues can be processed, and without building quality enough interaction to deal with the anxiety that the ripe issues have created. Without the channelling and moderating quality of Container, the presence of the leader can feel like self-serving 'stirring things up'. For example, we have seen how leaders who perpetuate vast e-mail exchanges about lack of co-operation and misunderstanding in a situation only make the matter worse. E-mail is perhaps not the most appropriate way to deal with interpersonal misunderstandings, whereas picking up the phone and setting up an interactive conversation to deal with the issue is perhaps more so.

Edge without the affirming presence of Container can also feel harsh and cutting. Bringing attention to performance shortfalls without any expression of confidence in how to work through the issues can just set tactical hares running through the organisation as people run fast to cover their backs. Edge with Container, however, can generate creative and confident energy to make radical change happen. And Edge without Attractor can feel meaningless. The tension seems to be created without any purpose or sense of context for where the organisation is trying to move. The Edge starts to feel like a personal hobby horse, rather than a galvanising 'call to arms' to raise the game and get closer to where the organisation's potential lies. Edge without Attractor can generate unrest and rebellion; with Attractor, it can create extraordinary excitement, passion and commitment to go through major change.

Working as an Attractor without Containment

Leaders who can serve as Attractors create such magnetic energy that unless it is bounded and appropriately channelled, can take their organisations off track. The excitement of moving into the unknown can take over the requirement to deliver certain 'non-negotiables' for the organisation. The atmosphere may feel pioneering and hugely meaningful, yet in the absence of contracting any boundaries and hard rules, starts to feel a touch messianic, dangerous, and risky. Working with the unfolding story can be alluring, however unless the chapter headings are clear and the organisation is allowed to process its anxieties as well as its purpose, the change starts to feel non-robust and all a bit self indulgent. Working towards an inspiring cause is fine; however it would also help to know who is authorised to do what in getting to purpose, to know how decision making is going to get done in transparent and effective ways, and to understand whether or not it's going to be okay to raise doubt and concern about how the change is progressing.

Attractor with Container on the other hand, can make organisations feel very rewarding, secure, and purposeful places to be. When these two practices are combined, inspiring purpose and movement gets channelled towards tangible and bounded outcomes, intentional awareness flows into day to day behaviour, and any niggles and upsets get dealt with, not ignored in a zealous march towards purpose.

Over Containment Generally

Container leadership, while wonderfully calm and clarifying, in and of itself will not create movement. When it is over used, or just practiced in isolation, it can feel obsessively concerned with process and structure. People might be aware of meeting ground rules and expectations, yet somehow the energy falls flat. Authorities and networks might get established, yet they have nothing to channel. Hard rules might get set and communicated, yet there is no game at stake to play. The leader is present and attentive, yet nothing seems to move around them, there is an air of complacency.

Containment needs Edge and Tension to make any new structures and processes vibrant and energetic, the combination gets people doing things differently. Without it, people may know their place in the organisation and what they have to deliver, however they stay enacting the same mindsets and behaviours that caused the reorganisation in the first place. Containment also needs Attractor to point the bearing and processing of any anxiety towards its appropriate direction. Otherwise, the Container focus on promoting quality interaction and dialogue can feel like self indulgent introspection. And without Transforming Space, Container leadership can feel like walking through treacle – its emphasis on process in the absence of any 'in the moment' movement can create meetings where people feel they are simply going round in circles. The two combined however can create safe places for people to make a break through in their thinking and change the way in which they operate together.

Creating Transforming Spaces without Attractor and Containment

We have already noted the danger of working with Transforming Space as an isolated practice. Leaders often feel impelled in change to design and implement interventions that will 'take people to a new place'. The internal change professionals might get involved, and/or external consultants engaged, and groups of people are brought together to 'live the change'. The risk of doing these kinds of interventions in and for their own sake is that the change process starts to become divorced from the essential purpose and work of the organisation. It becomes a separate 'programme' that you must go on to in order to be able to 'get' the change. These kinds of interventions require the intentional pull of Attractor such that changing mindsets and behaviour has a concrete purpose, and they require the safe channelling of emotion from Container leadership so that they are not seen to be potentially disturbing and irrelevant events.

With Attractor and Containment, Transforming Space leadership can powerfully make change happen in real time, on real work, and bring to life what it means to work on process (for example team dynamics, better quality conversation) in order to give rise to different outcomes.

Having explored some potential combinations of practices that could be out of kilter, you may wish to reflect a while, drawing from Table 9.1, on the extent to which the four practices are currently in balance in your organisation, or part of the organisation you are responsible for. *Once you have done that, pause and consider, to what extent is this picture a reflection of your own personal leadership?* Where might you be either over, or under, playing any of the practices? Again, we suggest you use this table with your leadership team to collectively diagnose the current state of play of your change process, explore how that might be explained by how you have led the change to date, and decide what changes in emphasis might now be necessary.

What can leaders do to combine the four practices to get maximum impact?

Having considered your requirement to work inter-dependently with the practices, and assessed where there might currently be a shortfall in any of them, in what ways can you and your leadership team combine them in single high impact interventions? In Figures 9.2 and 9.3 we identify some of the 'multi-hit' interventions we have seen leaders use that enable them to bring combinations of the practices to bear; they contain examples from the research transcripts where we coded a single intervention for 'hits' against several of the four practices. You could consider using these multi-hit interventions to enable your change process to move forward more effectively. Figure 9.2 covers the *formal* interventions you can

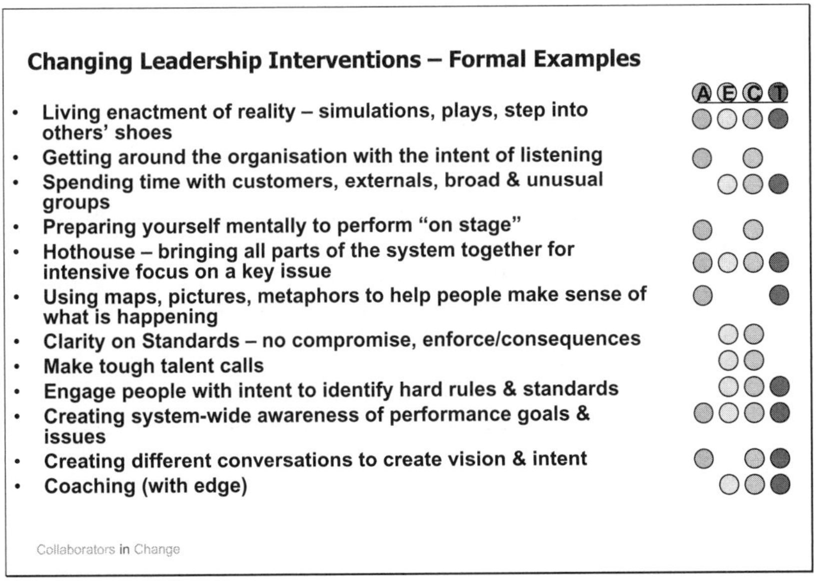

Changing Leadership Interventions – Formal Examples

Ⓐ Ⓔ Ⓒ Ⓣ

- Living enactment of reality – simulations, plays, step into others' shoes
- Getting around the organisation with the intent of listening
- Spending time with customers, externals, broad & unusual groups
- Preparing yourself mentally to perform "on stage"
- Hothouse – bringing all parts of the system together for intensive focus on a key issue
- Using maps, pictures, metaphors to help people make sense of what is happening
- Clarity on Standards – no compromise, enforce/consequences
- Make tough talent calls
- Engage people with intent to identify hard rules & standards
- Creating system-wide awareness of performance goals & issues
- Creating different conversations to create vision & intent
- Coaching (with edge)

Collaborators in Change

Figure 9.2 Changing Leadership Multi-Hit Interventions, Formal © 2008 Transcend Consultancy

make, in other words, those that are planned and designed. However you can also combine the four in *informal* encounters, in other words, during the day to day flow of events and interactions with others, examples of which are shown in Figure 9.3.

Different kinds of interventions help link different combinations of the four practices. Note how the informal interventions all provide opportunities for you to practice Container and Transforming Space leadership – working to change things in the moment can clearly be done on a day in day out basis, as long as you stay attentive to what is happening in front of you and can skilfully and confidently help others to become more aware of their behaviours in that moment. You don't

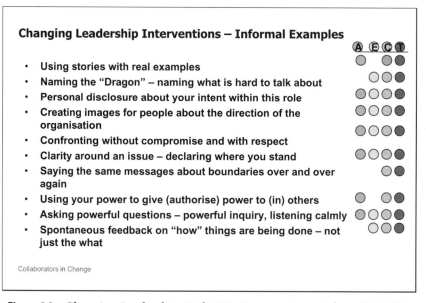

Figure 9.3 Changing Leadership Multi-Hit Interventions, Informal © 2008 Transcend Consultancy

need to orchestrate transforming 'off site' meetings to create transforming spaces! All of the informal interventions are essentially about how you conduct conversations around the organisation. Note also how Edge and Tension is always coupled with Container; whatever the intervention, you need to create a safe setting within which tough subjects can be processed.

Formal multi-hit interventions summarised

Living enactments of reality: designing activities that enable people to experience the changes required, for example simulations, plays and socio-drama, spending time in other people's roles; any creative intervention that has people walking the change, not just talking it.

Getting around the organisation with the intent of listening: dialogue engagements with groups of staff during which both yourself and your leadership team can get out and about in the organisation to inquire about the change and hear what is going on; for example interactive 'town hall' meetings. Avoid the temptation to talk and present at people!

Spending time with customers and other stakeholders: design and host gatherings of diverse and unusual groups, normally a cross section of the people who could impact the success of your change outcomes, who might bring external and helpful insights, and whose support you need in the implementation; record these encounters and bring their insights to the general attention of the organisation.

Preparing yourself mentally to perform 'on stage': before you do have to front an important engagement event or meeting, designed to help move forward your change process, take time out to fully contemplate the purpose of your intervention, consider why it is important to you personally, and visualise not just how you want to come across but how you want others to be impacted by your intervention. Prepare carefully for these moments, find your inspiration.

Hothouse (example follows): a planned event that brings together a 'diagonal slice' of people from across an organisation to work intensively together on a complex task, for example improving performance along an organisation's supply chain. Whatever the precise task, in all instances, the work of the hothouse is to create some form of breakthrough on a systemic issue facing the organisation, and produce tangible outcomes that will make a difference to how it will function in the future.

Using maps, pictures, and metaphors: creative ways to communicate and engage with an organisation that visualise the sense of the change and what is needed to be done differently. The development of the visuals should be done collectively, not issued from one central source, in order to build system wide capability to make sense of the change and create shared vision.

Clarity in standards: creating clear and uncompromising statements of the performance standards required to take the organisation to its potential. Ensuring that in the process of creating these standards the leadership team is fully aligned and aware of their implications for requiring the organisation to operate differently.

Engage people with intent to identify hard rules and standards: contracting with the organisation around these standards and taking action to ensure compliance. Working with your leadership team to create a framework of the 'hard rules', or essential behaviours that will be necessary to shift the culture and deliver different outcomes.

Making tough talent calls: identifying the roles that are 'mission critical' to delivering the change and ensuring that 'A player' talent is deployed in these roles. With your leadership team, regularly tracking performance of these individuals, planning for their development, and making calls on changing talent if needed.

Creating system-wide awareness of performance goals and issues: designing and implementing communication and educational devices to have performance targets and implementation progress clearly visible around the organisation; setting up and hosting interactive spaces within your offices (or virtually, for example on your company intranet) that track the change and can become meeting places for discussing implementation issues and learning.

Creating different conversations to create vision and intent: hosting unstructured and creative gatherings that can inspire people towards a collective purpose; for example using story telling and 'appreciative inquiry' techniques.

Coaching (with edge): for yourself, for your leadership team members, and for your leadership team as a whole, engaging the support of a coach/coaches who can 'keep you honest', act as a mirror to your behaviour and practice, and provide structured and explicit development support.

Informal multi-hit interventions summarised

Using stories with real examples: rather than speaking in abstract or general terms, illustrate what you are trying to say through the use of credible and compelling stories; keep notes of what you see around the organisation, or with other stakeholders such as customers, and continually refer to real examples of what's going on; encourage others to share their stories to join up with yours.

Naming the 'dragon': stay attuned to where there is discomfort in the organisation or in conversations, and openly voice what it is you sense people are finding hard to talk about; also use inquiry to help others voice what they are finding unsettling and what, if it could be named, would enable them to move forward with greater confidence and energy.

Personal disclosure about your intent within this role (example follows): a leader disclosing what they see to be the purpose of their leadership task, which when articulated, can help people around them line up in its energy, provide a sense of meaning to the collective endeavour, stretch their sense of the ambition, and create some boundary conditions within which others can find their source of inspiration. When done informally, it moves people around the leader since it creates a heightened level of attention and awareness on the present moment.

Creating images for people about the direction of the organisation: when you are tempted to explain things in meetings in words, can you pick up a pen and draw an image instead for what you are trying to convey. When you are opening or closing an important intervention, can you use a picture that conveys where you are trying to take the organisation? This is not about being a great artist; it can be an articulated image, not necessarily a drawn one.

Confronting without compromise and with respect: drawing your own and others' attention to unaware and unhelpful behaviour in ways that accurately describe what you see, yet is also done in ways that show respect for others; using moments in encounters with people around the organisation to bring edge to where the organisation is still falling short; practice 'not beating about the bush'.

Clarity around an issue, declaring where you stand: speaking from the 'I', in other words, using personal statements that authentically describe where you are coming from on an issue; encouraging others to do likewise.

Saying the same messages about boundaries over and over again: repeating time and time again as you go around the organisation, and have meetings with your team and other staff groups, what the 'non-negotiables' are about the change, i.e. what counts, and where you want people to place their attention.

Using your power to give power to (authorise) others: you know what your mandate is and where your authority lies; from that position, clearly articulate to others what it is you are expecting them to lead on and what authority they will have (and not have) to execute that leadership; clarify people's decision making power, and where they do not have to consult you.

Asking powerful questions: a constant theme throughout all the Changing Leadership practices, when you are trying to help other people move to a different place, consider the use of inquiry (rather than your own advocacy) as a way to generate new thinking, learning, and behaviour; use questions that can link the practices (for example when groups seem unable to take a big decision, 'if we were to stop doing further analysis, what decision would you now take to move us closer to our purpose?', which combines Attractor and Edge and Tension); listen calmly to the responses you get back to your inquiry to provide a safe processing space.

Spontaneous feedback on 'how' things are being done, not just the what: connect people's behaviour and intervention style to the outcome that was delivered, so that when you give any feedback you can help them become aware of their practice, adjust if necessary, and give you an opportunity to reinforce the message that process and practice is as important as what is being accomplished.

We next illustrate a couple of interventions from each category – both formal and informal – as examples of where leaders inspired people towards purpose, got tricky subjects out in the open, safely channelled activity and processed emotion, and in doing all of the above transformed the way in which things got done; in other words, they linked all four of the Changing Leadership practices.

'Hothouses'

We once helped to design and facilitate a hothouse for a large retail bank. The bank's business ambition was to become the number one in their market for consumer lending and transaction profitability, and for this ambition they had to create a revolution in their retail outlets. Staff at the 'frontline' needed to be equipped with the right information to sell, feel more authorised to take initiative and responsibility for customer lending decisions, and to accomplish all of this the regional leaders needed to create a more inspiring and high performance work climate. The Human Resources department were central to the change. They needed to move from seeing their role solely as a transactional support service to line managers to one in which coaching the leaders to implement change, and shift the culture, had equal importance.

The process through which the event was designed and implemented role modelled the desired change outcome. A 'microcosm' of the retail bank organisation was involved at all stages – including the design process. At the event itself the Managing Director was as fully engaged and present as the sample of frontline bank tellers invited. Never before had the whole hierarchy been represented in the room, never before had the HR department actively facilitated and coached a change process, never before had Regional managers been asked to share performance data so openly in front of their staff, and never before had a cross section of the organisation been asked to determine how the ambitious strategy was to be implemented. Each and every aspect of the hothouse was countercultural. This created discomfort. *And yet it precisely simulated the organisational conditions that were being planned.* During the event participants were encouraged to note down reflections of how they were relating to such new ways of working, including what they were needing to 'unlearn' in order to be able to function and perform in this different environment. Towards the end of the day these process insights were shared to produce invaluable learning for the organisation after the event on how to build capability to operate differently more generally across the organisation. Hothouses therefore pay as much attention to the processes through which the results are getting produced, as they do to the results of the event itself. Over the course of just one intense day this representative group of 50 people had worked up a set of robust proposals to revolutionise the ability of the retail outlets to profitably sell.

By bringing a cross section of the organisation together to share stories and create a new one, Attractor energy is instantly generated. The Managing Director did not have to do any fancy speeches. And the magnetic energy generated created a sustaining force in the organisation long afterwards. The organisation did not have to wait for descriptions of new values and behaviours to arrive before starting to try things out differently, which the hothouse participants catalysed when they returned to their work. The Attractor energy of compelling purpose was set alongside the performance data of the branches, which had never been seen before in such explicit comparative terms, raising the ambition levels of those present to identify ways in which to raise the game across all of the branches. The stretch goal to deliver the outcome in just one day forced the participants to have to speak and work differently with each other, creating Edge and Tension, and the Transforming Space urgency it generated simulated the speed at which the culture was going to have to learn more generally to operate. The structure of the hothouse, and its 'leader led' facilitation, created a Containing presence that guided people at speed to produce remarkable results together.

Overall, hothouses can therefore be extremely impactful and insightful ways to accelerate change – as long as its design and accompanying leadership practice are as attentive to process as they are to outcomes. Perhaps you have a pressing and complex systemic issue that would benefit from such an intervention? Who could you get involved and how?

Personal disclosure about your intent within your role

An example of an informal disclosure of leadership intent, and the power of its impact, was witnessed recently by one of the authors. A Chief Executive of a newly globalised business was hosting a dinner with his leadership team. It was only the second time they had all met face to face. The recent months had been an intense and stressful period. The team had had to integrate several companies into one, appoint people into a new organisational structure, figure out who should do what in the new global organisation, get the budget figures together for the current and new financial year for the main Board – when they still did not have integrated Management Information systems, and in the meantime still try to serve and win customer business out in the marketplace. Travel schedules had been punishing. Email traffic had reached gargantuan proportions as the organisation pushed up questions around still unclear authorities to the leadership team. All in all, any of its team members might have started justifiably wondering why he or she had so excitedly accepted the post on the leadership team that euphoric four months ago.

Over dinner, the Chief Executive decided to host an informal dialogue in the team about the 'what's in it for me' question – what would make his leadership team stay around for the next 12 months (which were showing no immediate signs of getting any less stressful!)? What was this all really for? His team members one by one volunteered a few sentences each – at the relatively 'polite' level of 'making a contribution', 'delivering growth', 'hitting target', 'supporting others'. Then their leader spoke. And his disclosure went along the following lines;

When I got off the plane from China six weeks ago I was seriously thinking about whether all the aggravation was worth it. Did I want to go off and prove myself somewhere else? Well, I decided not to start looking elsewhere. And here's why. We have the chance to build a global business in an industry full of regional players. This gets me excited. It's not been done before and it's going to require us building a very different organisation together. And I want to help do that. Our budget for next year is a real stretch. However if we get this new organisation up and running and operating differently I believe we can hit budget. And I want that to happen. I want to show that I can win in this role. I want to show to the investors that I can do it and that the strategic decision to build the business is the right one. This is important to me. And I want to support you all in achieving what you are hoping for. This is also important to me. I want to build a winning team for this organisation and I know I have the right players.

As he was talking the atmosphere around the table altered. People's movement seemed to slow down, they became still, focussed entirely on what was being said and what was going to come next, they were 100 % present – they were there and nowhere else. When their leader stopped talking there was silence. Eating had ceased. One team member said from his heart, 'I want you to win too'. He seemed to voice what everyone else on the team was thinking and feeling. And in the next few moments the team now knew and expressed that they all wanted each and every member on the team to 'win' – it had become a collective game. The atmosphere the next day in the team meeting was potent with potential. They progressed rapidly on a task to create a 'storyline' for their organisation, they became inspired together. When diaries had to come out to put time and attention behind the change process in the coming months it now seemed that that was the task they had to do together as a leadership team. Habitual grumbles had disappeared in their commitment to the collective endeavour. When they reviewed towards the end of the day how they had been performing as a team in the last few months the degree of candour and openness in confronting their 'low points' and 'bad behaviour' was striking. A circle of mutual support and trust had been built.

The team leader's disclosure the night before had been a transforming moment. He had confronted doubt as well as belief, which gave a place for everyone's sense of vulnerability (Container and Transforming Space). His desire to build a global organisation uniquely placed to take on the market held an inspiring purpose for the team (Attractor) and its challenge seemed to create excitement, not fear (Edge and Tension). His personal disclosure about wanting to win had created followership and a desire in the whole team to win together, an informal contract with each other had been struck (Container and Attractor).

Do you know what keeps you going as a leader in your role? Have you taken enough chances to convey that intent to your team and the wider organisation?

Summary

In this chapter we have shared the findings and insights from our own inquiry into how leaders can creatively link all four of the Changing Leadership practices. Our research showed that leaders who could do this successfully shared three striking characteristics: they possessed high levels of self awareness and based on this used their presence in very mindful ways in their organisations; this conscious use of leadership made them able to be attentive to what was happening in the moment, make visible the systemic forces that were giving rise to the present, and in so doing change any unhelpful or taken for granted mindsets and patterns of behaviour; finally, in order to be able to see the systemic issues getting played out in the current moment, they reached out to the wider context within which their organisation operated, and used this context to help the organisation make sense of the current performance improvement required. In this last aspect they also required their leadership teams to be able to see the wider context and based on this 'lead for the whole', not just their own part of the organisation.

If leaders possess these characteristics they will find it easier to integrate all four of the Changing Leadership practices. This is important because if any of the four practices are overdone, or not practiced with the complementary impact of the others, it can lead to organisational dysfunction. The corollary of this is that there is also a danger in any of the four practices being absent from a change process. Somehow the change won't move as effectively as it could do, it is not firing on all cylinders. Combinations of the practices are therefore vital, and leaders need to be able to read the 'visible signs' of what might be needed when, and adapt their leadership, and that of their leadership team, accordingly. Changing Leadership is a team game.

In order to leverage the whole framework, we have found examples of what we call 'multi-hit' interventions, in other words things leaders can do to bring combinations of the four Changing Leadership practices to bear. When designing formal change interventions and processes it is worthwhile to do a check on whether or not the design will bring forth Attractor, Edge and Tension, Container and Transforming Space leadership in combination. However, a leader can also bring all four to bear in their informal day to day leadership around the organisation – all it takes is a high level of self awareness and the skill to 'richly intervene'.

This requires a fair bit of practice and perhaps a struggle or two along the way. However linking the practices can produce extraordinary results, and an organisation far more ready, willing, and able to implement change that is sustainable. In the next chapter we move to sharing some strategies of how these practices can be learned.

10

Developing Changing Leadership

'I respect faith but doubt is what gets you an education'

Karl Weick

The starting point for learning can be described as a state of not knowing, or uncertainty. One Chief Executive we know actively seeks out people who tell her things 'I don't understand'. She respects people who know things she does not, since she acknowledges that this is the only way she will learn and grow as an organisational leader. To embark on any developmental journey is therefore to accept the existence of one's own ignorance. The developmental notion that 'not-knowing' is the necessary state of mind for learning has become to be known as the capacity for 'negative capability'. A term originally defined by the poet Keats as man being 'capable of being in uncertainties, mysteries, doubts, without any irritable reaching after fact and reason', it has since been used in the psychoanalytic and developmental professions as a term to describe one's ability to live with ambiguity and paradox and to contain the pressure to act from one's own ego impulses. This can be challenging for those of us with active and 'need to be able to explain everything' minds. *However, unless we can contain the uncertainty of not knowing our imaginations are not free to entertain new discoveries.*

In this sense we hope that the book has raised as many questions in your mind as it has given validation to what you already know. Perhaps you bought the book out of curiosity to learn more about leading change, and as you started to read it might have challenged your notion of leadership, and/or raised questions about your own practice. Some of the 'dark side' descriptions, or questions posed at the end of the chapters in Part II might have stirred up reflections about that which you didn't want to see or hear – about yourself, your 'shadow', or the situation around you. Did you stay with those reflections? Did something new emerge for you as a result? Were you tempted to do anything differently or think in a different way? In writing the book we were ourselves frequently in doubt, or mystery, as to what it was we were trying to convey. It helped to be writing this together, and to be able to express our still held 'not-knowingness' to colleagues, based on which precious new insights emerged. The uncertainty we therefore held in the process of writing enabled us to make new discoveries about Changing Leadership, since the uncertainty gave space for awareness about the subject matter that had not existed prior to writing.

What we do know, however, is that these leadership practices seem to 'work'. Knowing exactly why, and how, and in what combination, has been the focus of our own developmental journey. This penultimate chapter now shares what we have observed of how leaders can learn to master its practices. This has been informed by our own coaching work and, dare we say it, the struggles and attempts to master the practices ourselves. We begin this chapter with a fundamental look at whether or not these practices can be developed – given that it could be argued that certain personality styles are necessary to be able to practice them – and we share some of the underlying beliefs that seem to be vital underpinnings to its authentic practice. We will then take each of the four practices in turn and share what it is we have seen work in enabling leaders to develop them. We conclude with some generic thoughts on how these practices can be developed, using the framework to guide the design of learning interventions – for if the development process itself does not contain Attractor, Edge and Tension, Container and Transforming Space we could argue that no sustainable change in individual leadership capability will occur!

Can Changing Leadership be developed?

At practically every debrief through our research process participants would ask us the question, 'can these practices be developed?' This question was particularly fuelled by the finding that leaders who could practice all four were more likely to be successful in implementing high magnitude change. We still maintain that the Changing Leadership framework is not a 'competency profile' based on certain skills, attributes, and traits, but rather a way of categorising certain sets of behaviours that in combination define *what it is that leaders do* to implement change well. It does not contain, for example, competency levels around strategic thinking; however, it does describe what leaders do to engage their organisation in creating a new future story. It does not contain the skills and attributes required for managing conflict; however, it does describe how leaders can confront reality and raise difficult subjects in ways that create energy to improve things, and not lead to break down. In that respect therefore, one could claim that these are practices that anyone could pick up and learn, it's just a question of education, awareness and considered reflective practise.

We do not wish to enter too deeply into the big topic of whether or not leaders are 'born' or 'made'. The 'nature-nurture' debate can become very polarising and one which is not always that practical or relevant for leaders wishing to develop their capability. In the 'Where Next' chapter we do raise the question of future research into the relationship between the Changing Leadership factors and more 'in bred' personality styles as a fruitful avenue of inquiry. What we can say now however, and this relates to our observations through-out the book, is that the practice of Changing Leadership does require high levels of self awareness, authenticity, and the holding of certain beliefs. Without these preconditions it becomes very hard, if not impossible, to develop the practices.

Self Awareness

Low levels of self awareness are correlated with certain personality traits (e.g. Anxiety, Lack of Openness to Experience, High Control needs, Low Emotional Resilience, Low Self Belief). Levels can be increased though through the proactive and conscious attention to getting feedback from others and recognising your 'shadow' in the organisation, in other words becoming aware of how your unconscious needs and behaviour could be influencing how others perceive your presence – since it is their perceptions of your leadership that will influence how they behave, not the intention you might hold in the situation. When you are therefore frustrated or anxious about unhelpful behaviour you see around you in the organisation, the self aware leader will ask first, 'what is it about my own way of thinking about the situation, or what I might be projecting, and/or what is it about my own behaviour, that might be causing the dysfunction I see around me?' Asking those around you for their response to this question can be very enlightening, and increase your ability to see your true self and your part in the system – as long as you are open and receptive to what comes back! What we have found in our coaching work with our clients supports the paradoxical theory of change (see Beisser, 1970): that change occurs when one becomes what he is *(through increased self awareness)*, not when he tries to become what he is not.

Intention

Authenticity springs from your intention – and this can also affect your impact on others. We have already noted in this book how leaders can possess very high levels of self awareness, and appear to be engaging the organisation around them, yet in seeking to act in service of themselves, rather than in service of others, are unable to practice Changing Leadership with any degree of sincerity. Such leaders tend to have outer-directed needs towards recognition, esteem, reputation and entitlement, compared with inner-directed needs such as becoming purposeful, creative, and desirous of reaching what Abraham Maslow has called the state of 'self actualisation'. While leaders can learn to examine their intention, and question its appropriateness for facilitating organisational commitment and change (and we all have to recognise some degree of self interest in our intent), it can be tough to shift a dominant outer-directed orientation to any significant degree without some kind of life transforming experience that forces one to reconsider what your purpose is really all about (and we would not necessarily wish to plan that into any development programme . . .).

The following figure summarises how leadership impact can be viewed along the two axes of self awareness and intent. Clearly the most damaging and consciously manipulative 'dark side' behaviours occur in the Pseudo Leadership quadrant. It is in this area that developing Changing Leadership is most difficult and yet holds the greatest potential. Developing leaders' capabilities to move out of the Damaging and Ineffective quadrants can be achieved by raising their Self Awareness. In the former case this will help the leaders to understand the nature of the role of their intent and its limiting nature.

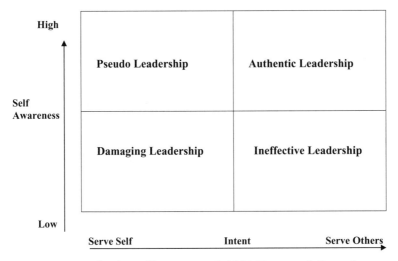

Figure 10.1 Leadership Effectiveness © 2008 Transcend Consultancy

Beliefs

We have found that it is hard to get out of the starting blocks with Changing Leadership unless leaders hold certain beliefs. We have observed how the presence or otherwise of these beliefs determines whether leaders either struggle with, or can more readily adopt, its practices. Without these beliefs, it is very easy for leaders to slip into a more Shaping style leadership behaviour. While our thinking is still evolving on this subject, the following beliefs appear to us to be fundamental to the skilful practice of Changing Leadership:

- *'I can never know all there is to know – and need others' help'*; we have already noted above the importance of 'negative capability', or the capacity to stay in doubt and work with uncertainty, to learning and development.

Without a belief that the world is incomprehensible to any one person, it is hard for leaders to create shared purpose and build collective meaning (Attractor), authorise independent action (Container) and open up one's vulnerability and 'not-knowingness' to inquire into something unsettling happening in the moment (Transforming Space).

- *'I try not to solve difficult dilemmas: I seek to reconcile them'*; a tendency towards black and white, or 'either/or' thinking, impedes a leader's ability to create an open and creative space to wrestle with perplexity (Container), hold the discomfort of uncertainty (Edge and Tension), and build a deeper and wider awareness of the uniting structures and range of options that can help reconcile the dilemma (Attractor). The developmental process of seeking to reconcile dilemmas fundamentally changes the space (Transforming Space) from which potential 'answers' arise.

- *'There is always a better way – but I treat it as a mystery to explore, not a problem to solve'*; Changing Leadership is about curiosity, not fixing things. Unless one can go to the source of what is most troubling, or in need of improvement, and believe that this underlying source is serving some purpose which needs exploring, not eradicating, then it becomes hard to confront the deeper recurring patterns in the culture (Edge and Tension) and create the safety to openly talk about what needs improving and why (Container).

- *'I believe in the untapped potential of others and the system as a whole'*; one leader described her mission with her people as being one in which 'everybody who leaves here leaves bigger'. A belief that people can only 'appreciate', and not 'depreciate', drives a leader to affirm people's place and build their confidence (Container), while still not avoiding pointing out the gap between current reality and potential (Edge and Tension), and making visible unhelpful behaviour in the system as a whole (Transforming Space). And it becomes hard to serve others and navigate an organisation into uncharted territory (Attractor) if you don't believe the system is able to move to a different place.

- *'I trust that if others take responsibility, we are more powerful'*; transformational change is not just about driving single handed towards new results, it's about building the capability and heartbeat of the organisation around you. Unless a leader believes that by giving away power they become more powerful, they will find it challenging to be open to serve what arises (Transforming Space), build commitment and ownership throughout the organisation (Attractor), and give clear mandates for others to lead (Container).

- *'I take responsibility for myself and my own needs and motives'*; while believing in the sharing out of responsibility, the leader still acknowledges that they are driven by their own impulses, which have a part to play in responding to any situation and contributing to its outcome. Unless a leader believes they are responsible for their own needs and intent (and not 'play the victim' or feel 'done to') it is hard to let other people know where you stand and thereby build their trust (Container) and it becomes nigh on impossible to responsibly and transparently intervene in the moment (Transforming Space). Indeed we believe, and would suggest, that this belief is a prerequisite for developing self awareness.

- *'I am clear I have a purpose'*; purpose creates energy and movement (Attractor). And unless a leader believes that there is a purpose that is guiding their action (even if it is not always crystal clear to them as to what that purpose is!) then they will be more likely to act out of impulse, not confidence, and get unsettled at those times when others most need them to be non-anxious (Container).

- *'My role is to help create a vision and a frame'*; acting in service of the organisation, the leader believes their role is to set the framework within which people can find inspiration and purpose – it is not to dictate what has to happen, *or,* to let anything go. If the leader believes otherwise, they will be tempted to push and prod the organisation, or become too democratic – the former compromises their ability to build ownership and commitment (Attractor), and the latter their ability to firmly contract boundaries and 'non-negotiable' expectations (Container).

- *'Nothing happens by chance – and every intervention counts'*; whatever arises is meant to have arisen; whoever shows up are the right people; whatever gets said is what was meant to have been said. Leaders who believe that the world is a connected system in constant flow recognise that there is no such thing as random behaviour – while things might look a bit messy and chaotic on the ground, when you step back you can see repeating patterns and deeper structures that hold things together. Unless leaders can see the world as such it becomes hard to work with what arises, because conversations, statements, or people who do not 'fit' will be discounted (leading to poorly done Edge and Tension and missed opportunities to work in the moment with Transforming Space); the space for rich interactions, generative dialogue, and processing awkward moments will be narrowed (compromising Container); and the leader will be unavailable to tune in to the ongoing 'noise' and stories in the organisation (limiting their Attractor energy).

It is not our intent here to 'change your beliefs'. All of our beliefs have been formed for a reason, and they serve us in making sense of the world and how we then act within that frame. What we are simply offering is our sense of the beliefs that are necessary to fully engage with the Changing Leadership practices. If you do wish to develop your ability to work with these practices then you might pause to consider the degree to which you hold these beliefs. In order to do this, notice your current actions: can you uncover the beliefs that led to these responses? What caused you to behave in that way and not some other way? How do your beliefs serve a purpose? Once you have taken stock of your beliefs, are some of the above beliefs challenging for you to hold? Consider, why might that be the case? What might it take for you to believe differently? If you *were* to adopt the belief, how would you see what is happening around you differently? And what new or different action might you then take?

To summarise, we do maintain that each and every one of us can learn to incorporate the four Changing Leadership practices into our behaviour, because they describe what it is that leaders do. However, we need to recognise that the degree of ease with which we can put them into action does depend on some fairly fundamental underlying characteristics. We need to raise our levels of self awareness, examine our leadership intent, and reflect on the beliefs we hold about leadership and how our organisations function. In taking these steps alone we will already have shifted our attention, and by definition opened up our leadership to new possibilities.

Learning Strategies for each of the Changing Leadership practices

In Table 10.1 we summarise what we have seen leaders typically do to practice Changing Leadership. You may wish to do a little self assessment in this table. Which practices can you readily say you do on a regular basis? Based on this review (which you might want to test out with a colleague who knows you well), what is your 'profile' against the Changing Leadership framework? Where do you think you might have the most development need(s)? Next, consider your change context and upcoming challenges. Where *should* you be applying more Changing Leadership (draw on your reflections from the previous chapter)? Take out your next three month schedule. What opportunities do you have coming up when you could explicitly start to do things in different ways? So, how might you now go about trying to learn how to do things differently?

Table 10.1 Changing Leadership; What It Is That Leaders Typically Do – Self Assessment

Consider – to what extent do you currently practice these behaviours?

Attractor
- Creates emotional connection – heart and gut ☐
- Tunes into the desires and ambitions of the organisation ☐
- Creates a shared sense of identity, purpose, and intent ☐
- Engages in visualising 'what if?' conversations ☐
- Creates a story for the organisation ☐
- Notices and reinforces progress ☐

Edge and Tension
- Tells the truth without compromise and with respect ☐
- Has the courage to make the tough calls ☐
- Challenges deeply held assumptions and beliefs ☐
- Focuses attention on the few big priorities ☐
- Sets goals to the limits of what's possible ☐
- Creates simple and compelling performance metrics ☐

Transforming Space
- Looks for movement in the here and now ☐
- Breaks repeating patterns ☐
- Takes personal risk to be open and vulnerable ☐
- Puts unusual and diverse groups together ☐
- Notices emerging legends as they happen ☐
- Pays attention to the quality of the physical space ☐

Container
- Uses own power to authorise others ☐
- Sets hard rules and boundaries ☐
- Makes explicit contracts with individuals, team, and the organisation ☐
- Applies consequences – rewards and sanctions ☐
- Gives encouraging and consistent signals ☐
- Is serene, confident, and self assured ☐

© 2008 Transcend Consultancy

While each of us has our own preferred learning style, and favourite 'techniques', in this section we offer our suggestions for how you might go about developing each of the Changing Leadership practices, based on what we have seen works. At the end of each practice we review the potential 'psychological risk' involved in stepping into its use. The psychological risk can be a powerful 'learning block'. Sometimes we feel uncomfortable about adopting certain behaviour not as a result of our levels of self awareness, our intent, or underlying beliefs, but because we fear that by taking certain action there could be consequences for how we are perceived by others. This fear might be unfounded in today's reality but be absolutely founded in very real life experiences we have had which have subsequently coloured our response to certain situations. If our family systems discouraged the open discussion of risky subjects, we might imagine now that if we used Edge and Tension we would be exiled from the community. If we had powerful parent figures that looked after us and shielded us from pain, then we might fear that by practicing Container we will have to take on all the responsibility for holding things together.

Increased self awareness enables us to recognise where these beliefs have come from and allows us to question how they might support us in the different circumstances in which we find ourselves. Each of the four practices holds a distinctive risk which could explain why we might avoid moving towards them. It could be helpful for you to reflect on these risks and consider if they apply to you. If they do, try to uncover the source of your assumption and see if you can loosen your hold on it – since commonly the risk is more in our head than in the situation around us. Others might actually *want* you to step more into that space. Recognise also the systemic context in which you currently operate, since you may be avoiding the practice because it would be counter cultural to 'how leadership happens around here'. Having said that, it could still be worthwhile trying it out!

How to learn Attractor leadership

Tuning in, observing, classifying, and journaling; can you take down notes in some quiet times about what you are noticing around the organisation – stories you see around you, both inside your organisation and the wider context. What stands out? Can you see recurring patterns and connections? What sense do you make of these? What appears to be missing? Jot down records of important conversations in your team – bringing those out in future conversations with your team helps weave together the story of change and progress your team are making – it can be a motivating and aligning force. Periodically, look back on all your notes – what's your sense of the story that is emerging in your organisation? What key legends are being built? Can you share these observations with others? Learning to see the emerging story as it unfolds is a key Attractor quality.

Self aware, knowing what you 'stand for'; in your journaling you might also notice something about your own sense of purpose or intent in the situation – note what actions you take and reflect on the values and intent that led to those actions. What do you feel your leadership represents? Do you know the answer to this question, and can you articulate that to others? If you do not yet know, how do you view your not knowing, make some notes about what others may think of your not knowing, both positive and less positive. There can be intention in not knowing. However it is hard to pull an organisation towards its purpose if you are unclear about your own. Have you asked others about how you come across? The 'mirroring' back of your leadership can help you feel more purposeful and inspired. And when others feel this in your leadership it becomes a magnetic force for them to find inspiration.

Powerful listening, questioning, and inquiry; before you leap into making plans for your organisation have you done enough tuning in? One senior church figure we worked with called this learning to 'hit the ground kneeling'! He was skilfully aware of how leaping into action could blind you to sensing where the true purpose in the organisation lay. Instead, if you can powerfully inquire into what people are hoping for and listen intently to their response they open up their hearts with their stories and aspirations. And as they tell their stories they will start sharing them with others and you start building collective commitment to change. When people have to do their own thinking it also builds ownership to the outcome. So try learning to notice when you are about to make a suggestion, pause and reflect and think instead of a big question that will guide people towards purpose and exciting new possibilities. Engage your curiosity!

Facilitating generative dialogue and storytelling; how often do you sit down with your team and have open unstructured conversations about what's going on around the organisation, and then use these stories to help navigate where the organ-isation is going? Such conversations hold a very different quality to reporting out on numbers and results. In stories people start to track the visible signs that are shifting in the organisation, such as mindsets and behaviours, which are necessary precursors to changing the numbers and results.

And as stories get shared so does the collective sense of the change become more apparent. It helps overcome uncertainty, and by facilitating such conversations your leadership will start to become a more powerfully aligning force in the organisation.

Creating a compelling manifesto, 'what we stand for'; based on all the above, the organisation starts to sense who it is they are trying to become. When you are with your organisation, 'doing the vision thing', can you build on your deeper sense of purpose, and what you have picked up in the stories around you, and use that as a platform to create a compelling and collective statement of intent and principles for the organisation? Do you rehearse your story before such interventions? One leader we have worked with learned to do this completely without any words or slides – just a few metaphors and visuals. In the picture of the rugby scrum the insurance brokers present immediately got how they had to work together as a strong interdependent team to move the competition out of the market place. Learning how to build shared vision from the energies and forces around you (and not from set speeches) will significantly increase your ability to practice Attractor leadership.

Overall, how do you feel about stepping into the Attractor practices? What might you risk if you develop this capability? Even when skilfully done, with the leader avoiding the ego driven impulse to draw attention towards them, but rather drawing the organisation towards its purpose, Attractor leadership does create a lot of magnetic energy. It's inspiring and special to be in a place that has Attractor leadership. At times, this can bring a degree of envy into the organisational system, as people sense the magnetic draw around the leader's presence. Things seem to happen around them, and even when they are not present, they exert an invisible influence. Their power might even be feared, or misunderstood by those around them. To step into Attractor leadership requires you to become both more visible *and* invisible. To help move an organisation into new directions requires you to be available, present, voicing where you sense the organisation needs to go; and yet if you take over and become the heroic saviour not the humble guide, then people will only follow you, not the purpose. In order to express your Attractor leadership you therefore need to reflect a bit; can you take the attention that this will bring and are you comfortable, not spooked, by the potential potency of your influence?

How to learn Edge and Tension leadership

Getting to the 80:20 and lining up the system on these; do you know what the few big priorities are for your organisation to perform to its potential, and does everybody in the organisation know what these are? One leader we worked with called this learning how to work on the 'left hand side of the decimal point', in other words, learning to not get bogged down in the myriad small details but find those few things that have the biggest leverage on the outcome. Once you know what those 'levers' are that generate most value for your organisation, that is where you can focus your Edge and Tension; setting stretch goals against them, identifying unhelpful assumptions that could block their achievement, and holding people to account to deliver performance. Learn to measure what matters.

Spotting limiting assumptions; people are often blocked from reaching their potential or from delivering a break through in performance because of their limiting assumptions. Can you learn to spot statements people make about that which they believe to be true and from which they draw conclusions, and yet which are unfounded in proof? Can you spot your own? Unless we can learn to identify, work with, and shift assumptions we will get stuck in the same repeating patterns of behaviour, maybe just trying harder, and yet hoping for a different outcome. Breaking out of this is known as 'double loop learning'. When you are in a meeting, start by noting down the assumptions which you inadvertently make in your inquiry, then note down those assumptions which you hear people making in the conversation. Assumptions can be dangerous things if they remain untested, and are often defence mechanisms against 'discovering the truth'. Edge and Tension is about uncovering and confronting reality, so learning how to spot the assumptions that might be distorting reality, and bringing this to the attention both of yourself and of others, is a key intervention to be mastered. The practise of journaling can be very powerful here – asking yourself how I limit myself can yield powerful awareness.

Making effective confronting interventions in the moment; the purpose of a confronting intervention is to raise others' consciousness about a limiting attitude or behaviour about which they are relatively unaware, which if revealed in the moment of its occurrence can create insight and movement.

How to do this *without creating a defensive reaction in others* can be tricky. What's essential to learn here is how to name and state what you see going on, without compromise (in other words don't hold back and become mealy mouthed about what you need to say), yet saying what you need to say with respect, lack of ego, and with the intention to serve the other (in other words, don't clobber the person or the group!). Knowing when to confront, and when not to, is as important as knowing how to confront. If you run around confronting everything people say, do or believe, then you'll just become an irritating 'opposer'. Confronting interventions are appropriate when you notice situations such as: unaware competition and struggles for leadership; unaware avoidance of anxiety arousing issues; aware or unaware 'undiscussables'; cultural oppression or dominance; lack of knowledge, competence, or group process skills; team members going for the easy option and avoiding risk; results not being delivered and 'explaining away' of the performance. Holding the purpose of confronting interventions in mind, having good data to back up your observation, building up a bit of courage, and doing all the above with the compassion to help others to learn, will all stand you in good stead.

Bystanding and asking the big questions that are being avoided; to practice Edge and Tension well requires you to step back a bit and notice what is going on. If you are too caught up in a debate or the day to day operations it can be hard to notice the real issues that are somehow 'in the room', but not being talked about or named. If you just practice Edge and Tension in the heat of the debate, rather than at the more systemic level of what might be causing the debate or discomfort in the first place, you will find it hard to create situations where people break out of their limiting assumptions. Learn to ask a few big questions that get to the heart of what might be being avoided, for example; 'If we were to stop skirting the issue, what would we be talking about?', 'what is it we are thinking and feeling but avoiding saying right now?' Learn also to use your personal experience of what is going on and share it, not for personal indulgence and ego building but in the belief that in voicing your own experience you may reveal something more. Such questions and expressions of personal experience can get the 'ripe issues' out on the table, and in so doing create the momentum to make visible and explore and address what really matters. So when targets are being repeatedly missed, and people seem 'stuck' in their habitual routines, or circling around issues, pause, and consider – what question could I now ask, or what statement could I make from my own experience, that goes to the heart of what seems to be most troubling us?

Coaching for achievement and performance; coaching can perform many roles, one of which is to help an individual, team, or organisation reach its performance potential. Coaching for achievement and potential therefore focuses on the delivery of tangible outcomes or deliverables, which rely on the individual or team to raise their standards and competence levels. To what extent do you spend time having conversations about stretch goals, setting standards, assessing people's capacity to deliver, giving targeted feedback around performance, and then making the tough calls on levels of achievement and ultimate potential? Again, consider the use of big powerful inquiry questions, such as, 'what is it we are not doing today, that if we could do, would make the biggest difference to realising our potential?', or, 'if this organisation were performing to its potential, what could be achieved?' Does each of your direct reports have focussed development plans around both results expected and learning goals? How much time do you spend on developing your leadership team, as a team, to get to high performance? Have you been coached on how to coach?

How do you feel about stepping further into Edge and Tension leadership? What might you risk if you develop your capability in, or increase your emphasis on, this practice? Are you okay about potentially being seen as the person 'rocking the boat'? Even when practiced with skill and positive intent, Edge and Tension leadership does not create comfortable situations. You might be seen to be the person holding things up just when the group think they are making progress. There is a risk that people will project onto you their own anxiety of being unable to confront the troubling subject and in so doing 'blame' you for their discomfort. Of course when Edge and Tension is practised with good Container leadership then people's fear and anxiety is appropriately 'held', and quite magnificent movement can occur. However even so there remains the real risk that you will cause discomfort. Is this something you can bear? Can you yourself be comfortable about feeling uncomfortable? Learning to overcome the potential fear of being disliked can therefore be necessary mental preparation for a leader stepping into Edge and Tension.

How to learn Container leadership

Understanding power and how it works and how to use it constructively; many social systems are designed to apportion power yet are destined to create powerlessness ('I have responsibility delegated to me yet no authority to make any decisions!'). And when people feel powerless they do not feel safe. They feel vulnerable. This leads to defensive behaviour (such as withholding information between departments and creating social distance between levels) that keeps the system 'stuck' in resistant, unhelpful, and dysfunctional patterns. Container leadership is about setting up structures in which people can feel powerful, and can take on leadership responsibility. Senior leaders in particular can create structures that make the whole system powerful. Can you learn to use your power to create powerful systems? To what extent do you pay attention to: creating simple, delegated authorities (that match people's responsibilities) so people know the scope of their own power; building communities that cut across organisational boundaries; promoting the free exchange of information; establishing joint task forces to lead on important performance improvement initiatives? All such initiatives create an organisation that feels powerful and able to collectively lead.

Powerful inquiry to understand where people are coming from; teams and organisations are not 'safe' places when it is unclear 'where people stand'. Even if people's motives, agendas and behaviour are well intended, it is easy for people to mistrust others when they are unsure as to where they are coming from, and are unclear as to what is expected of them. Clear and open contracts, expectations, and statements of intent create safe places. Can you learn to make needs and expectations more visible and explicit in your own team or organisation? Can you engage and test people's intentions? If done through powerful inquiry and declared interest in supporting the development of others you will build confidence and develop the courage to disclose. Inquiry elicits ownership, openness, and transparency, all of which are vital for effective containment.

Coaching and feedback – providing supportive frame; Container coaching is complementary to Edge and Tension coaching. While Edge and Tension seeks to raise levels of achievement, Container coaching encourages others and sends appreciative signals about things done well. 'Positive strokes' can build confidence and resilience to go through change. As a leader, do you simply assume that your people are going to do good things, or do you actively and visibly tell them when you are pleased with what's been accomplished? Can you learn to notice everyday yet significant accomplishments and then communicate to others not just 'well done', *but what you saw about how people approached the task that you particularly want to recognise, and how these tasks contribute to the overall intention of the organisation?* This helps reinforce the 'boundaries', or 'hard rules', about what kind of performance you expect. Do you send notes out to your team after a challenging team meeting and give feedback on what went well? And prior to a big event or meeting, do you let people know that you have faith in them and why?

Deep self and system awareness and self management; in the chapter on Container leadership we emphasised how critical it is for a leader to be able to recognise their own impulses and issues, restrain the natural tendency to let these 'spill over' into the situation, and be present and available to work with the dynamics of the situation in front of you. Can you learn, not to 'empty' yourself of your own feelings and internal responses – since these are critical 'clues' as to what might be happening in the system around you, but rather to notice them, restrain the impulse to act on them in habitual ways, and in so doing project a calm and confident presence to those around you? Sometimes, if you are an extrovert, this might simply mean learning to sit on your hands for a while and resisting the impulse to leap into the conversation! If you are an introvert, it might mean that you step forwards a bit more into the situation. It might also mean seeking out a coach, counsellor, or good friend with whom you can process turbulent feelings and emotions, learn to differentiate which are your own issues and those that belong to the system, and thereby develop the awareness not to project your own issues unwisely onto people and the situation around you. In learning this key skill people will feel much safer in your hands and more trusting in your leadership.

Creating detachment and space for self – holding one's own boundaries; some times the need to contain your own feelings and emotions creates a little pressure pot inside you that just has to let off steam there and then. Good Container leadership requires detachment. Unless you stay slightly on the edge of the system you can't by definition learn to hold it. Do you consciously pause and create time and space for yourself to be 'off stage', or do you let your diary and schedule take you over? Creating detachment can simply mean taking time out every now and then to pause and look after you. Indeed it is hard to deploy any of the Changing Leadership practices if you are emotionally exhausted. In the award winning animation film 'Chicken Run', the heroine chicken, Ginger (who if you have not seen this film exhibits excellent Changing Leadership skills), takes time out every night to go and sit on top of her hut to vent her emotions, cry a little, and analyse the situation from afar. She comes back to the other chickens the next day always calm, confident, and full of hope that today will be the day that the chickens will be able to fly and escape from the farm. Her detached yet containing leadership presence keeps them together and on track. Can you step out of your attachment to activity and do likewise?

Learning to 'contain' can be a life long task. It requires a robust yet purposeful reflective awareness of self. Our behaviour is a complex phenomenon made up of situational triggers and deep personal needs, motives, and impulses. Leaders who have low inhibition will always struggle to contain, in other words be able to monitor one's own impulses and avoid 'acting out' on them alone, in order to become more present to work with the needs of the situation. Yet leaders who *can* contain, become remarkable guides and facilitators of their organisations. They build confidence where there is doubt; they bring assuredness where there is uncertainty. Stepping into Container leadership therefore brings quite a responsibility for others. It can feel like giving up one's own ego needs in order to 'take on' and help process the dynamics and emotions of those around you. When you have become a strong containing force it can feel like there is nothing left of you, and this can feel exhausting and draining. Sometimes we therefore avoid stepping into containing out of fear we will have to 'carry' too much responsibility for the system. Moreover, upholding boundaries and 'rules', i.e. the structural side of containment, can feel like putting your head above the parapet which risks incurring the projected wrath of the organisation who would rather remain free to do what they like. As you consider developing your Container leadership it might therefore be helpful to do a little self reflection; what might you be sacrificing of yourself, and how can you continue to have your own needs acknowledged and satisfied? Paradoxically, the stronger and more comfortable you are about your sense of self, the less you will risk sacrificing and the greater your ability to practice Container leadership for others.

How to learn Transforming Space leadership

Understanding 'systems dynamics' to recognise key patterns; given that Transforming Space leadership is about 'disturbing' the system while in flow, it helps to learn how to see the world in systems. We have earlier referred to complexity theory and its endeavour to understand how 'complex adaptive systems' work. Can you learn to see your organisation, not as a set of unrelated parts and random events, but as a connected and dynamic web of relationships and interactions that produces certain patterns of behaviour? Through this lens you don't seek to change behaviour through changing the 'parts' ('let's tell people about the new values and behaviours'), you do so through changing the relationships between the parts and how they interact ('let's design a meeting that has unstructured dialogue and no pre-determined agenda so that responsibility and risk taking will emerge'). When you understand systems dynamics you look a bit more deeply into what you see around you – you connect the dots, and you look for the few (often invisible) structures that are driving behaviour, and in so doing you develop your ability to design and facilitate interventions that are high leverage and 'system changing'. In the process you also reveal how you see, thus supporting continued development and building of your own system sight. What opportunities do you have coming up at which you could develop greater system awareness?

Ability to see yourself in the system as an actor and player and use this as data; by definition every part in a connected system has a direct role to play, and participation (and non-participation) will impact how the system behaves. And what matters about participation 'in the moment' is not your rank, level, profession, or department, but how you play your part as an individual interacting with others and 'co-creating' the outcome. Transforming Space leadership feels more like improvisational theatre than rehearsed scripts and stage managed contributions. If you can learn to 'go with the flow', stay attuned to what arises inside you in the situation, and then make a move to intervene how the flow happens, *in other words stay present to the moment and not just relate to the outcome or any pre-rehearsed input,* your ability to practice Transforming Space leadership will be significantly enhanced. What meetings or conversations do you have coming up at which you could learn to work in a more improvised way?

Recognise big thresholds and how to navigate them; a threshold is a starting point for a new state or experience; and just as thresholds in a doorway help you move from one room into another, they offer support in moving through transition. In that sense thresholds mark boundaries. Organisational thresholds can take many forms, such as: integrating an acquisition into the parent company; changing the way you 'go to market'; re-branding the identity of your core service offering. Transforming Space leadership can recognise, if not anticipate, when these thresholds are happening and then navigate them *in the present moment*. These moments could be either planned, such as working at the first engagement event with the leaders of both an acquired and acquiring company; or unplanned, such as hearing the first time when leaders in the company start saying 'we', rather than 'us' and 'them'. Smallest detectable sensations (which are often physiological, such as heart beat and clammy hands) can give you clues that people are about to enter a threshold. And very often, signs that people are about to enter a threshold are signs of avoidance and withdrawal rather than the brave movement forwards. If there is hesitation in a group, it could be a sign that they are on the edge of moving into quite different territory together – can you see it as such, bring it to the attention of the group, and in so doing help them move through the transforming state, rather than stay where they currently are? If you sense that people have moved to a different place, can you bring that to their attention and mark it in some way? Learning to recognise and navigate threshold entry, transition, and exit will help you as a Transforming Space leader. Can you already note down any important thresholds that you are taking your team or organisation through? How could you recognise and mark them more explicitly?

Working with 'negative capability' – being open to doubt and not knowing; we opened this chapter with a definition of 'negative capability' and its role in fostering learning and development. In Chapter 8 on Transforming Space we referred to the practice of making yourself vulnerable and open in order to be able to open up oneself and others to new possibilities. Can you therefore learn about what you don't know? When you engage with your team do you articulate as much about what you don't know, as about what you do know? Rather than 'solve' what you don't know, can you stay open to its mystery and engage people around you in exploring the uncertainty and in so doing uncover new insights collectively? Learning to stay in curiosity is essential for Transforming Space leadership – since it opens you to being attentive to new possibilities arising in the moment, rather than explaining away everything through prior knowledge. If all you do is the latter, the organisation will never be able to learn about itself and act differently. Asking oneself a question as simple as, 'if I did not know anything about this – what then?' can help remove limiting assumptions (Edge and Tension) and enable Transforming Space.

Understanding 'field dynamics' and knowing how to intervene; Transforming Space leadership keeps attention on the space that is currently being worked in. This can be referred to as working with the 'field'. A field is an allocated space that has certain functions and properties. It has boundaries, it has marker positions, and it has depth – there are many layers in a field, and what you see on the surface could be a manifestation of what lies beneath. If you could learn to see your team as a 'field', how would you start to see it? You might start to notice its membership – who is in and who is out, and are there some people who come in and out on a temporary basis? What does that do to the dynamics of the field? What roles and positions do people take up in the team, who are the 'field markers' in the team, what are they marking, and how do they relate to each other? How do people take turns in conversations, and what is that saying about the implicit and explicit hierarchy in the team? When is the team at its most energetic and most stuck? And how does what happens in the team in some way reflect the wider field of the organisation? Can you learn to intervene in the field of the team so that it becomes more able to see its own dynamics, and in so doing, become conscious of how to impact the organisation around it?

Transforming Space leadership can feel a bit like going into freefall. Noticing, responding to, and intervening in what is arising are all unpredictable processes. People are often not conscious of what it is that is driving their behaviour in the moment, and drawing their attention to this can at best feel like getting in their way and at its most unsettling feel like you have made a gross error of judgment about what you are noticing and how you are intervening. Designing interventions that are meant to be transforming also has risk. While people might have signed up to it with their heads they can be unprepared for the emotional and behavioural discomfort it will bring. This discomfort (which of course is a sign that something is being transformed) could be too troubling for people to process and the threshold opportunity is lost. In all situations, you the leader who is trying to work with Transforming Space could be rejected by others as being a bit of a weirdo, not someone we necessarily like, and someone who in some way is confronting our sense of our identity and attachment to that which we currently cherish. It takes a healthy degree of conviction and personal ego strength to make visible the forces that are giving rise to the present. Are you up for doing this and then working with the consequences of the heightened attention? While this risk is mitigated if you bring in the other three Changing Leadership practices in your interventions, nonetheless Transforming Space leadership moments can be avoided out of fear of 'getting it wrong', damaging others, and being rejected.

General guidelines for developing Changing Leadership

We close this chapter with a few general comments on how to develop Changing Leadership. The guidelines in themselves incorporate its practices; we found it helpful to turn the framework onto the very learning process to develop it!

1. *Working with intent, intervention, and outcome;* developing a new practice is a conscious, mindful activity, which requires a degree of discipline and an explicit structure. If you wish to experiment with a new practice, and have an occasion coming up in which you believe you can do that, can you concretely and specifically explain: the intention of what you are doing; the processes you plan to use to achieve that intention; and the results you expect to see? After the event, can you go back to what you recorded against these three headings and note down what actually happened in the experience and what the outcomes were? Using the three part structure of *intent, intervention, and outcome* makes your learning process explicit and therefore able to be tracked. It helps you to assess how realistic your intention was, whether your intervention game plan made sense, and how skilful you were in doing it. Working

with intent builds Attractor energy into your learning process, noting down your expectations and plan of intervention creates a learning Container, and openly and transparently recording and learning from what actually happened brings a frisson of Edge and Tension.

2. *Learning what you need to unlearn;* doing something differently usually means we have to lose an attachment to how we have typically done something in the past, or see the attachment as having a potentially different purpose in the present. When one of the authors went to a professional tennis coach to raise their game they learned that how they had been gripping the racket for the serve had been limiting their ability to play the game with any power. To raise their service game it was therefore necessary to consciously stop gripping the racket in this way. Can you reflect on what you might need to let go of, be that an underlying belief, or a more Shaping style behaviour, in order to develop Changing Leadership? What assumptions and habits might you find it most hard to shift and what concrete and practical steps can you take to widen your awareness of whether or not you are being successful in unlearning them? Our attention can sometimes fail to register a great deal of what occurs; working with a coach, and/or seeking feedback from others, can help broaden our range of awareness and in so doing develop our ability to both unlearn old practices and learn new ones. Learning to unlearn requires both the guidance of safe Containment and the confronting reality of Edge and Tension.

3. *Practice, practice, practice;* one of us heard recently on the radio that it takes 10000 hours of practice to become

'world class' at any activity – be that a sport, playing a musical instrument, or mastering a profession. Clearly different kinds of activities contain different levels of complexity, and hence greater or lesser learning time, yet nonetheless this statistic brings general attention to the importance of simply repeatedly trying things out. Transforming Space teaches us the importance of enactment – working in the moment to change things, bringing one's attention to the present. In that respect, it's important to start jumping in and working with the Changing Leadership practices in order to help move your leadership. Take a look at your forthcoming calendar for the next three months. In what planned events could you take the opportunity to practice Changing Leadership, and perhaps reduce any natural tendency to 'shape'? Schedule some time ahead of these events to use the 'intent, intervention, outcome' framework and plan what different kind of interventions you wish to practice. Seek out a colleague with whom you can gain support for your intention.

4. *Seeing leadership capability building as a team game;* we have noted already that given the complexity of high magnitude change, it becomes necessary to see its leadership as a collective activity. Furthermore, given the time it can take to develop an individual leader, more rapid progress towards capability for Changing Leadership will come from working with the combination of styles and strengths that the leadership team brings. We have developed feedback questionnaires for the Changing Leadership practices at both the individual and team level, and it can be helpful for a leadership team to both self assess and get feedback

from the organisation around them on how well they currently balance all four of the practices. Team learning can happen without questionnaires of course, and we have worked with leadership teams who (a) regularly give each other peer feedback on the practices, (b) set up coaching 'buddies' within the team to provide support to each other on experimenting with more effective practice, (c) use face to face team meetings as opportunities to practice and learn about Changing Leadership, and (d) plan interventions in the organisation, as a team, that will play to their respective strengths on the framework. You might want to reflect on how you could move forward in developing your leadership team's capability to collectively master the framework.

5. *Seeking feedback to help you stay on course;* feedback generates awareness. Awareness can then be applied to generate new perspectives for action to achieve the purpose. Increased awareness is the life blood for learning how to practice Changing Leadership. This kind of transforming leadership cannot be learned through going on courses, or reading books. While some initial education about the framework and its practices is important, learning to put it into action is an ongoing, subtle, and at times frustrating activity about changing behaviour. Given this, a combination of Edge and Tension confronting feedback and Container encouragement and support can work wonders in maintaining your energy levels to stay on the development course. Where can you obtain this ongoing feedback from and how might you contract for its support?

Summary

In this chapter we have shared our thoughts on how Changing Leadership can be developed. We explored the fundamental question as to whether or not the practices can be developed, given one could argue that some of the practices need to be underpinned by personality styles that are a relatively unchanging aspect of one's character. We reiterated our belief that the practices can be learned, and that they are essentially what it is that leaders *do* to implement high magnitude change successfully. However, the relative ease with which they can be developed is determined by an individual's level of self awareness, their intent in the situation, and the holding of certain underlying beliefs.

Before embarking on attempts to develop the practices we suggested that it can be helpful to reflect on your levels of self awareness, intent, and beliefs, since these are the foundations upon which all four of the Changing Leadership practices is built. We then shared some learning strategies for each one of the four practices, based on what we have found has worked to build leaders' capability. For each of the practices we acknowledged that there could be a psychological risk in stepping more into its use and that this could become a learning block. However, more often than not the fear of being envied (Attractor), disliked (Edge and Tension), having to carry the entire load (Container) or being rejected (Transforming Space), is more about what is inside our heads than what is present in the organisation around us. If we can learn to overcome these blocks, then we just might be surprised at how positively responsive the organisation will be to our shift in leadership.

We concluded with some generic guidelines on how to build your Changing Leadership capability, which covered: working to a structured and explicit learning and review process; considering what you may have to unlearn in order to learn new practices; the importance of frequent practice; the insight that developing Changing Leadership capability at the level of the team can bring a faster return on the learning investment; and the vital importance of ongoing feedback to raise level of awareness. Throughout, the learning process for Changing Leadership should work with intent (Attractor), setting goals and obtaining accurate feedback (Edge and Tension), a guiding and supportive structure (Container) and the chance to simply go out and try new things (Transforming Space). In that way, you can increase your chances of developing your Changing Leadership capability.

We close this chapter with a final thought: have the courage to change what you can change; have the compassion to see what you cannot change; and have the wisdom to see the difference. A leader once gave us the following quote which very wisely expands on the above:

CHANGING THE WORLD?

When I was a young man, I wanted to change the world.

I found it difficult to change the world, so I tried to change my nation. When I found I couldn't change the nation, I began to focus on my town. I couldn't change the town and as an older man, I tried to change my family.

Now, as an old man, I realise the only thing I can change is myself, and suddenly I realise that if long ago I had changed myself,

I could have made an impact on my family. My family and I could have made an impact on our town. Their impact could indeed have changed the nation and I could indeed have changed the world.

Unknown Monk 1100AD

11

Where next?

In concluding this book we mark the end of one journey and the start of a new one. The journey travelled has been a testing yet rewarding one. We have discovered insights into change and its leadership that we would not have found without inquiry, comprehensive research, experimental practice, and the courage to keep exploring when we could have just said, 'that's it'. The inquiry has kept us curious, the research grounded, the practice relevant, and the courage pioneering. We sincerely hope that the book has accomplished its aims of stimulating thinking and changing leadership practice. Its writing has brought further rigour to our thinking, and its reading and editing has changed our consulting practice. The book had a collaborative life within our team, and while it fed into our consulting engagements, it was in turn enriched by them. The conversations we have had with leaders whose stories are featured have been helpful in recollecting precisely what it is about a leader's intention, and intervention, that can lead to the creation of remarkable movement in the organisation around them.

The biggest insight that emerged through its writing is the requirement that leaders become conscious. The more a leader is conscious and aware of their own impulses, and able to restrain acting on them, the less likely they are to project a dysfunctional shadow into their organisation. The less dysfunction there is in the system, the less 'stuck' the organisation becomes. And the less stuck the organisation, the greater the potential for movement, innovation, and improved performance. In order to become conscious, the leader needs to become aware. Once they are aware, they can recognise their shadow, and acknowledge its implications. Awareness brings increased insight which generates choice and an ability to respond differently. Self aware leaders therefore use their leadership presence in more mindful and creative ways. They become available to hear others, to tune into the systemic change requirement in the organisation around them, and connect their leadership intent and intervention to act in service of that. Once so engaged, the system then transforms. Increasing awareness is therefore the key to unlocking Changing Leadership.

Given that we have found that what leaders do determines half of change implementation success, we could argue that becoming more aware is almost a moral imperative for leaders tasked with stewarding organisations whose size and impact affect the well being of so many lives. How many of us are completely aware? What fear and anxiety stops us from increasing the range of our self awareness? Becoming aware takes courage. Very often the bits about ourselves that we don't like to look at are those that keep us most stuck. However what we have seen is that increasing self awareness is a necessary and powerful precursor to being freed from one's ego impulses. Once leaders are free from these shackles they can practice Changing Leadership with a potency and sincerity that does credit to their function, their teams, and themselves.

As we move forward on the next stage of our journey we are keen to engage in dialogue with the reactions this book has elicited. In anticipation of some of the potential topics we offer the following as fruitful avenues of inquiry.

The organisational conditions required for successful Changing Leadership

We are sanguine about the organisational context within which individual leadership occurs. Sometimes it is just not enough for a leader, or even a leadership team, to be able to impact an organisation that is systemically wired to stay stuck. We have encountered leaders whose Attractor capability gets picked up as dangerously undermining to an organisation that talks collective purpose but actually believes in unilateral control. We have felt the frustration and hurt of leaders whose Edge and Tension capability casts them as the 'wicked witch' in organisational cultures that are wedded to protecting the status quo. We have regularly seen organisations running scared from leaders whose ability to Contain have forced tough choices around strategic clarity in cultures that prefer to 'let anything go'. And we have witnessed the isolation of leaders whose unnerving ability to create Transforming Spaces, has cast them out of the 'in crowd' in organisations not courageous enough to walk change versus talk change.

If more leaders in a culture collectively practice Changing Leadership then obviously the organisational context will start to shift. However, what will make that easier is an organisation conscious enough to recognise the gap between its intent and its action. We would like to learn more about what it takes to create 'mindful' organisations that stay attuned to their own shadow and indeed encourage its exposure.

Do certain personality styles suit Changing Leadership more than others?

We are still at the early stages of understanding the relationship between the Changing Leadership practices and personality. It could help us inquire as to how and why some individuals find it harder than others to naturally pick them up. Aside from the potential impact of organisational conditioning alluded to above, what is it about individual make up that also influences its practice? Is Attractor Leadership most suited to individuals with the temperament that enjoys making others feel powerful, as opposed to satisfying their own needs to feel influential and in charge? Will Edge and Tension come most naturally to individuals who do not have an innate desire to be liked, or put harmonious relationships above everything else? Is a prerequisite for successful Container Leadership the possession of high inhibition that is coupled with strong self esteem? And how important is high intuition and low fear of failure, or loss of face, to the ability to sensitively and courageously practice Transforming Space?

As we work more intensively in our coaching practice with individual leaders, greater insights into these potential correlations should emerge. When we conduct further research can we test for personality styles, at the same time as we conduct Behavioural Event Interviews, and in so doing discover whether or not any relationship between Changing Leadership and personality does in fact exist. We would like to structure a rigorous inquiry into this topic, including an exploration of how self awareness can be developed in leaders, since it could have significant implications for the identification and development of those with the potential to lead and sustainably transform large organisations.

Have we missed anything?

While our research has given us confidence that the Changing Leadership framework is robust, we would certainly not claim that (a) we have the full 'answer', and (b) that it is universally applicable. The practice of leading large scale transformational change is so complex that no one framework will ever be the comprehensive solution. We might have been biased in our own coding and classifying of the interview data such that some practices were unconsciously missed, or, we are prepared to accept, consciously screened out. Our findings are also drawn from the sample of leaders available to us, selected from our own network and field of operation. We readily admit that that sample is not the most cross-culturally representative of the leadership population at large. While it contained leaders from four different Continents, the sample is not large enough to be able to detect cultural nuances or biases.

Does the Changing Leadership framework therefore travel globally? While the four practices overall might have universal relevance, and indeed findings from complexity theory research substantiate the need for their complementary energies in all living systems, does the way in which they need to show up in different cultures vary? We would welcome any insight, help, and dialogue on this subject since it holds crucial importance to the tackling of the very real change challenges facing the ever increasing global economy.

'Is change, changing?' 'Are leaders leading?' We would now answer 'yes', and 'maybe', to these two questions we originally posed. In seeking to answer them, how has the whole inquiry left us? Certainly wiser about change and its leadership, and more able to see the connection between what leaders do and the legacy they leave in the world. We are also wiser about ourselves, and our relationship to client work, recognising that what we say and do in our practice needs in some way to replicate the intent, beliefs, and self awareness required for Changing Leadership. We sometimes struggle with that (as we are sure leaders struggle too!), and yet learning the hard way always seems to bear more fruit. We have changed the way in which we contract assignments, drawing on sound Container principles. We have become bolder in our interventions, recognising that Edge and Tension is a powerful force for movement. And we stay far more alert to working with what arises in front of us, harnessing the 'dislodging' potential of Transforming Space. And finally, we stay working on our own story as we help create the unfolding story in our client organisations. The field between what we do and how we do it, and the lives and journeys of our clients seems connected and inextricably woven. We are grateful for all those shared experiences, since they have helped move us ever onwards towards our Attractor purpose.

Recommended reading list

Beer, M. and Nohria, N. (2000). *Breaking The Code Of Change.* Boston; Harvard Business School Press

Beisser, A. (1970) The paradoxical theory of change. In J. Fagan & I. Shepherd (eds.) *Gestalt Therapy Now.* New York; Harper

Bossidy, L. and Charan, R. (2002). Execution: The Discipline of Getting Things Done. New York. Crown Business

Denning, Stephen. (2001). The Springboard: How Storytelling Ignites Action in Knowledge-Era Organizations

Collins, J.C. (2001). *Good to Great: Why some companies make the leap – and others don't.* New York; Harper Business

Cooperrider, D. and Whitney, D. (2000). *A positive revolution in change.* New York; Bettett-Koehler Publishers

Fredrickson, B.L. (1998). What good are positive emotions? *Review of General Psychology, 2*(3), 300–319

Fredrickson, B.L. (2001). 'The role of *positive emotions in positive psychology: the broaden-and-build theory of positive* emotions.' *American Psychologist* 56 pp. 218–226

Goffee, R. and Jones, G. (1998) *The Character of a Corporation.* Harper Collins

Greenleaf, R.K. (1997). *Servant Leadership.* New York; Paulist Press

Hesse, H. (1974). *The Journey to the East.* Panther Books Ltd

Issacs, W. (1999). *Dialogue and the Art of Thinking Together; A pioneering approach to communicating in business and in life.* Bantam Doubleday Dell Publishing Group

Johnson, S. (2002). *Emergence: The Connected Lives of Ants, Brains, Cities and Software.* Penguin Books Ltd

Kotter, J.P. (1995). 'Leading change: why transformation efforts fail?' *Harvard Business Revies;* May–June, pp. 11–16

Pascale, R., Milleman, M. and Gioja, L. (2000). *Surfing the Edge of Chaos: The Laws of Nature and the New Laws of Business.* Texere Publishing

Scott, S. (2003). *Fierce Conversations: Achieving Success in Work and in Life, One Conversation at a Time.* Piatkus Books

Seligman, M.E.P. (1999). 'The President's address.' *American Psychologist* 54, 559–562

Shaw, P. (2002). *Changing Conversations in Organizations: A Complexity Approach to Change (Complexity & Emergence in Organizations).* Routledge.

Smith, K. and Berg, D. (1997). *Paradoxes of Group Life: Understanding Conflict, Paralysis, and Movement in Group Dynamics.* Jossey-Bass

Toffler, A. and Toffler, H. (1998). *Rethinking the Future: Rethinking Business Principles, Competition, Control and Complexity, Leadership, Markets and the World.* Nicholas Brealey Publishing Ltd

Waldrop, M. (1994). *Complexity: The Emerging Science at the Edge of Order and Chaos.* Penguin Books

Wheatley, M. (1993). *Leadership and the New Science.* San Francisco, CA; Berrett-Koehler

Weick, K.E. (1995). *Sense-making in Organisations.* Thousand Oaks, CA; Sage Publications

Index